EZEKIEL

STUDIES ON PERSONALITIES
OF THE OLD TESTAMENT
JAMES L. CRENSHAW, *Editor*

DANIEL IN HIS TIME
by André LaCocque

JOSEPH AND HIS FAMILY: A LITERARY STUDY
by W. Lee Humphreys

EZEKIEL: THE PROPHET AND HIS MESSAGE
by Ralph W. Klein

EZEKIEL

THE PROPHET AND HIS MESSAGE

BY RALPH W. KLEIN

UNIVERSITY OF SOUTH CAROLINA PRESS

Library of Congress Cataloging-in-Publication Data

Klein, Ralph W.
    Ezekiel: the prophet and his message.

    (Studies on personalities of the Old Testament)
    Bibliography: p.
    Includes index.
    1. Bible. O.T. Ezekiel—Criticism, interpretation,
etc. 2. Ezekiel (Biblical prophet) I. Title.
II. Series.
BS1545.2.K54   1988   224'.406   88-1280
ISBN 0-87249-553-1

CONTENTS

EDITOR'S PREFACE

Critical study of the Bible in its ancient Near Eastern setting has stimulated interest in the individuals who shaped the course of history and whom events singled out as tragic or heroic figures. For example, Rolf Rendtorff's *Men of the Old Testament* (1968) focuses on the lives of important biblical figures as a means of illuminating history, while Fleming James's *Personalities of the Old Testament* (1939) addresses the issue of individuals who function as inspiration for their religious successors in the twentieth century. Other studies restricted to a single individual—e.g., Moses, Abraham, Samson, Elijah, David, Saul, Ruth, Jonah, Job, Jeremiah—have enabled scholars to deal with a host of themes and questions: psychological, literary, theological, sociological, and historical. Some, like Gerhard von Rad's *Moses*, introduce a specific approach to interpreting the Bible, hence provide valuable pedagogic tools.

As a rule, these treatments of individual figures have not provided books accessible to the general public. Some such volumes were written by thinkers who lacked an expert's knowledge of biblical criticism (Freud on Moses, Jung on Job) and whose conclusions, however provocative, remain problematic. Others were targeted for the guild of professional biblical critics (David Gunn on David and Saul, Phyllis Trible on Ruth, Terence Fretheim and Jonathan Magonet on Jonah). Few such books have succeeded in capturing the imagination of a wide audience in the way fictional works like Archibald MacLeish's *J.B.* and Joseph Heller's *God Knows* have done.

The books in this series are written by specialists in the Old Testament for readers who want to learn more about biblical personalities without becoming professional students of the Bible themselves. The volumes throw light on the imaging of deity in biblical times, clarifying ancient understandings of God. Inasmuch as the Bible constitutes human perceptions of God's relationship with the world and its creatures, we seek to discern what ancient writers believed about deity. Although not necessarily endorsing a particular understanding of God, we believe such attempts at making sense of reality contribute something worthwhile to the endless quest for knowledge.

James L. Crenshaw
Duke Divinity School

PREFACE

When Professor James Crenshaw invited me to write a book on Ezekiel for this series, he was asking me to return to an old friend. Through the years I have lectured frequently on this important prophet to parish adult forums, to pastoral conferences and summer clergy institutes, and, of course, to the students I have taught at Concordia Seminary, Christ Seminary–Seminex, and Lutheran School of Theology at Chicago.

Ezekiel claimed a chapter in my theological interpretation of the sixth century BCE (*Israel in Exile*, 1979), and, in fact, that book was written in Göttingen, West Germany, where I had gone on sabbatical leave to study with Professor Walther Zimmerli, the doyen of twentieth-century interpreters of Ezekiel, and, happily, a powerful influence on my understanding of the Hebrew Scriptures.

What is needed on Ezekiel is not another commentary; Zimmerli's epic work has now appeared in English, and Moshe Greenberg is halfway through a brilliant alternate reading for the Anchor Bible. What Professor Crenshaw sought and what I hope to deliver in the following pages is a literary and theological study that will be of interest to the clergy, theologians outside the biblical field, seminary and college students, and the kind of lay person whom I meet at Sunday morning forums—eager to learn fresh approaches to the biblical record and hungry for something substantial to read. I also am bold enough to believe that my interpretation might have real value for other members of the guild of Old Testament scholars.

Ezekiel was a radical prophet. The word "radical" acknowledges that Ezekiel returned to the roots of Israelite faith in his hour of crisis, even if he also freely adapted that tradition for his new situation. It also refers to his unusual life style and the sharpness of his theological diagnosis—no prophet ever expressed criticism more radically. But the word *radical* also alludes to the freshness of his program for the future and the way in which this uniquely God-centered man organized his theology of hope around the presence of God.

Public thanks are due

—to the Boards of Directors of Christ Seminary—Seminex and Lutheran School of Theology at Chicago, who granted me a leave in the 1985-86 academic year to work on this manuscript, and to the Lutheran Brotherhood Life Insurance Company, which made that year financially feasible;

—to Professor James Crenshaw, for the stimulus and encouragement of his invitation, and to Kenneth J. Scott and staff members of the University of South Carolina Press, who have offered courteous and expert advice at every stage of this project;

—to all those who have listened to my presentations on Ezekiel, and who have asked leading questions and made important suggestions, or who have studied texts from Ezekiel in detail in seminary classrooms;

—to my current teaching assistants, Melinda Wagner, who worked through the manuscript with uncommon care and alerted me to many obscurities and grammatical infelicities, and Mark W. Bartusch, who ably assisted with the reading of the galleys;

—and to my daughter, Becky, who assisted me with the illustrations.

Finally, this book is dedicated to my wife, Marilyn, who for twenty-five years has ventured with me into a quest for the radical implications of the presence of Ezekiel's God. She has shaped me as a person and as a theologian in ways beyond telling. Without her understanding and encouragement this book could not have been written.

ABBREVIATIONS

ATANT — Abhandlungen zur Theologie des Alten und Neuen
       Testaments
  BHS — *Biblia Hebraica Stuttgartensia*
BZAW — Beihefte zur *ZAW*
  CBQ — *Catholic Biblical Quarterly*
HUCA — *Hebrew Union College Annual*
   Int — *Interpretation*
  JBL — *Journal of Biblical Literature*
JSOT — *Journal for the Study of the Old Testament*
 LXX — Septuagint
  MT — Massoretic Text
  VT — *Vetus Testamentum*
ZAW — *Zeitschrift für die alttestamentliche Wissenschaft*

EZEKIEL

INTRODUCTION

This book is not a biography of the prophet Ezekiel. As Brevard Childs reminds us, investigation into a prophet's personal circumstances or his psychological struggles may be an inappropriate way to interpret him, even in the case of a prophet like Jeremiah, where data about his life are readily available.[1] Rather, the way we read a prophetic book should be determined by the way the prophet himself, his followers, and the community of the faithful recorded, preserved, and reshaped the text. The prophetic message is to be found in the received text, not in the biography of the prophet.

In the case of Ezekiel data about the life of the prophet are notable by their sparseness, as the following paragraphs will demonstrate. Only twice do we even hear the prophet's name—in the title verse of the book (1:1) and in an address by Yahweh to Israel through the prophet (24:24). Everywhere else, some 93 times in all, Yahweh calls him "mortal," my translation for the title conventionally and literally rendered as "son of man." The meaning of the name Ezekiel (God strengthens or toughens), while not inappropriate to the type of relationship the prophet has with his God, is never invoked to clarify that relationship. It seems to be, simply, the name his parents gave him.

The title "mortal" does tell us something about how we are to perceive the relationship between the prophet and God. Ezekiel was profoundly influenced by the presence (or absence) of God and by the presence (or absence) of God's glory. In comparison with the glorious deity, the prophet himself is a mere mortal, a lowly, virtually anonymous channel through whom the word of Yahweh came. While earlier prophetic books often distinguish between the words of the prophet himself and the revealed divine words of judgment (contrast Amos 3:1a with 3:2), almost every pericope in Ezekiel begins with an expression like "The word of Yahweh came to me," thus explicitly identifying the whole body of words uttered through Ezekiel as the word of Yahweh. The name Yahweh, rather than the name or personality of Ezekiel, gives authority to the prophet's message.

The prophet and his successors, of course, shaped the message in accord with their traditional background, their distinctive vocabulary, and the needs of the day as they perceived them. But only rarely did they identify specific words as Ezekiel's subjective response to what had been revealed. During his visionary journey to the Jerusalem temple Ezekiel twice lamented, "Ah, Lord Yahweh, will you destroy the remnant of Israel when you pour out your wrath upon Jerusalem?" (9:8; 11:13). In addition, he cried out in protest when Yahweh asked him to eat what he perceived to be ritually impure food (4:14; cf. 20:49; 37:3). But there is nothing in this book even remotely similar to Jeremiah's confessions, in which the prophet expressed his reactions to Yahweh's overbearing presence (Jer. 20:7–9) or to the people's persistent failure to hear and obey (Jer. 15:15; 18:20–23).

We should not imagine that everyone accepted the prophet's message as God's truth. In fact, evidence for widespread rejection of Ezekiel is abundant. His unique designation of Israel as a rebellious house (2:5–8; 3:9, 26–27; 12:2–3, 9, 25; 17:12; 24:3; 44:6) refers both to the people's sins against Yahweh and to their rejection of the prophet and his message. In calling Ezekiel to be a prophet, Yahweh instructed him to be hard or tough and to deliver his message, whether the people would hear or refuse to hear. The large number of disputation words in the book indicates that many within Israel did refuse to hear, some out of an arrogance that denied their guilt (11:2–12, 14–17; 12:21–25; 18:1–9; 33:23–29), and some simply because their hearts failed them for fear when it came to believing his promises about the future (12:26–28; 20:32–34; 33:10–20; 37:11–13).[2] He could not have been pleased that he could be compared to one who sings love songs to an admiring but basically fickle audience (33:32), which heard his words but would not follow them. Still, Jeremiah's

4

plea for vengeance against those who persecuted him (Jer. 17:18; 18:21–23) finds no echo in Ezekiel's disputations.

PERSONALIA

We only know that Ezekiel was married because his wife's death became an occasion for a symbolic action (24:15–24). The prominent role played by the wife (or wives) of Hosea and his public anguish over her (their) infidelity offer a pointed contrast. The names of Hosea's and Isaiah's children are central to an understanding of the message of these eighth-century prophetic predecessors, while the Bible leaves us totally in the dark about whether Ezekiel even had any children. Such biographical facts about family life are spelled out clearly in the case of Jeremiah: he was commanded *not* to marry and *not* to have children (Jer. 16:2).

Ezekiel was by profession a priest, or, at the least, he was the son of a priest named Buzi. This background accounts for his interest in the temple, his knowledge about its ordinances, and for the close resemblance in his language to the Holiness Code (H)[3] and the Priestly portions (P)[4] of the Pentateuch. He was among those three thousand or more (Jer. 52:28) leading Judean citizens exiled in 597 BCE with King Jehoiachin, but we do not know for sure whether he functioned as a priest prior to that time or how old he was in 597. He mentions no other contemporary exiled priests by name.

More dates are provided for his prophecies than for any other prophet.[5] When translated into modern calendrical equivalents, they range from 13 July, 594 (or 593) to 10 April 574,[6] suggesting that the early part of Ezekiel's prophetic ministry overlapped with his Palestinian contemporary Jeremiah (whose activity as a prophet extended from 626 to somewhere in the 580s). Though he never mentions Jeremiah by name, there are numerous indications that he was aware of what Jeremiah was saying.[7] We do not know if Ezekiel met Jeremiah while he was still in Jerusalem. Carley believes that Ezekiel's knowledge of Jeremiah's words may derive from oral tradition in Judah and Babylon.[8]

The large number of dated oracles stemming from the years of the final siege of Jerusalem reflect the intensity of Ezekiel's activity before 587.[9] Many of these are also oracles against foreign nations, and they express his persistent attack on the idea that reliance on foreign nations

5

would help Jerusalem survive the Babylonian invasion. He continued to deliver messages for about a decade after Jeremiah, but his last recorded date is still twenty-five years or more before Second Isaiah. Ezekiel and Second Isaiah in fact represent different generations of the exilic experience. It was Ezekiel's responsibility to condemn the city of Jerusalem during its final years, deal with questions of relative guilt and innocence before and after its fall, and argue forcefully for the hope of a new Exodus; Second Isaiah's concerns reflect those of a prophet at the end of the exilic period when Jerusalem's fully justified fall was already a fading memory and when discouragement and/or falling away to Babylonian deities were more urgent concerns.[10]

THE GEOGRAPHICAL LOCATION OF EZEKIEL

The book places Ezekiel at Tel Abib, by the river Chebar. The latter has been identified with the Šaṭṭ en-Nil, a canal connected with the city of Nippur.[11] Tel Abib's exact location is unknown. The Babylonian equivalent of its name means roughly "The Hill of the Flood," suggesting that the Judean exiles were settled on a ruined site that local tradition thought had been rendered uninhabitable long ago by the great flood. Because Ezekiel claims to know current events in Palestine (he cites words of those still living in the land in 11:3, 15; 12:22; 18:2; 33:24), because a man in Jerusalem named Pelatiah dies during one of his sermons (11:13), and because his intended audience at times also includes the citizens of Jerusalem, a number of scholars have proposed that the historical prophet actually delivered his oracles in Jerusalem, either in whole or in part. But the book consistently locates him in Babylon, and his knowledge of contemporary Jerusalem can be explained either by his own earlier experience there or by reports that reached the exiles in Mesopotamia thanks to an apparently lively correspondence between the land of exile and the homeland.[12] The death of Pelatiah is a historical problem for any interpreter, regardless of the prophet's location; it may merely offer symbolic proof of the effectiveness of the divine word (cf. ch. 3). As far as Ezekiel's living conditions are concerned, we know only that he had a house where elders of the people would occasionally meet with him (8:1; 14:1; 20:1; cf. 33:21–22). According to 2 Kings 6:32 the prophet Elisha of the northern kingdom also met with elders in his house.

INTRODUCTION

THE HEALTH OF EZEKIEL

Modern interpreters have consistently expressed shock at the unusual and, at times, bizarre behavior of Ezekiel and at his priestly behavior. Some, like Samuel Terrien, have done little to disguise their dislike of the prophet:

> His contacts with sources of ritual impurity—especially corpses and foreigners—at the expense of his ethical sensitivity to social injustice and inhumanity. . . . His persistent concern—not to say his obsessiveness—with the ritual uncleanness of blood and sexual secretions played a part in the cultic degradation of womanhood in Judaism.[13]

I suspect that Ezekiel had many colleagues in creating a lower than desirable position for women in the cultic life of Judaism. Though his use of adulterous women as examples of infidelity to Yahweh in chapters 16 and 23 might lead the unwary reader to associate women with evil, the same charge could be laid against the use of this figure in Hosea and Jeremiah. Ezekiel's persistent concern for ritual purity, however, should be viewed in a more positive light. For someone so focused on the presence of God with his people—cognizant of the devastation to be brought by the departure of that presence and the radical transformation to be effected by its return—it follows as a necessary corollary that he would in every way try to make sure that ritual misdeeds in the future would not drive the divine presence away again. How could a priest responsibly act otherwise? That he emphasized ritual purity to the exclusion of emphasis on other moral issues—idolatry, social justice, and the like—is simply contradicted by the text (e.g., ch. 8; 16:49; 18:7–8; and often elsewhere).

A more widespread criticism of Ezekiel in scholarly literature is that his personality lacks balance, that he was beset with emotional problems, and even that he was afflicted with psychosis.[14] There can be no question that many of the words and actions of Ezekiel would mark him as strange if said and done in our social context. Many today would object to the wild imagery of his visions, or even to the notion of a normal person seeing visions at all. His symbolic actions consist of most unusual, bizarre, or even apparently humanly impossible feats—lying on one's side for 390 days, conducting a mock siege against a city drawn on a brick, shaving off one's hair, and showing no emotion at the death of a beloved spouse. Scholars have pointed to his occasional inability to speak and to what

7

they see as attacks of temporary paralysis as evidence for what they allege to be acute mental disorders. In the nineteenth century A. Klostermann diagnosed him as having catalepsy; E. C. Broome in the present century believed him to be a paranoid schizophrenic beset by catatonia, delusions of grandeur, hallucinations, and other signs of psychosis.[15]

The trouble with such analyses is that they often forget that we are talking about a man who lived twenty-five centuries ago when words and actions may have had vastly different connotations than the same words or actions would have today. They have also often neglected the question of what was original and what was secondary in the book, assuming a unified, unaltered account. Many recent scholars, for example, have labeled secondary the whole account of Ezekiel lying successively on his two sides, and have even argued persuasively that the original draft of this incident has been vastly expanded and changed in the current text of the Bible, with the switching from side to side and, perhaps, the duration of his lying down being secondary.[16] If these conclusions are correct, they render the prophet's lying on his side irrelevant to the diagnosis of the health of the historical Ezekiel. Some of his other reported words or actions are literary devices or theological commentary rather than accurate accounts of his actions. His digging through a wall in a vision and the fatal effect of his sermon on Pelatiah are probably to be seen respectively as a literary device and a theological comment. Many of his other symbolic actions, too, are products of literary activity. They are too complex—or even impossible—to have taken place literally.[17]

If all religious activity is merely a defense mechanism, then Ezekiel was abnormal; but if visions—and other religious activity—are plausible phenomena, though difficult for anyone but the visionaries themselves to validate, we should be cautious about making judgments about the prophet's emotional health.[18] Many religious activities of this kind are normal, even if unverifiable. On one occasion Ezekiel turned a sketch of the future temple into a visionary tour (ch. 40–42), just as his fourfold diagnosis of Jerusalem's sin has been stylized into a visionary trip from Babylon to Jerusalem (ch. 8–11). The text of visions and symbolic actions in general shows a very traditional, stylized form.[19] Even Ezekiel's translocation from one site to another in a vision, often through the power of Yahweh's spirit (3:14; 8:3; 11:1, 24; 37:1; 43:5), has important roots in the tradition of the prophet Elijah (1 Kgs. 18:12; 2 Kgs. 2:16). Carley attempts to distinguish between visionary, or imaginary, experiences (the visions of God, 8:3; 11:24; cf. 40:2) and true translocations from one place to another.[20] Even Paul had a hard time telling the difference: "I know a man in Christ who fourteen years ago was caught up to the third heaven—whether in the body or out of the body I do not know" (2 Cor. 12:2).

Though the vast majority of current exegetes would refrain from putting Ezekiel on the couch, Bernhard Lang persists in believing that the prophet was ill because of what he understands as states of temporary paralysis and aphasia.[21] In my judgment this diagnosis does not accurately reflect the biblical text. Ezekiel's lying on his side—whether original to the book or not—is primarily a literary image that expresses the prophet's vocation to bear the guilt or punishment of his people; the prophet's inability to speak on one or more occasions also has symbolic rather than historical or medical significance. When Ezekiel sat among his fellow exiles overwhelmed, for seven days, because of the significance of his call vision (3:15), this is no more unusual—or evidence for ill health—than the seven-day silence Job's friends observed before launching into their "dialogue" with him (Job 2:13).

Moshe Greenberg understands the silence of 3:22–27 to be the prophet's inability to speak except when Yahweh (repeatedly) opened his mouth to deliver a divine oracle.[22] In his view it is merely a literary way of emphasizing that everything the prophet said was divine revelation, and that the early message of Ezekiel was centered appropriately on nothing but lamentation, mourning, and woe. When Ezekiel's silence ended with the arrival of a messenger, who told of the fate of Jerusalem, this does not merely mean that a period of intense stress was over;[23] it also means that after Yahweh's judgment had descended on the people and the dimensions of their guilt were no longer in question, a new period in saving history could dawn, when the prophet could speak freely and effectively of the promises for a new Israel centered on the divine presence. Up until this moment Ezekiel could only speak when Yahweh filled his mouth with a word of judgment; once guilt had been established, there were no restrictions placed on the prophet's enunciation of words of hope.

The reaction of the prophet to the death of his wife was indeed unusual—a sorrow too sad for tears—but only such an image could adequately indicate Yahweh's own inexpressible sorrow at the loss of the temple. Ezekiel's quiet sighing, without going through the external mourning rituals, reflects his own and Yahweh's deep grief at their recent losses (24:17, 22–23). Similarly, Yahweh commanded him to eat bread with quaking and to drink water with trembling as an anticipatory image of the fearful times his fellow Israelites would go through in the last siege of Jerusalem

9

(12:17–20). Lang suggests that his words and actions were designed to attract attention and to get the people to consider repentance; Ezekiel is far removed from the distant, reflective, literary-intellectual prophet that some would have him be.[24] His public sighing was meant to evoke questions. The reason he sighed was because of news from the homeland; he anticipated the great suffering which all of those remaining in Jerusalem would have to go through (21:6–7).

The cords placed on Ezekiel, which prevented him from going out among the people, represent the effect of the constant hostility that the prophet experienced from his audience. While the literal meaning of these references to binding cannot be entirely ruled out, since Jeremiah did suffer similar abuse (Jer. 20:2; 29:26; 37:21), it seems more likely that the public reaction to him virtually drove him out of public areas into a kind of house arrest.[25]

When the prophet clapped his hands and stamped his feet (6:11), he flamboyantly displayed a kind of glee similar to Yahweh's triumphant settling of accounts with his enemies (21:17; 22:13) or Ammon's celebration of the destruction of Jerusalem (25:3, 6). While modern ethical attitudes might favor more restrained images of Yahweh's anger and less glee by the people of God over the destruction of their enemies, the prophet's actions seem well within the parameters of normal doxological responses to Yahweh's judgment in antiquity. The prophet also dramatically set his face toward those against whom he was prophesying (6:2; 13:17; 21:2; 25:2; 28:21; 29:2; 35:2; 38:2; cf. 4:7)[26] In doing so he seems to appropriate a gesture used by the preclassical prophets Balaam (Num. 24:1) and Elisha (2 Kgs. 8:11). His flair for the dramatic has him eating a scroll literally (3:1–3) rather than just swallowing the word of God symbolically (Jer. 15). When he shaves off all his hair in order to demonstrate that some Jerusalemites will be burned by fire, others killed by the sword, and still others sent into exile, he echoes from afar Isaiah, who had seen Assyria as a great razor hired from beyond the Euphrates to shave—that is, defeat completely—the southern kingdom (Isa. 7:20).

THE MESSAGE OF THE BOOK

In sum, Ezekiel, insofar as we can analyze him, was a more or less normal human being with a very important message about judgment and hope at a critical moment of Israel's history. Because of the radical times he embodied a radical message, drawing on deep wells of Israelite tradition and expressing in words and actions his shock at Israel's sin and coming punishment, as well as his hope for a new, more wholesome day when Yahweh's presence would take up residence again in the land. As I have shown, we have extremely limited data on which to construct a biography of the prophet—and much of that data functions to make literary or dramatic points. What we do have is the book of Ezekiel, the product of the prophet himself and disciples, editors, and redactors, which in its own unique way tries to come to terms with the first deportation and the impending second one, and then probes God's gracious future beyond the year 587.

I do not wish to go too far and speak of the "Personality" of the book, though the author(s) certainly used dramatic, priestly, and even outlandish human imagery at times to secure a hearing for a profound priestly diagnosis of Israel and for a soaring picture of future hope. What I hope to offer in the following chapters, instead, is a series of probes into that literary document, to see what it has to say about the following critical issues:

being a prophet (chapter 1);
dramatic actions directed to a nation in need of repentance and headed toward destruction (chapter 2);
the cultic bankruptcy of Jerusalem and its consequences (chapter 3);
the history of Israel as a history requiring judgment (chapter 4);
the disputed doctrines of retribution and repentance (chapter 5);
failed kings and their counterparts among the nations and within Israel, and their roles in the judgmental and restorative actions of Yahweh (chapter 6);
the problems involved with contemporary (chapter 7) and future (chapter 9) enemy nations;
formulas that announce a future beyond judgment (chapter 8);
the saving significance of Yahweh's renewed dwelling in the land (chapter 10).

Thus, this book is not a biography but a literary and theological analysis of a biblical document left by a nearly anonymous and mostly unknown prophet to the community of the faithful. It attempts to take seriously the present shape of the book,[27] to decipher its imagery, to comment on its technical vocabulary, and to relate its several parts to one another. Finally, and unashamedly, it is an appreciative reading of the book, recognizing at once that the book of Ezekiel, like any other theology, has its hermeneutical weaknesses, but that its passionate diagnosis of the incompatibility between the failings of Israel and the potential for its ongoing history also calls into question our assumptions about the inevitable viability of synagogue, church, and society. On the other hand, its nearly unbounded optimism about the radical transformations that can be expected when God dwells with his people has important implications for all heirs of this prophet in the community of the faithful who know that the name of their "city" is—or ought to be—"Yahweh is there."

NOTES

1. Brevard S. Childs, *Old Testament Theology in a Canonical Context*, 125–28.

2. For this division of the disputation speeches into the categories of arrogance and fear see Adrian Graffy, *A Prophet Confronts His People*, 120–23. In my judgment, however, 12:26–28 and 20:32–34 may express arrogance rather than disbelief.

3. See the list of parallels in S. R. Driver, *An Introduction to the Literature of the Old Testament*, 49–50, 145–48, and in Georg Fohrer, *Die Hauptprobleme des Buches Ezechiel*, 144–48. Cf. the discussion in Keith W. Carley, *Ezekiel Among the Prophets*, 62–65; Carley finds the parallels too brief to show clearly the direction of literary influence.

4. Cf. Fohrer, *Hauptprobleme*, 148–54. Walter Zimmerli, *Ezekiel* 1:52, acknowledges the difficulty of detecting the direction of dependency with regard to both H and P. On the latter he remarks: "P drew from the great stream of priestly tradition, from which also the priest-prophet Ezekiel (at an earlier point of time) had also been nourished."

5. The latest study of these dates is provided by Ernst Kutsch, *Die Chronologischen Daten des Ezechielbuches*. I have adopted Kutsch's chronological equivalences in this book. The points of difference between him and other modern commentators (such as Greenberg and Zimmerli) are usually about one year. Such differences, of course, do not affect the type of literary and theological study undertaken in this book.

6. The date in 1:1 refers to June, 569, but it is as yet unexplained. See the discussion in chapter 1 below.

7. Note that Israel and Judah are regarded as sisters in Jer. 3:6–11 and Ezek. 23:1–7 and that there are similarities between the new covenant in Jer. 31:31–34 and Ezek. 36:24–28. Note also the parallel between Jeremiah's metaphorical eating of the divine words (Jer. 15:16) and Ezekiel's literal eating of the scroll in a vision (Ezek. 3:1–2). Cf. the extensive study of this issue by J. W. Miller, *Das Verhältnis Jeremias und Hesekiels sprachlich und theologisch untersucht*.

8. Carley, *Ezekiel Among the Prophets*, 57.

9. The following passages have dates during the final siege: 24:1; 26:1; 29:1; 30:20; 31:1; 32:1, 17.

10. See Walter Zimmerli, "Der Wahrheitserweis Jahwes nach der Botschaft der beiden Exilspropheten."

11. Ernst Vogt, *Untersuchungen zum Buch Ezechiel*, 26–31.

12. Moshe Greenberg, *Ezekiel, 1–20*, 15–16, lists conveniently the passages requiring a Babylonian setting for Ezekiel. See also Carl Gordon Howie, *The Date and Composition of*

Ezekiel, 5–26. A Palestinian locale is defended in the recent commentary by W. H. Brownlee, *Ezekiel 1–19*, xxiii–xxxi.

13. Samuel Terrien, *The Elusive Presence: Toward a New Biblical Theology*, 212–13. Bernhard Duhm's judgment is that: Ezekiel "is completely lacking in poetic inspiration, a man of cold intellect and sober calculation" (cited in Klaus Koch, *The Prophets*, 2:86).

14. See the extensive review of the scholarly discussion in Bernhard Lang, 57–76. W. F. Albright, *From the Stone Age to Christianity*, 325, remarked, "Ezekiel was one of the greatest spiritual figures of all time, in spite of his tendency to psychic abnormality—a tendency which he shares with many other spiritual leaders."

15. A. Klostermann, "Ezechiel. Ein Beitrag zu besserer Würdigung seiner Person und seiner Schrift," 391–439; E. C. Broome, "Ezekiel's Abnormal Personality," 277–92.

16. See the important discussion in Zimmerli, *Ezekiel*, 1:163–68.

17. Robert R. Wilson, *Prophecy and Society in Ancient Israel*, 283.

18. See the insightful critique of E. C. Broome by N. H. Cassem, "Ezekiel's Psychotic Personality: Reservations on the Use of the Couch for Biblical Personalities," 59–70, and by Howie, *Date and Composition*, 69–84.

19. Zimmerli, *Ezekiel*, 1:18.

20. Carley, *Ezekiel Among the Prophets*, 31–34.

21. Lang, *Ezechiel*, 70.

22. Greenberg, *Ezekiel, 1–20*, 102–03. Zimmerli, *Ezekiel*, 1:160, argues against the iterative understanding of the verb *open*.

23. So Lang, *Ezechiel*, 74: "Ezekiel had not only been transplanted into a hostile environment and into a different climatic zone (marshy lowland instead of the [Palestinian] hill country), but he also had to exchange his vocational and social position: far from the temple he could no longer exercise his priestly calling. Finally, he experienced the death of his wife (24:18). In addition, it came as an added burden that Ezekiel, who had been exiled with the pro-Egyptian party, became a warner against revolt and therefore ran into rejection by many of his fellow exiles" (my trans.). Lang views this condition as burdened and pathogenic, but admits it is insufficient to account for Ezekiel's bouts with paralysis and with temporary aphasia. As my discussion indicates, I believe that the claims about paralysis and aphasia are overly literal diagnoses of the prophet's symbolic and dramatic behavior.

24. Lang, *Kein Aufstand in Jerusalem: Die Politik des Propheten Ezechiel*, 170–74.

25. See Zimmerli, *Ezekiel*, 1: 160–61; Greenberg, *Ezekiel, 1–20*, 102.

26. See Carley, *Ezekiel Among the Prophets*, 40–42.

27. The pendulum has swung in studies of Ezekiel, from scholars who ascribed almost the whole of the book to the prophet (Rudolf Smend); to those who denied almost all of the book to him (Gustav Hölscher and Volkmar Herntrich); to mediating commentators like Walter Zimmerli, who ascribed the book to the prophet and his school, both of whom had largely completed their work before the end of the exile; and finally to the recent work of Moshe Greenberg, who is reluctant to deny any line to Ezekiel and even eschews almost all textual emendation. My debts to Zimmerli and Greenberg are both deep and obvious, as will be demonstrated on each of the following pages. While I side more with Greenberg in trying to read the book as holistically as possible (though without his near refusal to emend the text) and in recognizing that apparent unevennesses and "inconsistencies" may have literary functions in the structures devised by the original author(s), I have also profited from Zimmerli's tradition historical studies, his philology, theology, and textual criticism—and occasionally from his contention that this or that paragraph is secondary.

ONE

A PROPHET IN THEIR MIDST

Ezekiel's call narrative keeps expectations to a minimum. No matter how rebellious or disobedient his audiences might be, this narrative affirms that they would at least learn one thing for certain, even if it was the hard way: this disturbing man was a prophet (2:5). Years later, when Jerusalem had fallen and the prophet's message had changed from judgment to hope, the narrator tells us that the people who heard his words still did not follow or obey them. By that time Ezekiel had become something of a sensation, the talk of the town (33:30), valued not only for his positive message but also for the tone of his voice and the quality of the instrumental music to which his prophecy was sung (33:32). What his audiences always ignored, however, early and late, was that the word of Yahweh—whether it announces judgment or salvation—also calls in every case for obedience. Similarly, they failed to see that the hope-filled message delivered by the prophet after the fall of Jerusalem would expose their disobedience even as it ushered in a glorious new day. By happening, this promissory word of Yahweh would also serve, finally, to validate Ezekiel: "They will know that a prophet has been among them" (33:33). To speak a word that would reliably produce results had long been one of the standard characteristics of a true prophet in Israel (cf. Deut. 18:22; Isa. 55:10–11; Jer. 28:9); it kept that function in Ezekiel.

Ezekiel's call to prophesy left no uncertainty about the source of his authority, the mood of his audience, or the tone of his message. Called "mortal" eight times in the call narrative alone, a title which clearly differentiated him from the dazzling references to the deity in chapter 1, and which underscored the unqualified obedience that was unexpected of him, Ezekiel was simply "sent" (2:3, 4; 3:5, 6). Like his Palestinian contemporary Jeremiah, he was to be without fear of opposing words or adamant faces (2:6; 3:9; cf. Jer. 1:8), but unlike Jeremiah, Ezekiel raised no objection to his prophetic call (cf. Jer. 1:6). Almost without exception throughout the book Ezekiel passed on the divine word with no personal comment or elaboration of his own. Ezekiel was sent by Yahweh to speak "my words" (3:4) and to begin his speeches with the common messenger formula, "Thus says Lord Yahweh," mentioned two times in the call narrative (2:4; 3:11) and 126 times in the book all told. The divine title "Lord Yahweh," used in 122 (or 123) of the messenger formulas, 81 times in the formula *n'm 'dny yhwh* concluding a divine speech, and 217 times overall, reminded his audience of God's sovereignty and their own rebellion against it.[1]

In one of his confessions Jeremiah had spoken metaphorically of his acceptance of God's message: "Thy words were found, and I ate them, and thy words became to me a joy and the delight of my heart" (Jer. 15:16). For Ezekiel this metaphor became reality.[2] Yahweh commanded him to eat a scroll so filled with divine words that the writing appeared on both sides of the leather, an unusual procedure in ancient scribal technology. The contents of that scroll were simply "lamentations and moaning and woe" (2:10). Thus, unlike Jeremiah, at least according to the canonical form of the latter's call, Ezekiel was not to both tear down and build up (Jer. 1:10) in the first phase of his ministry. Rather, he was to be at once submissive to the will of Yahweh and adamant—a diamond tougher than flint—against all attempted intimidations. Three times in 3:8-9 God promised him a tougher stance than his audience, perhaps punning on the name Ezekiel itself, which can be translated "God toughens."[3] Success was not to be the criterion of his faithfulness. Three times in the commissioning speech he was reminded that his mission was to go on regardless of whether Israel listened to him (2:5, 7; 3:11). When he actually ate the scroll with its bitter message, it became sweet as honey in his mouth. The reader is left to guess the implication of this surprising turn of events. Was this a divine kindness making the leather easier to swallow and keep down (Greenberg)? Was this an echo of Jeremiah's delight in eating God's words (Zimmerli)? Or was this a sign that any kind of divine communication, even an angry message of judgment, was better than divine silence? Ezekiel's reasons to be joyful were minimal indeed.

His audience was to be "Israel," a holistic term in the book of Ezekiel, almost always referring to the entire people (4:5 is an apparent exception, but see the discussion of 4:4–8 in chapter 2 below). In 2:3 "Israel" connotes both the people back home in Jerusalem as well as the exiles (3:11) among whom the prophet lived. Two different Hebrew verbs—*mārad* and *pāša'*—make the people's rebellious character unmistakably clear, and Ezekiel coins for them a unique critical designation, "rebellious house," whose 15 occurrences are scattered throughout the entire book (2:5–8; 3:9, 26–27; 12:2, 3, 9, 25; 17:12; 24:3; 44:6). His opponents are characterized as nettles, thorns, and scorpions (2:6), and their stubbornness takes shape in their tough brows and their hard hearts (3:7). They and their parents (2:3) are rebels in God's eyes, according to Ezekiel. He demonstrates this theme of total corruption throughout Israelite history and frequently returns to it (e.g., chs. 16, 20). Still, this audience is to be considered by Ezekiel as "your people," "the house of Israel" (5 times in the first three chapters and 83 times throughout the book), people who speak the prophet's own language (3:5–6). But this linguistic advantage is contradicted by the people's disposition: "The whole house of Israel refuses to listen to you [Ezekiel] because they refuse to listen to me [Yahweh]" (3:7). It would have been easier for Ezekiel to have been sent on a foreign mission, because an alien nation would at least have listened (3:6). We shall have other occasions later to note similar references to the moral and spiritual superiority of the nations to Israel in the book of Ezekiel.

THE VISION BEFORE THE COMMISSION

The divine monologue in the commissioning speech (2:1–3:11) is preceded by a sensational theophany in chapter 1 that implies a great deal about Ezekiel's authority and even the content of his message. Its complicated symbolism makes it quite forbidding, at first, to the modern reader, but this symbolism and the traditions it represents tell us much about the man Ezekiel.

The divine vision began with the opening of the heavens (1:1) and continued with the description of a stormy wind from the north, replete with clouds, fire, and brightness. From the midst of the storm emerged four living beings (animals), who, though generally human in shape, had four wings and four faces. They apparently stood upright, like humans rather than animals, but a calf's foot was at the end of each leg and human hands were under their wings. Since each animal faced in a different direction, the throne chariot could move toward each of the four compass points by going straight forward, with no need for the animals to turn or reverse themselves. Each animal had four faces: a human face in the front, a lion face on the right, a bull on the left, and an eagle toward the rear. The "spirit" associated with the animals determined which way they would go. Burning coals, fiery torches, and lightning characterized the appearance of the animals.

Four wheels made of chrysolite were paired with these animals; the movements of animals and wheels, in fact, were always in tandem, since the spirit of the animals was also in the wheels. The design of the wheels was a "wheel within a wheel," and the brows, or rims, of the wheels were covered with eyes (vv. 15–21).

Over the heads of the animals was a plate, called the firmament or the sky, that appeared to be made of ice. Beneath the sky plate each animal extended a wing toward a wing of the animal on either side of it, but used its other set of wings to cover its body. The movement of their wings produced a loud noise that was comparable to the breakers of the sea, the voice of the Almighty (traditional translation; Hebrew *Shadday*), or the sound of an army (vv. 22–24).

Above the sky plate was something that looked like a throne made of lapis lazuli.[4] Seated on the throne was someone who resembled a composite human being. From what seemed to be the region of his hips and upward he seemed to be made of electrum, while from his hips downward he seemed to be composed of fire. All around him was a glowing radiance, much like a rainbow. The person represented the glory of Yahweh, and Ezekiel fell on his face at the sight (vv. 25–28).

A similar vision is recorded in Ezekiel 10, and the principal differences between the two accounts will be noted in the discussion of chapters 8–11. The description of the call vision above glosses over the repetitious character of the biblical account and a number of textual, grammatical, and lexical difficulties better treated in a commentary. Moving beyond these technical details, the interpreter is often hard pressed to understand how each part of the vision fits into a coherent whole. While Greenberg treats chapter 1 as an original unit, with the exception of verse 14 and

17

occasional words elsewhere, Zimmerli reconstructs a much shorter and more consistent account composed of verses 1, 3b, 4a, 5–6, 11b–13, 22, 26–28.[5] The most serious question about the integrity of the chapter deals with the account of the wheels. It is not clear how we are to conceive the connection of the wheels to the animals in general and to the legs in particular, and Othmar Keel has argued, convincingly in my judgment, that the wheels represent a shift from the basic idea of the vision.[6] The interpretation of the pictorial images in the following paragraphs will honor his literary critical judgment, though the final description of the impact of the chapter and its significance for Ezekiel's call will recognize that someone, presumably early in the tradition history of the book, found it appropriate to add wheels to the visionary scenery.

A few modern readers have interpreted the vision as if it were not a symbolic divine encounter at all, but merely the sighting of a space vehicle.[7] In addition to lacking any historical credibility, such bizarre interpretations miss the significance of this chapter for Ezekiel's self-understanding. At least two alternate and more reliable methodological approaches, based on archaeological and literary studies, are possible today. They unlock the code of the vision and allow the modern reader to experience a greater measure of its power.

COMPARISON WITH ANCIENT NEAR EASTERN ART

Artistic materials relevant for understanding the imagery of this chapter are provided by monumental remains discovered by modern excavators and by glyptic art, the minute engravings on gems used as cylinder seals. Even a casual perusal of these data makes clear that Ezekiel employed artistic images from his contemporary world, but a more careful analysis helps to clarify the content and significance of what he saw.[8]

Sometimes a deity in ancient Near Eastern art is depicted as seated on a throne that is located on a kind of plate resting on the backs of animals (Divine Depiction A; see Figure 1). The plate seems to serve a separative function, like the firmament in Genesis 1:6–7, and so we call it a sky plate. Figure 1 is a drawing of a basalt sculpture found at Carchemish and dating to the first half of the first millennium BCE. It shows two lions held by a bird-headed creature. Above the lions is a sky plate (not easily seen in the drawing), on which rests a throne supporting a bearded

Figure 1

deity. While there are similarities between Divine Depiction A and Ezekiel 1, there are also striking differences. There are only two animals in this depiction, and they do not have a human shape. In addition, they lack the four wings and the multiple faces of Ezekiel's vision.

An alternate iconographic tradition is represented by Figure 2 (Divine Depiction B). The deity in this Achaemenid (Persian) seal is the winged figure at the top, the upper portion of whose body differs from the lower portion. The deity's body ends in a kind of feathery tail which might correspond to the flames of fire that comprise the lower half of the divine figure in Ezekiel's vision. The wings projecting from the deity probably symbolize the sky or heaven, in which the god is thought to dwell.[9] Holding up the sky are two "sky-bearers," who have human faces and stand erect as humans do, but they also have four wings and their hind legs end

19

Figure 2

in calves' feet. These "sky-bearers" are common features of ancient art from the fifteenth century on, and from the eighth to the sixth centuries they usually have four wings.

Figure 3 is a depiction of the Egyptian goddess Hathor with three identical faces on her one head—or four, if the artist conceived of the goddess having a face directly opposite the one staring at the viewer. Keel notes that some sky-bearers have double (human) faces, which fits their additional function as guards of heaven who protect the holy regions from the profane.[10] Figure 4 shows three views of pairs of sky-bearers standing alongside a mountain god. In the top picture the sky-bearers have lion heads, in the middle frame oxen heads, and in the bottom panel eagle heads, precisely the three animal faces represented in Ezekiel's vision. Although the top of each drawing is not preserved, it is logical to suppose

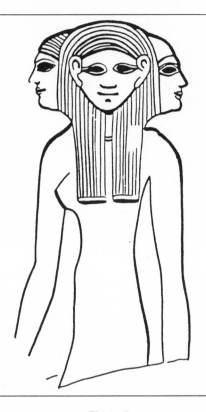

Figure 3

that the mountain deity who is in the center of the panel holds up the sun god while the sky-bearers support the wings of heaven.

Ezekiel's call vision in chapter 1 is a combination of what we have called Divine Depictions A and B. On the one hand, it contains an artistic sequence from bottom to top of animals, sky plate, throne, and an enthroned deity. But the animals Ezekiel describes have characteristics of sky-bearers—four wings and multiple animal faces. In addition to supporting the sky plate with their heads (vv. 22, 25), the animals may represent an attempt to defend Yahweh against contamination by contact with an unclean land (cf. 4:13). Yahweh's power is reflected in the majestic animal faces—eagle, lion, and bull—of his attendants. The symbolic winged sky held up by the sky-bearers in Divine Depiction B, however, has been replaced by a sky plate characteristic of Divine Depiction A.

Abb. 183

Abb. 184

Figure 4

22

Thus Yahweh dwells above the sky plate, not within the heavens as our pictures of the sky-bearers would suggest. The sky plate represents the boundary between the realm of creation and the holy and unapproachable sphere of God; the animals' wings and their four faces represent, among other things, God's omnipresence. Interestingly enough, the vision of chapter 1 has no iconographic ties to Jerusalem. The point of the vision, therefore, is not that Yahweh has now moved from Jerusalem to Babylon—though such a line of interpretation is appropriate to chapter 10—but that the God who rules over all and resides in heaven above the sky plate, or firmament, is also now present in Babylon.

The wheels in the present form of the call vision add a feeling of mobility to the whole account. Figure 5 shows a divine chariot from the Akkadian period (2300 BCE). The weather god wields a whip from a four-wheeled chariot drawn by a winged animal. The four wheels correspond to the number of wheels in Ezekiel 1. But the prophet's vision has God seated on a throne that is above the sky plate, and this means that the wheels would represent an empty chariot. A stela from Van in the region of Urartu, dating to 800-750 BCE, contains a drawing of just such an empty divine chariot.[11] Beneath the horses pulling the chariot lie two slain soldiers, silent testimony to the power of the unseen deity. The "wheels within wheels" in Ezekiel may represent an interpretation of the concentric circles formed by a heavy rim and the hub and other parts of ancient wheels.[12] The eyes on the rims presumably connote the all-seeing charac-

Figure 5

ter of the omnipresent deity, though their location on the rims is not readily explained. Perhaps the very notion of eyes represents a misunderstanding of nails that were driven into the rims of ancient chariot wheels to give
them added strength. Egyptian Bes figures were often inlaid with copper
nails, but certain late examples of this figure have eyes replacing the
nails.[13]

THE TRADITIONS IN THE VISION

While the preceding paragraphs have dealt with the connotations of
the visual images of Ezekiel 1, the vision itself is described in words that for
the most part have a long tradition of use in the Bible and a predictable
set of connotations. The connections between the traditional theophanies
and Ezekiel 1 are easily demonstrated. Yahweh was accompanied in the
theophanies by ten thousands of holy ones and flaming fire (Deut. 33:2) or
by brightness and earthquake (Hab. 3:4–6) in his march from his southern mountain. The psalmist furthermore proclaims:

Clouds and thick darkness are round about him;
   righteousness and justice are the foundation of his throne.
Fire goes before him,
   and burns up his adversaries round about.
His lightnings lighten the world;
   the earth sees and trembles.
The mountains melt like wax before the Lord,
   before the Lord of all the earth (97:2–5).

A survey of the words used to describe the divine theophany in Ezekiel 1
suggests two dominant emphases: the authentically divine character of
what Ezekiel saw and the real presence of this divine being in Babylon.

God Appeared

The vocabulary makes unmistakably clear that it was really the all-
powerful God who appeared to Ezekiel. As we saw in the quotation from
Psalm 97, aspects of the storm are common in theophanies. In Ezekiel 1
we read of a stormy wind,[14] a great cloud, and fire (vv. 4, 27), and of lightning, torches, and burning coals of fire (v. 13). Brightness (vv. 4, 13, 27,

28) is all around, comparable to that of a rainbow on a rainy day (v. 28), in addition to shining metal, such as electrum (vv. 4, 27) or burnished bronze (v. 7). Also present are precious stones—wheels made of chrysolite (v. 16) and a throne of lapis lazuli (v. 26). The firmament or plate that separates the deity from the profane realm is made of awe-inspiring ice (v. 22). The firmament in the Psalms declares God's glory (Ps. 19:1) and is his dwelling place (Ps. 150:1). In Exodus 24:10 there is a pavement of lapis lazuli, clear as the sky, under the feet of Yahweh.

The faces of the animals are those of a human, the highest of God's creatures; a bull, the king of domestic animals; a lion, king of the wild animals; and an eagle, supreme among the birds. Presumably only the finest of animals are appropriate for the faces of the sky-bearers, above whom rests Yahweh's throne. The cherubim of Solomon's temple, on which Yahweh was invisibly enthroned, had two wings, one that was stretched out to touch the wing of the other cherub and another to touch the wall of the Holy of Holies. In Isaiah's call vision (Isa. 6) the seraphim had six wings—two to cover their faces, two to cover their feet (or genitals), and two for flying. Ezekiel's sky-bearers have four wings—two for flying and two for covering their bodies in modesty (vv. 11, 23). When these wings move in flying they give off awe-inspiring noise like that of ocean breakers ("many waters"), an army in combat, or even the deity (Shadday) himself (v. 24). When Ezekiel resumes the account of the vision after the commissioning speech, he notes that the sound of the wings and the wheels was like that of a great earthquake (3:12–13; cf. Isa. 29:6).

In the verses describing the throne and the deity, the prophet uses measured, careful speech. He does not directly see a throne, God's hips, or even a rainbow, but only the likeness (4 times) or the appearance (7 times) of these phenomena. This resistance shows his priestly awe in the presence of the reality of God. What appeared to him was not just the glory of Yahweh, but the "appearance of the likeness of the glory of Yahweh" (v. 28; cf. 3:12, 23).[15] The reference to the glory of Yahweh, of course, makes explicit what all the details of the vision underscore in their own connotative ways. The opening line of the vision account shows that it was the deity whom Ezekiel saw. The event started when "the heavens opened," a term not used before in Scripture though fairly common in disclosures of God in the New Testament (e.g., Matt. 3:16; Acts 7:56). In Acts the opened heavens provide an opportunity for Stephen to gaze into God's dwelling place, but in Ezekiel they make possible the departure of God's throne chariot from its celestial home. After noting the opening of the heavens, the prophet adds, "I saw visions of God" (cf. 8:3, 40:2).[16] These explicit identifications of what he saw at the beginning (visions of God) and ending (glory of Yahweh) of the vision report form a literary inclusion (envelope construction) that ties the whole together. Ezekiel reacted to this divine appearance in the only appropriate way: he fell on his face, as he also did at a number of subsequent divine appearances (3:23; 9:8; 43:3; 44:4).

God's Presence in Babylon

The prophet Ezekiel leaves no doubt that what he had seen was the God of Israel in all his divine reality, but a second implication of the visionary language was that he had seem him *here*, in the land of Babylon. The hand of Yahweh was upon him in the land of Chaldeans (the Aramaic peoples in control of the Neobabylonian empire), by the river Chebar, a canal near the city of Nippur where the exiles had settled.[17] The Massoretic Text (3:22) adds that it was precisely "there" that the divine hand settled on him, though the adverb *there* is absent from the ancient Greek translation called the Septuagint.

Reinforcing this second theme of God's presence in Babylon is the motif of mobility as represented, for example, by the four faces of the animals. Each of the four compass points was straight ahead for one of the living creatures, so that the group could head off in a new direction without turning. This freedom of movement is echoed by the various kinds of propulsion referred to in the vision. The animals had wings and legs, and rolling along beside them were wheels. The animals and wheels could proceed along the ground, or they could rise up in the air. The directing force in the animals and the coordinating power between them and the wheels resided in the "spirit" (vv. 12, 20, 21), a word meaning something like "inner will" in this chapter, but with connotations of divine origin and a relationship to the glory of Yahweh.

Through myriad mental images and through the colors and sounds of Israel's theophanic tradition, the prophet was shown that the one who called him was the God of Isreal now present in far-off Babylon. This vision illustrates what I have termed elsewhere the faithfulness and freedom inherent in Ezekiel's doctrine of God.[18] The new combination of images and words makes evident that Yahweh is not limited to heaven, to the Jerusalem temple, or even to the land of Israel, but that he, in all the fullness of his divine majesty, is available to the prophet and to the exilic people. Ezekiel's authority comes from this awesome and awe-inspiring God. But this God outdoes his appearances in any previous call narratives, such as those of Moses, Isaiah, and Jeremiah. The prophet Ezekiel was faced with a most difficult task in a foreign land and with a rebellious people, who were tough-browed and hard-hearted, and who might question the ability of Yahweh to function effectively in Babylon at all. Yahweh had chosen, however, to become a sanctuary to them in a small way (or for a little while) in the country to which they had been exiled (11:16). This reuse and reapplication of old theophanic traditions to meet the needs of a new situation is what I mean by saying that Ezekiel's God is faithful and free.

I find it very difficult to agree with Greenberg's assessment that the meaning of the theophanies in chapters 1 and 3 was for the prophet alone.[19] However private Ezekiel's reception of the vision may have been, he did record and publish it and connected it indissolubly to the divine call speech in chapters 2–3. In fact, Greenberg's position seems to run counter to the holistic approach to the book he displays elsewhere so magnificently. The interpreter's task is not to seek what the vision might have meant in a putative context other than that of the book, but to uncover the meaning it has in the only context that we know for certain, that of the book itself.

Zimmerli has shown that there are two types of call narrative in the Bible. One of them places almost all emphasis on the divine speech (Moses, Jeremiah), while the second has the speech connected to a throne vision (1 Kgs. 22; Isa. 6).[20] Ezekiel's call narrative is of the latter type, though with clear connections to the call of Jeremiah as well. Ezekiel's elaborate development of this call narrative—both in the vision itself and in the commissioning speech—exceeds anything before him in length and complexity. This expansive literary characteristic is paralleled elsewhere by his elaborate and repetitive development of the theme "The end has come" in chapter 7, taken from Amos (8:2), and the theme of Israel as Yahweh's unfaithful wife in chapters 16 and 23, taken from Hosea and Jeremiah.

The awestruck prophet was raised to his feet by a divine word and by the spirit (2:1–2), a divine force apparently related to that same spirit that gave direction and coordination to the living animals and the wheels. After the commissioning speech it was this spirit (3:12) that took him back to the exilic community where he sat, dumbfounded and overwhelmed, for seven days (cf. Saul/Paul, after his vision on the road to Damascus, Acts 9:8–9). Ezekiel's distraught state once more reminds the reader that the prophet had really seen God, and had seen him right there in Babylon. Abraham Heschel proposes that Ezekiel's bitterness and rage (3:14) reflected God's own feelings toward Israel,[21] though Greenberg notes that these emotions might just as well also express his own distress over his dismal, thankless, and dangerous task. At about the time of his call, 13 June, 594/593 (1:2),[22] the community back in Judah was engaged in foolish conspiracies with the surrounding countries of Edom, Moab, Ammon, Tyre, and Sidon in an endeavor to avoid recognizing the divinely planned rule of Nebuchadrezzar (Jer.27). Ezekiel's "Thus says Lord Yahweh" exposes the people's manifest guilt; and, through word and deed (see chapter 2 below), Ezekiel announces Yahweh's inevitable and unremitting siege of Jerusalem. Whether the people would hear or refuse to hear—and the book reports mercilessly that the prophet's audience followed the second option—the words of 1:1–3:15 make clear that a properly commissioned prophet had indeed been in their midst.

Called to Be a Watchman[23]

Joined to the report of Ezekiel's call vision is another paragraph giving him divine designation as a watchman (3:16–21).[24] This passage is duplicated to a degree by a much longer paragraph in 33:1–9. Many scholars have found the second location to be the original one, since the content of the verses seems to them more appropriate in the context of the fall of Jerusalem, which is reported in 33:21–22.[25] Eichrodt believes that Ezekiel's activity in this later period was aimed entirely at individuals; he and Von Rad saw in it pastoral functions, the cure of souls.[26] Did the prophet become at some point in his life a pastor to individuals?

Close comparison of the structure of 3:16–21 and 33:1–9 and careful attention to the literary context of each passage offer new possibilities for interpreting these two pericopes. In 3:16–21 a chronological notice puts this "second call" seven days after the first, suggesting that it is a modification or explication of the previous call narrative. The word of Yahweh in 3:16–21 is addressed privately to the prophet, whereas in 33:1–9 the words about the watchman are to be proclaimed to the whole people (vv. 2, 4). The latter context is dominated by the question about the possibility of repentance and change for a people overwhelmed by the power of their sins (33:10–20). In sum: The first watchman paragraph, in chapter 3, is linked to the prophet's call and is a private message to him; the second paragraph, in chapter 33, is linked to the question of forgiveness and is part of the prophet's public message. Rather than conceding that the watchman theme is original in chapter 33 and secondary and anachronistic in chapter 3, I propose to interpret each in its present context in order to see how this theme defines the role of Ezekiel in the present redaction of the book.

The Watchman in Chapter 3

The following series of possible actions by the people and possible responses by the watchman are discussed in chapter 3:

Situation A. God sentences the wicked to death, and the watchman *does not* issue a warning. The wicked will die because of iniquity, and the prophet will be held responsible for their death (v. 18).

Situation B. God sentences the wicked to death, and the watchman *does* issue a warning. The unrepentant wicked will still die because of iniquity, but the watchman's life will be spared (v. 19).

Situation C. Righteous persons who backslide and who are *not* warned by the watchman die when God puts a stumbling block before them, and God holds the watchman responsible for this loss of life (v. 20).

Situation D. When righteous persons who are about to backslide *are* warned by the watchman, they do not backslide, and both they and the watchman save their lives (v. 21)

These four alternative scenarios in chapter 3 define and limit what was intended by Ezekiel's call to be a prophet, and they provide negative and positive motivations for the prophet to act. Ezekiel was called to give a warning to the people, regardless of whether his message would be heeded. In fact, the watchman paragraph in chapter 3 does not envisage possible change among the wicked, though the watchman's intervention in situation D, between the temptation of the righteous and their actual sinning, can lead to the sparing of life. Ezekiel's faithful giving of a warning would be motivated negatively by the fear of capital punishment if he failed in this calling (situations A and C), and positively by the hope of saving his own life (situations B and D) and by the opportunity to prevent righteous persons from falling (situation D). The watchman warns the entire nation, but the response to him is described in terms of what individuals do.[27] Hence a "pastoral" or individualistic interpretation of the office of watchman is a misunderstanding.

The Watchman in Chapter 33

The use of the watchman motif in chapter 3 contrasts dramatically with the parallel account in chapter 33, where the overall theme is God's desire for the people's repentance (v. 11). The chapter begins with a parable: A nation faced with divine attack picks a watchman, who is to issue proper warnings on his trumpet to the entire people. The possible actions by the people and responses by the watchman can be described as follows:

> *Situation B.* Persons who have not taken proper precautions when they are warned will fall by the sword, and the responsibility will be solely their own (vv. 2–5a).
>
> *Situation E.* If such persons take proper precautions, their lives will be spared (v. 5b).
>
> *Situation A.* If the watchman does not give a trumpet warning, the people will parish, and God will hold the watchman responsible (v. 6).

Verses 7–9 (see what was said about situations A and B under ch. 3 above) apply the parable about the secular watchman to the prophet, though, remarkably, Yahweh is identified as the one who selects the watchman. Thus Yahweh, who is the one bringing the military attack on Israel, is the same one who wants the prophet to give a warning about the impending judgment. This illustrates that Yahweh does not desire the death of the wicked, but only that they turn from their wicked ways and live (v. 11). Situation E, in verse 5, stands as a clear contradiction to the people's complaint in verse 10 that their sins were so onerous that they simply could not live. Rather, all those who heed the warning will save their lives. Since Ezekiel tells the people (v. 2) that Yahweh will send a watchman to warn of his own ominous approach, and since that warning when heeded leads to life, the watchman motif in chapter 33 serves to prove that God always desires the repentance of his people. The people need not despair over their guilt or their sense of powerlessness.

A Prophet in Their Midst

The Watchman Reconsidered

This line of interpretation notes the relationship of the watchman pericope to the context in two quite different chapters, distinguishes between the public and the private nature of the paragraphs, and takes account of the differences in detail between the two passages. It permits a reading of the book that makes obsolete the resort to textual surgery in chapter 3 to remove the account of the watchman. The response of the whole people in 3:17–21 and in 33:4–9 is described in terms of individuals only in order to clarify the principle of accountability, not to suggest the emergence of individualism with Ezekiel. Throughout both passages the prophet is to be a watchman for the house of Israel (3:17; 33:7), and he is to warn "them" (3:17; 33:3, 7) about God's impending judgment. In chapter 33, for example, the city's watchman does not give a separate trumpet warning to each individual. Whoever wrote, or added, these paragraphs has given additional nuance and subtlety to the portrait of Ezekiel and his theology at two stages of his life—at the time of his call and at a time well on into the exilic period.

SUMMARY

The call narrative, as we have seen, indicates that Ezekiel was to hand on obediently to the people whatever message was revealed to him, a message characterized as lamentation, mourning, and woe. The call narrative warns of the people's fierce resistance to any idea of change and indicates that the success of the prophet would not depend on the receptivity of the people. The watchman paragraph in 3:16–21 limits the prophetic calling to the giving of a warning about God's oncoming assault on the city. Theoretically this warning could be met either with change and repentance ("they would hear") or a decision not to change ("they would refuse to hear," rebellious house that they were). The task of warning might indeed appear to be dismal, thankless, and even dangerous, but, adds the watchman paragraph in chapter 3, carrying it out would result in the prophet's own deliverance (vv. 19, 21). In addition, some righteous persons, tempted to backslide, might even be spared from actual sinning, thanks to a timely warning by the watchman/prophet.

31

Though the watchman paragraph in 3:16–21 offers no hope that any wicked person would change, situations A and B suggest that the implicit reason for giving a warning is to subvert the need for the onrushing judgment of God. The phrase "whether they hear or refuse to hear" (2:5, 7; 3:11, 27) prepares the reader for the news that the people will refuse to hear throughout chapters 1–24. But the hypothetical notion that some might in fact hear provides a theological "germ" (Greenberg) that could grow elsewhere into calls for repentance and conversion. Nevertheless, the deafening silence about the conversion of the wicked in 3:17–19 shows that for now all the prophet/watchman can expect realistically is that the people will miss their great opportunity. But they will also come to know through this whole experience that a prophet has been in their midst.

NOTES

1. For this interpretation of the double divine names see Greenberg, *Ezekiel*, 1–20, 64–65. The statistics are taken from L.J. McGregor, *The Greek Text of Ezekiel*, 60–61, 219–21, and Zimmerli, *Ezekiel*, 2: 556. McGregor believes that the two divine names were rendered in the original LXX as *kurios* and *yhwh*. When later revisers replaced *yhwh* in the Greek text of Ezekiel and other books of the LXX, they were puzzled by the sequence *kurios yhwh* and resolved it in a variety of ways, one of which was a single use of *kurios*. The presence of *kurios* alone in the LXX, therefore, does not legitimate the deletion of '*dny* from the Hebrew Bible (contra *BHS*).

2. Zimmerli, *Ezekiel*, 1:136, notes a series of similar realistic understandings of metaphors: 4:3, 4–8; 5:1–2; 37:1–14; and 47:1–12.

3. Greenberg, *Ezekiel, 1–20*, 69.

4. Most English translations have "sapphire," a transliteration of the Hebrew word. But that word refers in fact to lapis lazuli, a semiprecious stone imported from northern Afghanistan, which was common in Egyptian and Mesopotamian jewelry and other artwork. A king from the Isin Larsa period made a throne for his god partly of lapis lazuli. See Othmar Keel, *Jahwe-Visionen und Siegelkunst*: 255–60.

5. Zimmerli, *Ezekiel*, 1: 100–06. His analysis is actually much more complicated since he also considers parts of many of these verses to be secondary. See also C.B. Houk, "A Statistical Linguistic Study of Ezekiel 1:4–3:11," 83.

6. Keel, *Jahwe-Visionen*, 144, 180–88. But T.N.D. Mettinger, *The Dethronement of Sabaoth*, 105, argues for the originality of the wheels because of the close connection between the cloud and the chariot in a number of biblical texts. According to W. Boyd Barrick, "The Straight-Legged Cherubim of Ezekiel's Inaugural Vision (Ezekiel 1:7a)," 550, the addition of wheels to the account also led to the depiction of the living creatures' legs as "straight," since they were no longer used for purposes of locomotion.

7. Erich von Däniken, *Chariots of the Gods?*, 54, remarks: "To our present way of thinking what he saw was one of those special vehicles the Americans use in the desert and swamp terrain"; cf. p. 56: "[The 'gods'] took him with them in their vehicle."

8. Much of the following material is drawn from Keel, though with differences in detail. Keel's method of interpreting texts in the context of ancient art may be sampled in English in his *The Symbolism of the Biblical World*.

9. Mettinger, *The Dethronement*, 104 fig. 5, cites an analogous depiction of the god Ashur. His head and torso are human in form, but his lower parts consist of flames of fire.

10. Keel, *Jahwe-Visionen*, 233–34.

11. See Keel, *Jahwe-Visionen*, 186–87 fig. 129.

12. See Keel, *Jahwe-Visionen*, 266 figs. 191, 192.

13. See Keel, *Jahwe-Visionen*, 270 figs. 193, 194.

14. Cf. Job 38:1; 40:6; Isa. 29:6; Jer. 23:19; 30:23; Zech, 9:14.

15. Mettinger, *The Dethronement*, 106–09, suggests that the term *glory* has assumed spatially the position occupied by Yahweh Sabaoth in older theology, since the latter term had come to represent and guarantee God's presence in and protection of Jerusalem.

16. The common properties of the three visions in which Ezekiel views the glory of Yahweh are spelled out by H. Van Dyke Parunak, "The Literary Architecture of Ezekiel's *Mar'ôt 'Elōhîm*."

17. Ernst Vogt, "Der Nehar Kebar: Ez 1."

18. *Israel in Exile*, 69–96.

19. Greenberg, *Ezekiel, 1–20*, 80–81.

20. Zimmerli, *Ezekiel*, 1: 108–10.

21. A.J. Heschel, *The Prophets*, ch. 18.

22. Ernst Kutsch, *Die Chronologischen Daten des Ezechielbuches*, 71. The fourth month is inferred from the preceding verse. The date in v. 1, June, 569, is unexplained. According to Kutsch, 54, the throne chariot vision of ch. 1 should be dated to 569, and was originally independent from the commission in chs. 2–3. The throne chariot vision, then, marks the conclusion of the activity of the prophet. I seriously doubt whether ch. 1 should be separated from chs. 2-3. Zimmerli, *Ezekiel*, 1: 114, believes the date in v. 1 is a gloss meant to harmonize the other dates to the duration of the exile or to the age of the prophet. Carl Gordon Howie, *The Date and Composition of Ezekiel*, 41, following Spiegel and Albright, thought the date referred to the time when the oracles were published. Other conjectures are discussed in W.H. Brownlee, *Ezekiel 1–19*, 3–4.

23. My understanding of this concept has been greatly influenced by Greenberg, *Ezekiel, 1–20*, 87–97.

24. Jeremiah also refers to God's appointing prophetic watchmen whose warnings about impending disaster were met with rejection (Jer. 6:17).

25. Walter Eichrodt, *Ezekiel*, 444, suggests that the passage in ch. 33 originally consisted of 33:1–9 and 3:20–21, but in the course of adding the watchman idea to ch. 3, the equivalent of 3:20–21 was lost from its original context. Georg Fohrer, *Ezekiel*, 23, 184, holds that the equivalent of 3:16b–21 originally followed 33:1–6. 3:16b–21 was added in its present position to make Ezekiel a watchman and pastor from the beginning, and 33:7–9 later replaced 3:16b–21 in ch. 33 in order to get rid of the idea that the righteous might need to be warned. Zimmerli, *Ezekiel*, 1:71, 143, proposes that 33:1–9 is a secondary insertion and that it and ch. 18 are the source of 3:16b–21, which was added by the final redactors of the book.

26. See Donald E. Gowan, *Ezekiel*, 21–24.

27. Greenberg, *Ezekiel, 1–20*, 95.

TWO

EZEKIEL WILL BE A
SIGN FOR YOU

Signs in the Bible are designed to help people know and believe in Yahweh.[1] The Deuteronomist, for example, writes: "Has any god ever attempted to go and take a nation for himself from the midst of another nation, by trials, by signs, by wonders, and by war, by a mighty hand and an outstretched arm, and by great terrors, according to all that the Lord your God did for you in Egypt before your eyes? To you it was shown, that you might know that the Lord is God" (Deut. 4:34–35). The signs referred to here are the great and miraculous deeds of Yahweh against Pharaoh and at the exodus from Egypt, events of the past which were made contemporary with the audience either by this sermonic recital or by cultic drama.

For the prophets signs often served to legitimate their words. Even seemingly miraculous signs, of course, were not to be believed if the message of the prophet who announced them contradicted the faith of Israel (Deut. 13:1–3). But when Isaiah offered a sign to King Ahaz, and urged him to ask for something as marvelous as lightning or an earthquake (Isa. 7:11), the king's refusal to believe was met with prophetic anger and the deliverance of the ominous Immanuel sign. The child soon to be born would have a name meaning "God is with us," a sign with predominantly negative connotations in its context (7:17–25; 8:5–8).

While many signs have a miraculous character, their symbolism does not necessarily have much to do with the message that is being conveyed.

Isaiah told Hezekiah, for example, that the shadow on his sundial would turn back ten steps, but this sign actually indicated that the King would recover from his serious illness and live an additional fifteen years (Isa. 38:8). In contrast, the symbolic or dramatic sign actions of the prophets are usually materially related to the events they symbolize. The prophet Ahijah tore his garment into twelve pieces and gave ten of them to Jeroboam as a sign that he would become king over the ten northern tribes (1 Kgs. 11:29–31). Zedekiah, a "false" prophet, made iron horns to illustrate or actualize an accompanying divine oracle to Ahab: "With these you shall push the Syrians until they are destroyed" (1 Kgs. 22:11). At the divine command Isaiah walked naked and barefoot for three years as a sign that the king of Assyria could carry off the Egyptians and Ethiopians, "naked and barefoot, with buttocks uncovered" (Isa. 20:2–4). What happens symbolically in the sign act is parallel to what is proclaimed through words.

The prophetic sign actions make clear that the words of the prophets will lead to real events. Zimmerli observes that the prophet guarantees the coming event by accomplishing a symbolic action.[2] While the carrying out of the sign action is not always reported in Ezekiel, since the accounts are cast as words of Yahweh to the prophet, it seems reasonable to hold that they were in fact always carried out in some fashion, and that without this action the sign act would be meaningless.

Sign actions in Ezekiel are really only alternate forms of the prophetic word. They are not to be confused with sympathetic magic since their authority is clearly that of the divine word. By actualizing that word and by dramatically anticipating the event it proclaims, the symbolic actions lend credibility and urgency to the prophetic message. A recent scholar compared them to street theater, so familiar from modern social justice movements.[3] One might even assert that in the symbolic actions the medium has become the message.

Biblical readers throughout the ages have been perplexed about whether biographical conclusions can be drawn from such symbolic actions. Discussions of Hosea's relationship to Gomer have been so voluminous that it took a recent author two hundred pages just to report on the history of this investigation.[4] An emphasis on the character of the symbolic actions as alternate forms of the divine word has correctly stymied such biographical quests in recent years and discouraged psychological probings into Ezekiel's mental stability. The dramatic and radical characteristics of these events, however, are surely not without significance for understanding the setting of the prophet. Twelve such events are reported for Ezekiel, slightly more than for his contemporary Jeremiah and far surpassing the number in earlier prophecy.[5] The number of these sign actions and their concentration during the period prior to the fall of Jerusalem[6] indicate the strong resistance to the prophet's message among his rebellious audience. Reports of his suffering and anguish also suggest the empathetic involvement of the prophet with his message. The sign is not some extraneous, miraculous happening, nor merely an action related in a direct way to the proclaimed word. In Ezekiel, perhaps more than in any other prophet, the prophet himself is the sign.

EZEKIEL'S REACTION TO HIS WIFE'S DEATH

Nowhere is the prophet more clearly a sign than in 24: 15–24. The outline of this symbolic action is typical, although many of the other accounts lack one or more of the following parts:

command to carry out a symbolic action (vv. 15–17);
report of the carrying out of the action (v. 18);
request by the audience for an explanation of the sign act (v. 19);
explanation of the sign action in the form of a divine oracle (vv. 20–24).

The account begins with God's announcement that he will take away in sudden death the prophet's wife, who is described as "the delight of your eyes." The prophet's reaction is to be stoic—no lamenting, no crying, no tears. Instead of letting his hair hang loose in mourning, he is to put on his usual turban and don his shoes. He is not to cover his head down to his upper lip (an ancient custom designed to make the mourner unrecognizable to the returning ghost?) nor eat the usual meals of lamentation. His only word is to be a groaning in deathly stiffness. After the prophet's wife had died on one evening, Ezekiel carries out the suggested actions the next morning.

Ezekiel's reactions resemble in some ways those of Jeremiah. Though the latter was forbidden to marry at all, he too was commanded not to participate in mourning rites for others (Jer. 16:5). The reason for this prohibition is not clear. In part it seems to symbolize that many of those killed will lie permanently unburied (Jer. 16:4), but it also seems to be an appropriate response to the righteous judgment God is exercising in these killings and the unbelievable extent of the catastrophe itself (16:9). In withdrawing from normal life, Jeremiah reminds his audience that Yahweh had withdrawn from the life of his people.

The request of the audience for an interpretation is a characteristic feature in some of the symbolic actions in Ezekiel (cf. 12:9; 21:7; 37:18). In his explanation the prophet relates his action very closely to the divine word; there is no inherent magical importance in the symbolic action. The divine taking of the prophet's wife is compared to God's defiling of his own sanctuary, identified as "your [plural] proud stronghold" and "the delight of your eyes and of your inmost being." The sons and daughters left behind in Jerusalem by those exiled in 597 are also to fall by the sword. When that happens, the exiles are to copy Ezekiel's stoic response—no usual mourning rites, but only pining away in their own wickedness and silent groaning with one another.

In this way "Ezekiel will be a sign to you." His own behavior dramatizes his message and makes it credible. No mere spectator, the prophet brings the future disaster very close to reality by carrying through the symbolic action. This verse is the only place in the entire book where God mentions Ezekiel by name. *Ezekiel* will be a sign to you! This living, breathing, radical-acting, flesh-and-blood prophet—he is the sign. His actions at his wife's death will be echoed by the exiles when the temple falls and when their own relatives perish by the sword. The temple is as precious to Yahweh as a dearly loved spouse, but that emotional tie will not result in his sparing the condemned sanctuary. The temple is the delight of the exiles, too, but their desire for it and their love for their own families back in Jerusalem are doomed to disappointment. In the coming destruction of their pride and joy, they will learn that God's essence is revealed also in his judgment. Through it they will know that he is Yahweh. He who stepped out of his hiddenness at Sinai and identified himself by the name Yahweh will be recognized in his integrity when Jerusalem burns. The exiles' groaning and their pining away (cf. 4:17; 33:10; Lev. 26:39) comprise a confession of guilt and an implicit justification of Yahweh's actions. Bewailing the dead—the doomed temple and the doomed people—is beside the point and inappropriate.

SYMBOLIC DUMBNESS

A second symbolic action is mentioned three times in the book, and its interpretation is the center of heated controversy. In 3:22–27, at the time of his call, Ezekiel is told by God to shut himself in his house, where he would be tied up with ropes to prevent him from leaving. God himself promised to silence the prophet's tongue, preventing him from offering reproval to the rebellious house. Only when Yahweh opens Ezekiel's mouth is he to say, "Thus says Yahweh."

The second reference to this dumbness is in 24:25–27, immediately after the symbolic action dealing with the death of the prophet's wife. This second paragraph on Ezekiel's symbolic dumbness picks up a number of thematic words from the previous verses dealing with the death of Ezekiel's wife. Note "their stronghold" (v. 25; cf. v. 21); "the desire of your eyes" (v. 25; cf. vv. 16, 21); the death of sons and daughters (v. 25; cf. v. 21); and the understanding of Ezekiel as a sign (v. 27; cf. v. 24). According to this pericope Ezekiel will regain his speech when news of the fall of Jerusalem reaches him. Then, too, he will be a sign to the people, and they will thereby recognize the revelation of Yahweh.[7]

The third reference to dumbness, in 33:21–22, reports the arrival of a refugee from the captured city of Jerusalem, on the fifth day of the tenth month of the twelfth year of the exile (19 January, 586). This was more than five months after the temple and the city had been burned on the seventh day of the fifth month of the nineteenth year of Nebuchadrezzar (29 July, 587; 2 Kgs. 25:8–9; cf. 2 Kgs. 25:2–3). The previous evening the hand of Yahweh had come on the prophet so that he was no longer dumb by the time the messenger arrived.

Apart from the questions this incident has raised about Ezekiel's psychological condition, students of Ezekiel have asked how it is possible for Ezekiel to have been dumb from 594/593 to 586, when chapters 1–24 are full of his words drawn primarily from this same time period. Some have limited his dumbness to the months immediately preceding and following the fall of Jerusalem and so treated most or all of 3:22–27 as secondary (e.g., Zimmerli, Eichrodt, Wevers).[8] The difficulty with this approach is that it solves the problem by excising part of the evidence and also leaves the present shape of the text unexplained. Robert W. Wilson suggested that the word usually translated "reprover" (*môkîaḥ*; 3:26) actually means "intercessor." Thus the prophet's dumbness before the fall of Jerusalem consisted in his inability to intercede for the people. Moshe Greenberg, however, has pointed out that this word elsewhere only means "reprover, arbiter, or judge."[9]

Greenberg himself offers a novel interpretation that resolves the apparent conflict. Most scholars have taken 3:27 in a momentary sense: "At the moment when I [Yahweh] speak with you I will open your mouth and you will say to them, 'Thus says Lord Yahweh.' " The implied moment is that referred to in 24:26 and 33:22, the arrival of the refugee from Jerusalem. The Hebrew verb in 3:27, however, can better be understood in the frequentative sense of "whenever."[10] An overall interpretation of this symbolic action, based on this insight, would run somewhat as follows:

The prophet should expect opposition that will confine him primarily to his own house. This virtual house arrest is expressed metaphorically by the expression "They will put ropes upon you" (3:25), and by the divine command to shut himself in his home (3:24; cf. his prophesying at his home in 8:1; 14:1; 20:1; 33:30–31). The human rejection of the prophet is matched by God's limitations on the prophet's activity. He is only able to speak, even as a reprover, when God permits or empowers it. And whenever God does this, the prophet says "Thus says Yahweh" to the rebellious house, which is prone not to listen to him.

With the fall of Jerusalem, Ezekiel's task changes fundamentally. After 587 his words primarily offer hope to a despairing people who are no longer in need of judgmental speeches from the prophet.[11] So the dumbness previously imposed by Yahweh ceases, and Ezekiel is able to move more freely among the people (the last reference to his confinement at home is in 33:30–31), speaking to them a more fully orbed divine message. While God allowed Ezekiel to be a reprover on a limited number of occasions before 587, the prophet's periodic dumbness ceases after the news of Jerusalem's fall, and he speaks more words of hope than any other prophet up to this time

The periodic dumbness, therefore, is a reminder to Israel of the consequences of their rejection of Yahweh and his prophet; the prophet will be kept quiet and confined except when he is empowered to deliver one of his oracles of judgment. Similarly, the prophet's mute response to the death of his wife anticipates and sets the pattern for the people's reaction to the loss of the temple and of the children left behind in Jerusalem. But the removal of dumbness from the prophet will also be a sign to the people (24:27). When Ezekiel speaks words of promise after the fall of Jerusalem, he will be disclosing the positive, promissory character of the deity. From this promissory word, too, the people will recognize Yahweh's true identity, his revelation of himself. Thus the first two sign actions we have studied—Ezekiel's stoic reaction to the death of his wife and his symbolic dumbness at the beginning of his prophetic ministry—offer two explicit identifications of the prophet as a sign. In 24:24 he is a sign of God's *judg-*

ment and its consequences; in 24:27 he is a sign of God's *grace* and its consequences.

AT THE PARTING OF THE WAYS

In a third sign action, 21:18–23, God asks the prophet to draw a map of two roads from one country (Babylon) and to set up signposts indicating that one road leads to Rabbath of the Ammonites (modern Amman, the capital of Jordan) and the other to the fortress of Judah, namely Jerusalem. The rest of the pericope is in the form of an address to the prophet, which reveals and interprets the actions of the king of Babylon. When the king (Nebuchadrezzar) comes to the parting of the two roads, he uses three kinds of divination to see which way he should go first: shaking arrows,[12] consulting teraphim,[13] and investigation of a liver.[14] When the lot for Jerusalem comes into his hand, he proceeds immediately to set up a siege against the holy city.

This symbolic action obviously antedates the beginning of the final siege of Jerusalem. No doubt many of the exiles in Babylon hoped that Nebuchadrezzar would choose to attack Rabbath of the Ammonites first, giving Jerusalem a temporary or even a permanent reprieve. The prophet's sign action and the subsequent divine oracle reveal, however, that the king of Babylon will march on Jerusalem without delay. This is consistent with Ezekiel's message elsewhere that Yahweh will not spare Jerusalem in even the slightest way.

Although the people in Jerusalem despised Nebuchadrezzar because his methods of divination seemed inappropriate and false—"and to them[15] it will seem like a false divination"—even this normally forbidden type of oracle confirmed God's judgment on Judah and Jerusalem and so revealed their guilt. The issue is not the morality or immorality of Nebuchadrezzar's method of determining the divine will, but solely the inevitability of Jerusalem's capture.

ACTING OUT THE SIEGE OF JERUSALEM

Chapters 4 and 5 of Ezekiel contain a series of five sign actions and a prophetic speech.[16] Though the individual units of these chapters may have originated over a long period of time and may be attributable to several hands,[17] the discussion here will attempt to interpret the present dynamic structure of the chapters, resorting to theories of secondary growth when necessary.

At the center of these chapters are three sign actions dealing with the siege of Jerusalem. In 4:1–3 Yahweh instructs the prophet to inscribe a picture or map of Jerusalem on a mud brick and then bring up against this model city various kinds of siege equipment. The irresistible character of God's attack is indicated by an iron griddle, which the prophet holds between himself and the city. Normally griddles were made of ceramic ware.

Within this sign action there is a command for the prophet to fix his face toward the city (4:3; cf. v. 7). By setting his face toward the city—that is, by glaring at it as he presses the siege—the prophet expresses God's own anger.[18] Although none of the other classical prophets speaks of setting his face toward his addressees, this expression is found in the Balaam stories, where the seer sets his face toward the valley where the Israelites are encamped (Num. 22:41; 23:13; 24:1).[19]

This mock siege is meant as a sign for the "house of Israel," a reference to Ezekiel's Israelite contemporaries in Babylon. The sign points to a forthcoming reality and, as an alternate form of the divine word, implicitly calls on the exilic community to reflect on this situation and take appropriate action. The fact that Ezekiel's actions serve as a sign implies that the prophet had an audience when he carried out the divine command to initiate the siege.[20] Throughout these two chapters Yahweh repeatedly addresses the prophet with commands, prefaced with a sharp "and you" (4:1, 3, 4, 9; 5:1), indicating to the reader that Yahweh is the real instigator of these actions. In his siege activities the prophet seems to represent Nebuchadrezzar and/or Yahweh.

Guilt-Bearing

The first sign action about the siege of Jerusalem (4:1–3) is given theological interpretation by the sign action reported in 4:4–8. Its content can be outlined as follows:

> The prophet is to lie on his left side for 390 days and bear the iniquity of the house of Israel. The 390 days represent 390 years (vv. 4–5).

The prophet is to lie on his right side for 40 days and bear the iniquity of the house of Judah (v. 6).

The prophet is to set his face toward the siege of Jerusalem and prophesy against the city (v. 7).[21]

Yahweh places ropes on the prophet so that he cannot turn from one side to the other until the siege is over (v. 8).

A number of features in this sign action require comment. First, it is most unusual for Ezekiel to refer to the northern kingdom as the "house of Israel" (but see 9:9; 37:16). Second, the 390 years assigned to the northern kingdom would seem to represent the years during which they sinned, while the 40 years for the house of Judah seem to represent the period of punishment. The Septuagint, which reads 150 in verse 4 and 190 in verses 5 and 9, is an attempt to correct the original 390 so that the figures for the north, too, will refer to the years of punishment. The northern kingdom, which had endured roughly 150 years of punishment before Jerusalem fell, would still face 40 more years of punishment, contemporaneous with the years of Judah's punishment.[22] Third, the number 390 has no clear referent if it refers to the northern kingdom, since this kingdom's entire life span was about 200 years. Fourth, verse 8, which tells of Yahweh tying the prophet (a theological interpretation of 3:25?), would seem to make the turning from side to side, presupposed in verses 4–6, impossible.

The best solution to these difficulties is to identify verse 6 as a gloss, designed to have Ezekiel "bear guilt" for both kingdoms. The glossator construed "house of Israel" as a reference to the northern kingdom, whereas the sign action originally understood this term as a reference to all Israel. The prophet has been instructed by Yahweh to bear the guilt of Israel for 390 years, a time span that could refer to a period from the beginning of the monarchy and/or the erection of the Solomonic temple to the fall of Jerusalem.

What is meant by "bearing guilt," and whom does the prophet represent in this sign action? The medieval Jewish exegete Rashi suggested that Ezekiel here represented God, who had put up with Israel's effrontery for 390 years. Zimmerli feels that the prophet represents only himself and that his "guilt-bearing" is first of all an accusation that the 390 years of Israel's history with the monarchy or the temple were sinful. In this view the prophet bears the guilt of the people as their substitute. Ezekiel publicly identifies with the people when he, like the servant of Isaiah 53, bears the guilt of many. Though his actions in beginning the siege (1–3) might suggest he was distancing himself from the people in an arrogant way, this act of public identification places him in solidarity with the people in suffering the consequences of sin.[23] Greenberg believes that Ezekiel represents Israel itself, suffering for its iniquity during the 390 years of its sin. In this understanding, God's siege of Jerusalem has been going on for 390 years, so that the periods of sin and punishment are contemporaneous. Greenberg finds an analogous interlacing of periods of sin and punishment in Leviticus 26:14–39. From this perspective verse 9b, which Zimmerli understands as a secondary harmonization of 4:4–8 with 4:9–11, would seem to reflect the view that the siege of God against Jerusalem had been going on for 390 years.[24] It is difficult to choose between the interpretations of Zimmerli and Greenberg, but this much they have in common: The sign action originally had the prophet lying on only one side, and the figure 390 once referred to the period in which all Israel sinned. This period of sin began either with the founding of the monarchy or with the building of the temple.

Verse 6 must have been added before 547, 40 years after the fall of Jerusalem, since a redactor would not knowingly create a historical inaccuracy by implying that the exile would last only 40 years if in fact it had already lasted longer than that. In selecting the number 40 he may have been guided by Numbers 14:33–34, where, after the sin of the spies, the Israelites were condemned to 40 years of wandering. Whereas in Numbers a year of punishment is assigned for every day the spies had spent in the land, in Ezekiel each day of lying down stands for a year of sinning.

If one were to understand the numbers 390 and 40 in the present text as sequential, the total of 430 would recall Exodus 12:40–41. According to this passage from the Priestly source, the exodus from Egypt happened exactly 430 years after the stay in Egypt had begun. Both the number 40 and the total 430 in Ezekiel, therefore, could be understood as referring to a limited period of exile, and the second number would imply that a new exodus would come after the Babylonian exile (cf. Ezek. 20:33–44).[25]

More Siege Signs

A second sign action relating to the siege of Jerusalem appears in 4:9–11. The prophet is told to bake bread from flour made of wheat, barley, beans, lentils, millet, and emmer. The use of so many kinds of flour symbolizes a besieged people scraping the bottom of all their barrels. This interpretation is made explicit by the divine word in 4:16–17, where God announces that he is breaking the staff of bread in Jerusalem (cf. 5:16; 14:13; Lev. 26:26) and that an anxious and desolate people will thereafter eat food of limited weight and drink water of limited measure.

Naturally, food shortages became acute during a siege. As a prisoner Jeremiah was granted only a roll of bread a day, and that lasted only until all the bread of the city ran out (Jer. 37:21). The meager rations here described—eight or nine ounces of bread and two-thirds of a liter of water—seem fairly substantial in comparison with other biblical accounts of sieges. According to Lamentations 4:10 women boiled their own children for food during the final siege of Jerusalem. Ezekiel's judgment speech in chapter 5 predicts that parents will eat their children, and children will eat their own parents (v. 10).

The symbolic action in 4:12–15 changes the setting from the siege of 4:9–11 to living in exile, although both these sign actions deal with bread. A divine command calls on Ezekiel to bake publicly (in their sight, v. 12) a barley cake, the food of the poor, on fuel consisting of unclean pellets of human dung (cf. Deut. 23:14). In verse 13 Yahweh interprets this action as corresponding to the way Israelites will have to eat their bread unclean among the nations. To this the prophet objects, stating he had never violated ritual food laws, such as eating an animal that had died of itself or that had been torn by wild beasts (Exod. 22:31; Lev. 22:8; Ezek. 44:31), nor had he consumed sacrificial meat that had been kept beyond an appropriate time period (Lev. 7:18; 19:7; Isa. 65:4[26]). How then could he eat bread baked on unclean fuel? The deity does make a small concession to Ezekiel: the prophet may bake his bread on animal dung rather than human dung. The Bible does not indicate elsewhere whether cooking on dried animal dung would be ritually defiling for lay people or even for priests. In any case, since foreign lands were unclean in themselves (Amos 7:17), all consumption of food in exile would take place in a condition of uncleanness. It is worth noting that Yahweh makes no concession on the threat of exile itself.

A Sign for After the Fall

The third symbolic act relating to the siege—and the fifth symbolic action in chapters 4 and 5—takes place after the siege had ended and the city had been destroyed (5:1–4). The prophet is commanded to play the role of a barber and shave off the hair of his head and his beard. It seems likely that the source of this imagery is Isaiah 7:20, where Yahweh announces that he will hire a razor, the king of Assyria, to shave the head hair, the beard, and the genital hair of Israel. This metaphorical description of a judging razor is taken quite literally by Ezekiel, just as was the swallowing of the scroll at his call (cf. also 4:3). Though no comment is made about the propriety of Ezekiel shaving, biblical laws actually forbid it for those in the priesthood (Lev. 21:5; Ezek. 44:20). As was shown in the symbolic action dealing with the barley cake and human dung, however, Yahweh did not find it inappropriate to ask the prophet to do something that would make him ritually unclean.

The prophet's shaved-off hair represents the surviving inhabitants of Jerusalem. Ezekiel is to burn one third of it in the midst of the city at the conclusion of the siege. One third of it he will smite with a sword in the vicinity of Jerusalem (cf. 2 Kgs. 25:4–7). A final third will be dispersed with the wind, and Yahweh will pursue this third with his sword. A similar idea is expressed in Amos 9:1–4, where it is said of the inhabitants of the destroyed city of Bethel, "Not one of them shall flee away, not one of them shall escape." Were the escapees to dig into Sheol, hide themselves on Carmel, or even go into captivity, Amos says, God would command his sword to slay them.

Verse 3 introduces into this devastating picture the idea of a remnant.[27] Yahweh commands the prophet to take a few hairs (people) and bind them in the hem of his garment. Even some of these few survivors among the exiles are to be thrown into the fire. Leviticus 26:36–38 also mentions a remnant among the exiles that will perish. Jeremiah quotes a grim curse that will be used by all the exiles from Judah in Babylon: "The Lord make you like Zedekiah and Ahab, [false prophets of the exile], whom the king of Babylon roasted in the fire" (29:22). Jeremiah thus knew of specific individuals among the exiles who had perished by fire.

A PROPHETIC SPEECH ON THE SYMBOLIC ACTIONS

At the conclusion of the symbolic actions in 4:1–5:4, a prophetic speech is appended (5:5–17) that comments on the whole series of symbolic actions in general (This is Jerusalem! v. 5) and on the symbolic action dealing with Ezekiel's hair in particular (vv. 10–12). Verses 5–7 provide reasons for Jerusalem's punishment: Though she was given an elect position in the middle of the nations (cf. 38:12), she had rebelled against God's ordinances and statutes more than these nations. In fact, she had not even kept the ordinances of the nations, which were presumably inferior and/or easier to keep. An indictment in the next section of the speech, verse 11, refers to the people's defiling of the sanctuary with their idolatries, thus anticipating the burden of chapter 8.

The next section of the prophetic speech, verses 8–17, consists primarily of a series of announcements of judgment.[28] Only the highlights need be mentioned. The "judgments" (*mišpāṭîm*) which Yahweh promises to perform in the midst of Jerusalem (v. 8; cf. vv. 10, 15) form a pun on the "ordinances" (also *mišpāṭîm*), which Israel had not kept, according to verses 6–7. (The word *ordinances* appears five times in these latter verses.) Israel will receive unprecedented punishments, such as parents eating their children and vice versa, and God displaying an eye that will not pity or have mercy.[29] The divine wrath reaches fever pitch in verse 13: "My anger will be complete and I will sate my fury on them without taking any break. Then they will know that I Yahweh have spoken in my passion, when I complete my wrath on them." Passion is the kind of emotion displayed by an irate spouse who suspects unfaithfulness in his or her mate (cf. Num. 5:14–31; Prov. 6:34). This kind of anger guarantees that Israel, who sinned more than the nations, will become a source of reproach and reviling among the nations. The nations who witnessed her sins (v. 8) will also witness her great punishment (v. 14). God's chastisements will be chastisements of fury (v. 15), not of love (Prov. 3:12).

Throughout these verses there are allusions to the preceding symbolic actions. The reference to God's scattering the survivors to every wind is a theological comment on the prophet's scattering his hair (the people) to every wind. Verse 12 restates the threefold fate of those who survive the siege of Jerusalem in the final symbolic action (cf. vv. 1–2). The references to famine and the breaking of the staff of bread recall the symbolic action in 4:9–11. The divine sword threatened in verse 17 parallels the references to a sword in 5:2–3.

GOING INTO EXILE

In the symbolic action 12:1–16 Ezekiel acts out a trip into exile. In the divine command of verses 3–6 special emphasis is placed on the peo-

46

ple watching the prophet. Six times there are references to the eyes of his audience. This forms an ironic contrast to verse 2, which informs us that the people have eyes and ears, but neither see nor hear (cf. Isa. 6:9; Jer. 5:21). Even when Ezekiel performs this symbolic action in their sight, it is not at all sure they will see him since they are so rebellious.

Yahweh commands Ezekiel to make an exile's pack, whose shape we can deduce from wall reliefs of Tiglath-pileser III.[30] With this pack the prophet is to go into exile in the evening, digging through a wall to escape and covering his face with a disguise. The irony dealing with the emphasis on eyes continues, since the fleeing prophet cannot see.

Verse 7 reports the carrying out of the symbolic action (cf. 24:18)— bringing out the exile's pack, digging through the wall in the darkness, carrying the pack on his shoulder—in full view of his audience.

Verses 8–16 are a divine speech which interprets the actions of the prophet. Faced with an inquiry about what he is doing, the prophet is commanded to tell the exilic audience that he is a sign ("I am your sign"): Just as he has done, so it shall be done to or by those in Jerusalem—they will go into exile or captivity. The "prince" (nāśî, literally, "the lifted one") will lift the pack on his shoulder. His retainers will dig through the wall for him, but he will cover his face and be unable to see. In verse 13 Yahweh himself assumes the role of captor and threatens the prince with exile. He spreads a net over him and brings him to Babylon, where he will die. Those around the prince will be scattered to the wind by Yahweh, whose sword will pursue them even in exile (cf. 5:2, 10, 12). This dispersion among the nations will convince those going into exile that Yahweh is who he says he is.

Verse 16 adds the promise to spare a few from the sword, famine, and pestilence so that they can tell their abominations among the nations. This will vindicate Yahweh in the eyes of the nations; that is, the nations "will know that I am Yahweh" (contrast 36:20–21, where the nations mock the people of God who are in exile).

This symbolic action anticipates and actualizes the people's journey into exile and includes the king (prince) in the threatened judgment. In one detail, however, it seems to be a prophecy after the fact. We know from 2 Kings 25:7 and Jeremiah 39:7 that when Jerusalem fell, Zedekiah, the last king, was taken into the presence of Nebuchadrezzar at Riblah. After witnessing the execution of his two sons, his own eyes were put out so that the brutal fate of his children was his last earthly sight. Clearly, the present text of 12:1–16 has been adjusted to reflect this reality, though there is no reason to interpret the entire symbolic action as a prophecy after the fact.

The question is: How much has the text been changed? Some have seen the references to "the dark" in verses 6, 7, and 12 as evidence that the author knew that Zedekiah's flight took place at night (2 Kgs. 25:4; Jer. 39:4; 52:7). But accusing the king and the Jerusalemites of trying to escape in the darkness is plausible before the fall of Jerusalem as well. Such a tactic would be needed to escape captivity by the Babylonians.[31] Despite the parallel in 2 Kings 25:4, the references to digging through the wall are also not impossible before the event. Even the threat that the prince would die in exile is plausible pre–587. In Jeremiah 22:10–11 the prophet foretold that Shallum (Jehoahaz) would die in the land of Egypt, a prediction that turned out to be true (2 Kgs. 23:34). It would not be surprising if Ezekiel felt that the same fate awaited Zedekiah. Therefore, only the specific references to the king's blindness seem surely secondary. This adjustment of the text to correspond with reality may have been facilitated by original references to the king's disguise, which made it difficult for him to see (cf. v. 5).[32]

SHOCK OVER THE COMING DISASTER

In 12:17–20 Ezekiel is commanded to eat his bread with quaking and to drink his water with trembling and anxiety. This command is interpreted by a speech he is instructed to give to the "people of the land," who are his companions in the exile. This use of "people of the land" may be ironic, since the exiles are clearly people *without* land!

In his address to the people, Ezekiel's symbolic actions are related to the future behavior of those who dwell in Jerusalem. They will eat and drink in anxiety and desolation, and they will have ruined houses and a desolate land. The reason for this impending destruction is the violence they have perpetrated.[33] It is not clear whether their anxiety stems from knowledge of their violence or from anticipation of their destruction—or from both. In any case, when the inhabited cities are ruined and the land has become desolate, the exilic companions of Ezekiel (the people of the land) will recognize Yahweh as the one who judges righteously.

The final symbolic action to be discussed here[34], 21:6–7, deals with a similar theme. Yahweh commands the prophet to groan publicly (before their eyes; per contra 24:15–24) in his bitterness and as he loses strength. When his exilic companions ask him about his behavior, he replies that he is anticipating their own reactions to a report about the attack on Jerusalem that they are about to receive. The report will make every heart melt, all hands grow weak, and every spirit faint, and all knees become wet with urine. Clearly, his fellow deportees will experience all the effects of the attack on the city, and their fearful reaction resembles the characteristic condition of those who have experienced Yahweh's might in holy war.[35] The message that an attack is coming ("Behold, it is coming, it will happen") recalls a similar expression in 7:5, 6, 10, which proclaimed the sure coming of the day of Yahweh.

These final two symbolic actions describe the effect of Jerusalem's fall on the city's inhabitants and on their exilic comrades respectively. Those in Jerusalem will quake at their sin and the extent of the disaster; they will lose all bodily strength and control. Those in exile, on the other hand, will groan, weakly and bitterly, over the terrible news that comes from Jerusalem. But for them, at least, the coming calamity has revelatory possibilities. When Jerusalem falls, they will know that Yahweh is living up to his name (12:20).

CONCLUSION

Through all of these symbolic actions—the stoic response to the death of his wife, his dumbness, his drawing the road for Nebuchadnezzar's attack, the five signs dealing with siege and exile in chapters 4–5, his mock escape into exile, his shaking and his groaning—Ezekiel is a sign. He is preaching in a medium different from, but supplementary to and always reinforcing, the word of Yahweh. The symbolic actions concretize his message, and they make the advent of the events they describe more sure. Ezekiel is explicitly a sign (24:24):

That there will be a siege against Jerusalem (4:3);
That the prince and the other inhabitants of Jerusalem will go into exile (12:6, 11);
That the loss of the temple, like the loss of his wife, will be a sorrow beyond tears, but that in Yahweh's act of judgment his identity will become known to the exiles (24:24);

That the end of his dumbness will initiate a new phase of proclamation, full of promise, through which Israel will also learn that "I am Yahweh" (24:27).

NOTES

1. Ernst Jenni and Claus Westermann, eds., *Theologisches Handwörterbuch zum Alten Testament*, 1: col. 93.

2. Zimmerli, *Ezekiel*, 1:156.

3. Bernhard Lang, *Ezechiel*, 87.

4. Stephan Bitter, *Die Ehe des Propheten Hosea.*

5. Zimmerli, *Ezekiel*, 1:28. Georg Fohrer, *Die symbolischen Handlungen der Propheten*, 25–70, numbers the symbolic actions in a different way. He combines 4:9–11 with 4:12–15, and he identifies 24:1–14 as a symbolic action, though it is better understood as a parable referring to a working song. Fohrer counts two sign actions in Hosea, three in Isaiah, and ten in Jeremiah.

6. The one symbolic action with a positive message, 37:15–28, is to be dated after the fall of Jerusalem and will be discussed in chapter 8 below.

7. Zimmerli, *Ezekiel*, 1:508, suggests that this account of Ezekiel's dumbness originally consisted only of vv. 25 and 27, which made the end of the dumbness come on the day of Jerusalem's fall, whereas 33:21–22 states that this happened only when a messenger arrived some five months later. V. 25 was partially "corrected" by v. 26, which suggests that the messenger arrived on the same day that Jerusalem fell.

8. Zimmerli, *Ezekiel*, 1:161; Walther Eichrodt, *Ezekiel*, 75. John Wevers, *Ezekiel*, 57, argues that the dumbness in 24:27 was temporary and ecstatic.

9. Robert R. Wilson, "An Interpretation of Ezekiel's Dumbness"; Greenberg, *Ezekiel, 1–20*, 102.

10. Wevers, *Ezekiel*, 58, raised the possibility of this understanding. For him, however, this verse is an attempt by a glossator to relate this passage to the original commission in 2:4–5 and 3:11.

11. The only reference to Israel as a rebellious house after ch. 24 is in 44:6, where the prophet calls for a reform of the preexilic cultic practices.

12. A practice known as belomancy; cf. Hos. 4:12. Perhaps this was similar to the casting of lots or the use of Urim and Thummin. See Burke O. Long, "Divination," 242–43.

13. Teraphim are strongly rejected in 1 Sam. 15:23 and 2 Kgs. 23:24.

14. A practice known as hepatoscopy. Divination via examination of a liver was widely practiced in Mesapotamia, but liver models, which offered guidance to diviners, have also been found in Palestine at Hazor and Megiddo.

15. The MT has a longer reading modifying "them," namely, "who have sworn solemn oaths," which is lacking in the LXX, Old Latin, and Syriac, and presumably secondary. The purpose of adding this clause was to link Judean unfaithfulness to the kinds of treaty infidelity discussed in 17:13–14. See Wevers, *Ezekiel*, 168.

16. In 4:1–3 a sign action points to the beginning of the siege against Jerusalem; in 4:9–11 the lack of food during the siege is dramatized; and in 5:1–4 a sign action announces what will happen to those who survive the siege itself. A complex sign action in 4:4–8 provides a theological interpretation of the siege, while the command to prophesy in v. 7 points forward to the prophetic speech in 5:5–17. The discussion of food shortages during the siege in 4:9–11 is supplemented by a sign action related to the problem of preparing and eating

food in the ritually unclean land of exile (4:12–15). This paragraph, which many would judge to be a late addition to the text, separates the divine speech of 4:16–17 from the sign action in 4:9–11, which it was meant to interpret.

17. Zimmerli, *Ezekiel*, 1:154–57, has worked out a typical and careful diachronic analysis of this passage.

18. On eight other occasions the book of Ezekiel reports that the prophet set (*śîm*) his face against a thing, a nation, or a person in order to announce judgment: against the mountains of Israel (6:2); against the false prophetesses (13:17); against the forest in the south (20:46); against Jerusalem (21:2); against Ammon (25:2); against Sidon (28:21); against Pharaoh (29:2); against the mountains of Seir (35:2); and against Gog (38:2).

19. Cf. Zimmerli, "The Special Form and Traditio-Historical Character of Ezekiel's Prophecy," 520.

20. Occasionally eyewitnesses are mentioned or clearly presupposed in his sign actions: 4:12; 12:7, 19; 21:6; 24:19; 37:18.

21. Note that the prophet is active in this verse (cf. v. 3) rather than passive as in the remainder of vv. 4–8. The command to prophecy anticipates the prophetic speech in 5:5–17. Do these factors indicate that this verse comes from a redactor?

22. Greenberg, *Ezekiel, 1–20*, 105–06, interprets the LXX's 150 as symbolizing 110 years of prior punishment, which are to be followd by 40 years of punishment contemporary with that of Jerusalem.

23. Zimmerli, *Ezekiel*, 1:165.

24. Greenberg, *Ezekiel, 1–20*, 124–25.

25. S. Kreuzer, "430 Jahre, 400 Jahre oder 4 Generationen—Zu den Zeitangaben über den Ägyptenaufenthalt der 'Israeliten,' " proposes that the calculations of Ezek. 4:6 served as a *Vorlage* for the writer of Exod. 12:40–41.

26. In this passage eating outdated sacrifices is compared to eating swine's flesh.

27. The idea of the remnant in Ezekiel is discussed in chapter 5 below.

28. The "therefore" at the beginning of v. 7 would lead one to expect an announcement of judgment, but this verse continues the indictment of Israel, almost as if the prophet were supplying additional reasons for punishment as an afterthought.

29. This motif appears also in 7:4, 9; 8:18; 9:5, 10. Contrast the confession of Jonah: "That is why I made haste to flee to Tarshish; for I knew that thou art a gracious God and merciful, slow to anger, and abounding in steadfast love" (4:2).

30. James B. Pritchard, *The Ancient Near East in Pictures Relating to the Old Testament*, 128 fig. 366.

31. Some have suggested that they left on their journey at night in order to avoid heat in their travel. Medieval commentators attributed the flight at night to the shame of the Jerusalemites over their defeat.

32. In v. 5 the original text also had to be updated with a reference to "the land"; in v. 12 the expression "he cannot see with the eye" is glossed with "that is the land"; in v. 13 the clause "and he will not see it" (the land of the Chaldeans) also reflects a revision of the passage to reflect the fate of Zedekiah.

33. For other accusations of violence see 7:23; 8:17; 9:9; 11:6; cf. 28:16 and Gen. 6:11, 13.

34. Other gestures and expressive movements of the prophet are discussed above in the introduction.

35. For the discouragement and terror of enemies in holy war, see Gerhard von Rad, *Der heilige Krieg im alten Israel*, 10–11.

THREE

YAHWEH DOES NOT SEE US;

YAHWEH HAS ABANDONED THE LAND

(EZEKIEL 8–11)

There are four major visions in Ezekiel. The vision in chapters 1–3 centers on the call of the prophet; the vision in 37:1–14 deals with the resurrection and restoration of the people; and the vision in chapters 40–48 reveals a blueprint of the new temple and the new community in Palestine. The vision complex in chapters 8–11, the focus of the discussion in the following pages, might well be captioned "A Vision of Judgment."

What we have termed a "vision complex" consists of the following parts:

Introduction to the vision (8:1–4).
The cultic sins of Jerusalem (8:5–18).
The coming destruction of the city (9:1–10:7).
A description of the divine throne chariot (10:8–17, 19–22).
Yahweh's move from temple to cherubim (10:18).
An ancillary vision in which a saying of the people is disputed (11:1–13).
Another saying of the people disputed (11:14–21).
Yahweh abandons the temple and the land; vision concluded (11:22–25).

This vision complex provides opportunity for Ezekiel to contest three sayings of the people, the first of which is repeated twice:

1. "Yahweh does not see us. Yahweh has abandoned the land" (8:12; 9:9).
2. "It is not the time to build houses; the city is the pot and we are the flesh" (11:3).
3. "They have gone far from Yahweh; the land is given to us as a possession" (11:15).

It is unlikely that this vision complex was created at one time by one person. The ancillary vision in 11:1–13, for example, takes no notice of the presence of the divine glory at the very gate where this vision takes place, nor does it presuppose the slaughter by sword or the destruction by fire that are described in 9:1–10:17. Nevertheless, it is not the principal assignment of the interpreter to peel off secondary verses in an attempt to reconstruct an original vision.[1] What we have before us in chapters 8–11 has been artfully arranged and has been structured in an intricate way to enunciate clearly the message of Ezekiel.[2] We shall, therefore, explicate the canonical text of the vision complex in chapters 8-11, attempting to see the message of its individual sections as well as the meaning of the vision as a whole.

INTRODUCTION TO THE VISION

The vision begins at Ezekiel's home, where the elders of Judah had gathered on 28 September, 593. Two similar gatherings, both with the explicit intent of inquiring of Yahweh, are reported in 14:1, 3 and 20:1. Jeremiah also refers to the exilic elders in his famous letter to those in captivity (Jer. 29:1). These exilic elders play no further role in the vision complex of Ezekiel 8–11, unless they are to be identified with the exiles to whom the prophet reports "all the words of Yahweh which he had shown me" (11:25). The date of the vision is significant because it antedates the beginning of the final siege of Jerusalem.[3] What the vision reports about the words and activities of the people in Jerusalem takes place after the first deportation of 597, when Ezekiel and many other leading personalities had been taken off into exile, but before the encircling presence of the

53

Babylonian army would have undercut the greedy optimism that characterizes the people, especially in the sayings quoted in chapter 11.

The hand of Yahweh fell on Ezekiel (8:1) in the presence of the elders. Such a divine hand also accompanies the visions of 3:22; 37:1; and 40:1–2. The use of the verb *fell* with *hand* is unusual in this book, though the word *fall* is also used to denote the spirit's coming in 11:5. What the prophet saw initially, under the power of the divine hand, was a human-like figure,[4] much like the one enthroned above the firmament in chapter 1. The bottom half of its body was composed of flames, while the upper half shone as if it were made of electrum. This figure extended what appeared to be a hand and took hold of the prophet by a lock of his hair, but it was a divine wind (v. 3; cf. 3:12) that actually carried Ezekiel to Jerusalem and its temple region. In the apocryphal book of Bel and the Dragon, an angel of the Lord similarly took the prophet Habakkuk by the crown of his head and set him down in Babylon "with the rushing sound of the wind itself" (Bel 36). In the temple precincts Ezekiel saw the glory of the God of Israel, which he identified with the figure he had seen in his first vision (v. 4; cf. 10:15, 20, 22). The movements of the glory of Yahweh (or the glory of the God of Israel) play a central role in the vision, though it is not completely clear how the glory of Yahweh is related to the "man" (see n. 4) who had seized Ezekiel by the hair.[5]

THE CULTIC SINS OF JERUSALEM

The balance of chapter 8 consists of a visionary tour of four areas in the Jerusalem temple area, where the prophet observed cultic aberrations.

The exact location of the first area is hard to pin down. The spirit brought Ezekiel to a gate facing north (v. 3), which is either the gate leading to the inner court (Eichrodt, Greenberg) or the north gate of the city (Zimmerli).[6] To the north[7] of this gate was a "statue of passion which provokes to passion," that is, an idol which called forth the passionate anger of Yahweh.[8] Manasseh had erected a statue of the Canaanite goddess Asherah in the temple area (2 Kgs. 21:7), and the noun used for this statue in 2 Chronicles 33:7, 15, *pas hassēmel*, resembles the vocabulary in Ezekiel (*sēmel haqqin'â*). While the statue erected by Manasseh was removed and ground into dust by Josiah in his reform (2 Kgs. 23:6), it is not impossible that Ezekiel may have been holding the people to account for the sins of this previous generation, or even that another statue had been erected after the destruction of the first one.

More important than the precise identification of this cultic sin is the word of Yahweh commenting on it (v. 6). For the first of four times the prophet is asked, "Do you see?" (c. vv. 12, 15, 17), a question finished in this case by "what great abominations they are doing?" Yahweh announces that by such abominable activity the worshipers are making themselves distant from the sanctuary (cf. 9:6; 11:15–16). What is more, the prophet is told that he will "see" additional abominations (see vv. 9, 13, 15).

After Yahweh brought him to the entrance to the (inner?) court of the temple (v. 7), the prophet was instructed to dig through a wall in order to reach the second area where cultic sins were taking place. These "abominations" (ḥattô'ēbôt) or detestable images (šeqeṣ; Lev. 11:10–42) consisted of various idolatrous figures9 carved on a wall, before which seventy elders of Israel stood, each with a smoking censer in his hand. Jeremiah also refers to the use of incense in idolatrous worship of the stars (19:13), though incense in itself was appealing to Yahweh (Deut. 33:10).

The reference in this scene to the elders is significant since it was their exilic counterparts who were present in Ezekiel's Babylonian home at the beginning of the vision. The number 70 seems to identify them as an official political body (cf. Exod. 24:1, 9; Num. 11:16, 24), making the enormity of their sin all the greater. The mention of Jaazaniah the son of Shaphan in verse 11 may fit in with such imagery as well, since a certain Shaphan was a royal scribe who had been involved in Josiah's reform a generation earlier (2 Kgs. 22:3). If Jaazaniah's father was the same Shaphan, it would be another indication of corruption at the highest levels. Judging by 2 Chronicles 26:19, an account of the sins of King Uzziah, the elders, in using incense, may have been impinging on the domain of the priests.

For the second time Yahweh asks the prophet, "Do you see?" (what the sinners are doing, v. 12), but in this case he also quotes their self-justifying comments, which also serve as an accusation against the deity: "Yahweh does not see us. Yahweh has abandoned the land." While this saying of the elders is not explicitly disputed, as are the sayings in chapter 11 and in other passages later in the book, chapter 8 can be seen in a number of respects as an implicit rebuttal of this saying. The elders felt free to worship as they pleased since Yahweh did not or could not see them, but the prophet is asked four times, "Do you see?" with the obvious implication that even he could indeed see them! Three times he is also told that he will "see" additional abominations. If the prophet is able to "see" so much from his exilic home hundreds of miles away, or when present in the temple only in a vision, how much more will Yahweh be able to see all that the elders and the others are doing. The harsh saying, "My eye shall not spare" (8:18; 9:5, 10), also indicates Yahweh's ability to see what is going on in Jerusalem.

The other half of the elders' saying—"Yahweh has abandoned the land"—is untrue, but ironically prophetic. Verse 4 reminded the reader at the start of this vision that the glory of the God of Israel was in fact in the temple area; but the sins of the Jerusalemites force Yahweh to leave the land by the end of the vision complex in chapter 11.

Yahweh next took the prophet to a third area of sinning, this time to a north gate near the temple (v. 14),[10] where he found women worshiping the god Tammuz. Tammuz was a Mesopotamian deity, who was thought to die and descend into the netherworld each year. His cult was a favorite of women and featured various kinds of mourning rites.[11] At the conclusion of this scene, when Yahweh again asked the prophet whether he saw this, Yahweh promised Ezekiel that he would see *greater* abominations (v. 15)—not just additional ones (vv. 6, 9, 13).

The fourth area to which the prophet was brought is easiest to identify. In the inner court, between the temple and the main altar,[12] he found twenty-five men, who had turned their backs on Yahweh and were worshiping the sun (cf. 2 Kgs. 23:11, where horses and chariots dedicated to the sun are mentioned). The charge of turning one's back on Yahweh would appear to be a literal adaptation of an earlier metaphorical expression (Jer. 2:27; 32:33). This fourth "abomination" is compounded by the violence that these people have perpetrated in the land (v. 17). Violence and bloody crimes are part of Ezekiel's accusations elsewhere (7:11, 23; 12:19; 45:9), even within this vision complex (9:9). It is probably a mistake to view the accusation of violence as a second charge, completely independent from the cultic sins that have occupied the prophet throughout chapter 8. Rather, he is indicating that a necessary fruit of idolatry is injustice and violence in society. Violence and idolatry are mutually reinforcing sins. Both sins alike goad Yahweh into fury.

The last clause in verse 17, "They have put the branch to their [or my[13]] nose," apparently indicates the last straw in their provocative behavior. The prophet may be employing radical or even vulgar language to describe this offense. From ancient Near Eastern art and texts scholars have reconstructed a rite called *labān appi*, a gesture in which worshipers stand before a deity holding something, perhaps a phallic symbol, to their nose. The sun worshipers, therefore, have included pagan gestures in their liturgy.[14] Another interpretation takes the word *branch* as a euphemism for "breaking wind" or flatus. Thus, in worshiping the sun the twenty-five men are "breaking wind" in the divine nose.

Either meaning is probably sufficient to explain the harsh announcement of judgment in verse 18. Yahweh states that he will act toward them with fury (cf. 5:15). His eye, which had in fact "seen it all," would not spare them, nor would he have pity (cf. 5:11; 7:4, 9; 9:5, 10; 16:5). Even if they should pray with a very loud voice, he would not listen to them (cf. Jer. 7:16; 11:11, 14).

Are the descriptions of cultic aberrations in the temple of Ezekiel's day accurate historically? The contemporary books of Jeremiah and Lamentations, which pull no punches in criticizing Judah's sinning, mention no comparable rites. Jeremiah is unsparing in chastising Jehoiakim for social injustice and for thinking of his own creature comforts when the need of the hour was for improved national defense (Jer. 22:13–17), but Jeremiah is silent about any syncretism in his day. Some, therefore (Torrey, Greenberg), believe that the public rites reflect the historical conditions under Manasseh. But some of these offenses had been observed by Ezekiel while he was still in Jerusalem, and the rest could have been reported to him in letters from Judah or by word of mouth. From a literary or theological perspective, in any case it is clear that Ezekiel saw no guarantee of security in the temple (cf. Jeremiah's temple sermon in Jer. 7 and 26), and in fact believed that temple activity was part of the problem rather than part of the solution.[15]

THE DESTRUCTION OF THE CITY

Echoing the last verse of chapter 8—"They call in my ears with a great voice"—the next scene of the vision begins with Yahweh calling in Ezekiel's ears with a great voice (9:1). The divine shout summoned six executioners, each with an instrument of destruction, or a wrecking tool, in his hand.[16] With them was a man clothed in linen, presumably a priestly figure, with scribal equipment hanging from his belt. These seven men came and stood by the bronze altar erected by Solomon (1 Kgs.

57

8:64), which King Ahaz had once moved when he installed an altar he had copied from the Arameans in Damascus (2 Kgs. 16:14).

Yahweh first instructed the man in linen to go through the city and mark with a *taw*[17] all those who sigh (cf. 21:1, 6, 7) or groan (24:17; 26:15) over the abominations that are being done in the city. Four of the five other uses of the verbs *sigh* and *groan* are in reference to the prophet himself, perhaps suggesting that only those who are like Ezekiel truly grieve over what is going on in Jerusalem.[18] Such a mark on the forehead might indicate that the person was the property of Yahweh (cf. the mark of Cain in Gen. 4:15). In any case, all those who were so marked would be spared punishment.

While the prophet Ezekiel did not believe it possible for Jerusalem to escape judgment, the book itself does have a few passages which indicate that a remnant might survive the destruction. We have already seen an adumbration of the remnant idea in the symbolic action dealing with Ezekiel's hair (5:3–4): a small number of the survivors of Jerusalem would be bound in the hem of the prophet's robe, but even some of these would be burned in fire.

According to Ezekiel 6:8–10, those left after Yahweh's act of judgment would remember him in exile and acknowledge that he is Yahweh, precisely in that he carried through on what he said he would do. His word was no idle threat, since it broke their wanton hearts and blinded their idolatrous eyes. Those who are the surviving remnant would themselves rue their own wicked behavior. Such remorse would also be experienced by those Israelites who would survive the exile and be restored to their homeland (16:61–63; 20:43; 36:31).

The remnant, according to Ezekiel, would even confess their faults in exile. This might lead the nations to see the justice of God's ways and acknowledge that he is Yahweh (12:16), or it might convince the earlier groups of exiles that it was the sins of the citizens of Jerusalem in the city's final days that led to its fall. In any case, the surviving remnant would make Yahweh's judgment appear righteous—he did not destroy Jerusalem without reason (14:22–23).

References to a remnant elsewhere in Ezekiel do not connote in themselves a saving word. The remnant, rather, would justify God's ways to earlier exiles or to the nations, or it would come to loathe itself in exile or after the restoration. The remnant idea in chapter 9, on the other hand, indicates that those who sigh and groan over Jerusalem's abominations will not have to suffer alongside those who actually did the abominations (see ch. 18). By sparing such a remnant Yahweh indicates his fairness, even if his eye will by no means spare those who are guilty. When the man clothed in linen had written all his *taws*, he reported, "I have done just as you commanded me." No hint is given of the number of those who are so marked, and the implication is that their number would be few indeed. After all, even responsible groups, like the seventy elders of the house of Israel, are ringleaders in the idolatry.

The six executioners themselves are dispatched on a ruthless mission—to smite old and young, unmarried and married women, and even children. Only those marked with a *taw* are to be spared, and the judgment is to start right at the sanctuary. Despite the many cultic activities going on at the temple—or better, because of them—the executioners are given permission to initiate their defiling ravages there. When Queen Athaliah was deposed and assassinated, she was first dragged out of the temple before being killed (2 Kgs. 11:15). No such ritual considerations deter the executioners Ezekiel sees. The religious elite retain their priority in being the first to experience the divine judgment. Jeremiah, too, had found the expressed allegiance to the temple to be deceptive and threatened it with a destruction similar to that meted out on Yahweh's ancient sanctuary at Shiloh (Jer. 7:4, 14).

As Ezekiel watched the carnage, he was left alone, a remnant of one. Does this suggest that none of those marked with a *taw* were in the temple precincts? In any case, he fell on his face in shock (cf. 1:28; 3:23) and interceded with Yahweh: "Oh, Lord Yahweh, will you destroy the entire remnant of Israel when you pour out your wrath on Jerusalem?" (9:8). The poignancy of this petition is emphasized by its being one of the truly rare words of Ezekiel that is not dictated to him by the deity (see 4:14; 11:13; 20:49; 37:3).

The response to his prayer can be broken down into five units. First, Yahweh calls attention to the greatness of the iniquity of the house of Israel, including their shedding of blood and their injustices (v. 9). Second, he quotes for the second time the self-justifying maxim that both accuses Yahweh and discloses a childish relish in disobedience: "Yahweh has abandoned the land, and Yahweh does not see us." Third, he reaffirms the harsh attitude into which their behavior has forced him: "My eye will not spare and I will not have pity." Fourth, he reminds the prophet that the victims are not suffering unfairly: it is *their* way he has put on their heads (v. 10; cf. 11:21). The fifth response comes from the narrator, rather than Yahweh himself, who tells of the return of the man clothed in linen and his words to Yahweh about his accomplished mission: "I have done just as you commanded me." Yahweh's response to Ezekiel's desperate lament and intercession, therefore, might be paraphrased as follows: Yes, I am going to afflict Israel severely, but with due cause. Yet those who sigh and groan over these abominations will be spared. I will not, in fact, destroy the entire remnant of Israel.[19]

During Ezekiel's tour of the four sinful areas in the temple (ch. 8) and his listening to the commands for judgment (ch. 9) the narrator repeatedly refers to the location of the divine glory. After his initial reference to its presence "there" (8:4), in the general vicinity of the temple, the narrator notes that the glory moved from the cherubim in the Holy of Holies, where it was usually enthroned, to the threshold of the temple (9:3) at the time when Yahweh issued his orders to the man clothed in linen and to the executioners. After the fivefold response to Ezekiel's lament the prophet himself observed the presence of the throne chariot (10:1) and described it in words very similar to 1:26, except that the "living creatures" of chapter 1 have been replaced by "cherubim." The reason for this change in terminology may stem from assimilation to the type of animal that normally formed the throne of Yahweh in the temple (cf. 1 Kgs. 6:23–28). This iconography can be illustrated by Figure 6, which shows a goddess (on the right), surrounded by stars and standing on the back of a leonine dragon. Throughout chapter 10 the narrator takes special pains to identify the throne chariot seen in Jerusalem with that seen by the prophet by the river Chebar (see esp. vv. 8–17, 20, 22).

After describing Ezekiel's seeing the throne chariot, the narrator reports that the man clothed in linen was dispatched on a second, more ominous mission. At the command of Yahweh he went into the wheelwork (*galgal*) beneath the cherubim to get coals of fire in order to set fire to the city. The location of these coals within the throne chariot emphasizes that Yahweh is the real cause of the immolation, just as he rained down fire and brimstone on Sodom and Gomorrah (Gen. 19:24) and as he promised to do generally on the wicked (Ps. 11:6; 140:10).

As the scene unfolds, we learn that the throne chariot was stationed just south of the temple and that, because of the presence of the divine glory at the threshold, both the temple and its courtyard were filled with the divine cloud and with brightness. The noise of the cherub wings (cf. 1:24) could be heard by the prophet in the outer court. The narrator, sensitive to the sacredness of the throne chariot, does not have the man clothed in linen reach in and get the fire himself, but the cherub has a

Figure 6

hand that fetches the fire and places it in the man's hands.[20] Zimmerli quotes the Babylonian Talmud, which finds in this intermediary hand a sign of surprising mercy: "If the coals from the hand of the cherub had not become cool in the hand of Gabriel, so would . . . no remnant and no survivors be left."[21]

THE THRONE CHARIOT DESCRIBED

When the man clothed in linen departed, with his hands full of fire, the account pauses to describe further the throne chariot and to make additional connections with the vision of chapter 1. Greenberg has noted the appropriateness of the location of this excursus.[22] The narrator cannot follow the man with the fire on his rounds lest the unity of setting in the temple area be lost, but one can imagine that he is carrying out his grim task during the description of the chariot. At the same time, the description of the throne chariot must be completed before the glory actually leaves the temple (10:18-19).

The description begins in verse 8 with the hand, which had just been mentioned in the narrative at verse 7 (cf. 1:8). Verses 9-11 refer to the wheels, with many similarities to 1:15–18. The chariot in chapter 10, however, is provided with four wheels (cf. Figure 5 in chapter 1 above), instead of the two that are implied in the earlier account. The "wheelwork," within which the man clothed in linen found the fire, was identified in the hearing of the prophet with the wheels from chapter 1 (v. 13). Not only the rims (1:18), but also the hands, the wings, and the wheels themselves were full of eyes.[23] Each cherub had four faces, as did the living creatures in chapter 1, but they consisted now of the face of a cherub, the face of a man, the face of a lion, and the face of an eagle.[24] Cherubim with the heads (rather than faces) of a man and a lion, and with a tail that ends in an eagle head, are known from late Hittite art, 950–700 BCE. Figure 7 shows such a creature from a relief found at Carchemish.

Halperin and Keel may be correct that 10:8–17 is secondary to the book of Ezekiel.[25] The purposes behind such an expansion might be first, to harmonize the divergent terminology used for the divine throne chariot in chapters 1 and 10. Especially distinctive in chapter 10 are the presence of the cherubim and the mention of the wheelwork. Another factor leading to an expanded description of the throne chariot in chapter 10 might be an attempt to underscore its divine character—for example, by assigning eyes to other parts of the chariot in addition to the rims of the wheels. A third reason might be the desire to make explicit items that were only implied (e.g., the number of wheels). But even if a diachronic analysis of 10:8–17 is correct, this descriptive paragraph serves important purposes in the present shape of chapter 10. It allows the reader to meditate on the details of the divine presence before that presence departs, and it provides an interlude during which one can imagine the man setting out to begin the burning of the city.

After the description of the throne chariot had been completed, the glory of Yahweh moved from the threshold of the temple and took its place on the throne chariot (v. 18). The prophet watched as the chariot paused at the eastern gate of the temple court (cf. 11:22–23). The living creatures, which he had seen beneath the God of Israel at the river Chebar, were now recognized by the prophet as cherubim. The faces too were the same faces he had seen by the river Chebar. As the throne chariot hesitated at the edge of the temple precincts, the narrator makes it crystal clear that the God who pronounces judgment against Jerusalem and its temple is the same one who had called Ezekiel to be his prophet in the exile (vv. 20–22).

Figure 7

AN ANCILLARY VISION: A WORD DISPUTED

In 11:1–13 the prophet experienced another vision. Note the references to the spirit lifting and bringing him, and the typical vocabulary of
visionary reports ("behold"; "I saw"). This vision seems to be distinct
from the one in chapters 8–10 since it ignores the glory of Yahweh, which
had paused at the east gate, and since it shows no evidence of the destruction wrought by the six executioners or the man clothed in linen. The
judgmental content of the vision is nevertheless congruent with the arro-

gant attitude displayed by the Jerusalemites in chapters 8–9. Both this vision and the following pericope (11:14–21) emphasize the hesitancy of the divine glory in leaving Jerusalem. This ancillary vision does not report additional cultic sins or judgmental activities. Rather, it centers on a word spoken by the people (v. 3) and how that word is refuted by a divine oracle. Such disputation speeches are common in Ezekiel.[26]

Ezekiel saw twenty-five men (cf. 8:16) standing at the east gate, among whom were Jaazaniah, the son of Azzur (to be distinguished from Jaazaniah, the son of Shaphan in 8:11), and Pelatiah, the son of Benaiah. The latter person reappears in verse 13, and these two references form an inclusio around the vision report.

These twenty-five men are credited with a two-part saying in verse 3: "No need now to build houses;[27] it is the pot and we are the meat." The second half of the saying compares Jerusalem to a cooking pot or soup pot, and the people apparently imagine themselves as pieces of meat stewing contentedly and safely within the iron walls of this pot. It is this part of the saying that is disputed in the following verses.

Yahweh commanded Ezekiel to prophesy against these people, and the prophet experienced the divine spirit falling on him (cf. 8:1). The subsequent divine oracle indicated that Yahweh knew the unexpressed thoughts of the group gathered by the east gate (cf. 14:3; 20:32). Verse 6 repeats the charge of violence that has also been raised elsewhere in this vision complex (e.g., 8:17; 9:9). The people whose thought is here under discussion—now identified as the house of Israel—have filled the streets of the city with their victims.

The announcement of judgment, which begins in verse 7, also serves as the refutation of the thoughts of the evil men. Jerusalem, to be sure, is considered to be a safe cooking pot, but the pieces of meat bubbling in it are the speakers' victims, not the speakers themselves. Yahweh will bring out of the city the people who trust in their own security. Although they were afraid of the sword, they will have to face the sword, and the sword of Yahweh at that. Yahweh will turn them over to the power of foreigners (cf. 7:21; 1 Sam. 31:4) and execute his own punishment on them in the territory of Israel (cf. 5:10). Through the agency of the sword, and especially through Yahweh's own act of judgment, the speakers of verse 3 will recognize Yahweh. One should note how forcefully the accusation is expressed in verses 7–10 by the repeated use of the word *you* in the divine address to the house of Israel.

A second refutation is provided by verses 11–12.[28] Again Yahweh denies that the Jerusalemite leaders will be the meat, but now he also challenges the idea that Jerusalem will be a safe cooking pot. He will judge within the territory of Israel those who spoke the offensive words of verse 3, and this will lead them to recognize him as Yahweh.

The final part of verse 12 ("whose precepts you did not follow and whose ordinances you did not keep, but you acted according to the ordinances of the nations") seems to be a secondary addition to the text (see n. 28). It suggests that Yahweh would be recognized not because of his own actions, but because of the sins of his people. This accusation resembles 5:7, though with one major difference. In the latter passage the prophet charged Israel with not even keeping the (supposedly easier and inferior) ordinances of the nations. In 11:12 he indicts them for living in accord with the (supposedly easier and inferior) ordinances of the nations.

As Ezekiel was prophesying and disputing the word of the people, Pelatiah fell dead. This incident has led to a great deal of speculation about Ezekiel's magical or supernatural powers.[29] The context, however, makes it clear that if anyone is to be credited with Pelatiah's death, it is Yahweh. He is the one who seems, to Ezekiel at least, to be making a full end of the remnant of Israel. The real significance of Pelatiah's death may lie in the victim's name itself, which means something like "Yahweh delivers" (Pelatiah), the son of "Yahweh builds up" (Benaiah). If a man with such a name cannot escape the judgment of Yahweh, who can?

In response to this death Ezekiel cried out "with a loud voice." The reference to great volume distinguishes this verse from the similar cry in 9:8 and repeats a motif used in 8:18 and 9:1 (the people call out to Yahweh with a loud voice, and Yahweh calls out to Ezekiel with a loud voice). It is difficult to decide whether the prophet utters an intercession in 11:13 nearly identical to the one he used in 9:8 ("O Lord Yahweh, are you making a complete end of the remnant of Israel?" cf. RSV), or whether in this case he rephrases the words to become an accusation: "Oh, Lord Yahweh, you are making a complete end of the remnant of Israel."[30] The replacing of the participle "destroying" (*mašḥît*, 9:8) with "making a complete end" (*kālâ... 'ōśeh*, 11:13) and the reference to the loud voice in verse 13 may tip the scale toward taking his words as an accusation. In any case, the work of the executioners and the deadly judgmental word of Yahweh force the prophet to say something on his own volition. As we have noted several times, these self-expressions are very rare in Ezekiel; almost all the words he says in the book are put forth as divine oracles.

A SECOND DISPUTATION SPEECH

The divine words of 11:14–21 are not really part of either the main or the ancillary vision, though they have been made to fit very smoothly into the overall structure of the vision complex. The oracle begins with a reference to the ever-widening circle of those to whom the prophet is related: "Your brothers, the men of your family, the whole house of Israel entire." The Hebrew words translated "the men of your family" are 'anšê gĕ 'ullātekā and so could be rendered as "the men of your redemption" or, more paraphrasti-cally, "the men who would be able to exercise the right of redemption of your property." This anticipates the property question that will be raised in the subsequent verses. Note that "house of Israel" in verse 15 refers to the exiles in Babylon, whereas in verse 5 it denoted the inhabitants of Jerusalem.

The prophet quotes a saying by the Jerusalemites in verse 15 only in order to refute it. They have said that Ezekiel's family and the whole exilic community are "far from Yahweh," and that the land has been given to those in Jerusalem as a possession.

It is surely ironic that those back in the land of Israel are accusing others of being far from Yahweh, when it was their abominations, accord-ing to 8:6, that were distancing them from the sanctuary. The charge that Ezekiel, his kinsmen, and the whole exilic community were far from Yahweh could refer to both their spatial distance from the temple and their spiritual distance from Yahweh (cf. 44:10; Jer. 2:5). Yahweh refutes this charge in verse 16. First, he concedes that the exiles are spatially dis-tant from Jerusalem, but this results from the fact that *he* has made them distant and has scattered them among the lands. Nevertheless, he has become for them a small sanctuary (perhaps by providing them places to pray, or by revealing himself through Ezekiel). The word *small* can also be construed in a temporal sense, "for a little while." In this case it would mean that Yahweh has become close to them (for prayer or for revelation through the prophet) for a brief time, perhaps until the time when he would reestablish his true sanctuary in Jerusalem. Whichever under-standing is correct, it is clear that Yahweh is affirming that geographical distance from Jerusalem does not necessarily mean distance from God.

The charge by those back in the land that the exiles were morally far from Yahweh is tempered by the statement that the divine judgment that made them distant from Jerusalem has been countered by Yahweh's renewed presence with them in Babylon.

If the Jerusalemites thought that since the previous owners had departed and were not going to return, the land would become theirs, they were also mistaken. Verse 17 contains the promise that Yahweh would gather the exiles from the various lands to which they have been dispersed, and he would give them the land.[31] Yahweh's promise to give them the land is related very closely to the word of the Jerusalemites that is being disputed. They had said, "The land is *given* to us as a possession," with the implied agent of the passive verb being Yahweh. Thus, in effect: The land has been given to us by Yahweh as a possession. The one who has the right to decide this dispute, however, is the Donor himself, and he promises the land to his exilic people. Those who return home will remove all their detestable things (cf. 8:10) and all their abominations (a key thematic word in ch. 8). This removal will be matched by Yahweh's removal of their old stony, unresponsive heart and his gift of a heart of flesh.[32]

Yahweh's promise to be a small sanctuary for them (v. 16) resembles the so-called covenant formula: "I will be their God, and they will be my people."[33] The covenant formula is cited in its normal form in 11:20, though it is made conditional there on the people keeping Yahweh's statutes and ordinances. Verse 21 states that those who choose detestable things and abominations—that is, who act in a way contrary to the way of the exiles—will receive punishment for their ways on their own heads.[34]

This second disputation speech, in 11:14–21, also responds to Ezekiel's accusation in verse 13: "O Lord Yahweh, you are making a complete end of the remnant of Israel." The words of promise in verses 16–20 put the lie to this charge, since the vastness of the diaspora in verse 17 shows that the remnant of Israel is in no danger of being completely destroyed. Note how the similarly worded question of the prophet in 9:8 was also met with a fivefold critical response.

YAHWEH ABANDONS THE TEMPLE AND THE LAND

The accusation of the elders had been: "Yahweh does not see us. Yahweh has abandoned the land" (8:12; cf. 9:9). In the final verses of chapter 11 the entire vision complex is brought to a conclusion that offers ironic fulfillment of these words. The glory of the God of Israel leaves the east gate and moves to the Mount of Olives, where it again pauses (11:23). The next we hear of the glory is when it returns from the east to occupy the new temple in Ezekiel's final vision (43:1–3). That glory was the same one he had seen when it came to destroy the city (chs. 8–11) and which he had seen by the river Chebar (chs. 1–3). Where the glory had been in the meantime is not made explicit.[35] Perhaps the glory resided in heaven, or it was the means by which Yahweh became a small sanctuary in Babylon.

The spirit meanwhile picked up the prophet (11:24; cf. 11:1; 8:3) and brought him to the Chaldean exiles, who had been assured that the future lay with them (11:16–20). To these exiles, perhaps represented by the elders who had come to his house (8:1), the prophet told all that he had been shown. This open sharing of information contrasts markedly with Ezekiel's dumbfounded silence after the call vision with its message of lamentation, mourning, and woe.

What can we conclude at the end of the complex vision of judgment in chapters 8–11? What response had been given to those who charged: "Yahweh does not see us. Yahweh has abandoned the land"? The charges were untrue or grossly misleading. From the beginning to the end of this vision complex Yahweh had in fact seen what was happening in Jerusalem, and had even shown it to his prophet. While he abandoned the land at the end of the vision complex, this had not yet happened when the Jerusalemites thought it had, nor for the reasons of divine infidelity they had imagined.

The bad news inherent in the dread word about the departure of Yahweh's glory was not the only meaning of the vision complex. As the divine response (11:16–21) to the people's complaint (11:15) makes clear, Yahweh had already become a sanctuary for the exiles in Babylon, and the exiles would surely also experience in the future a different kind of day, a day of new Exodus, of a new bestowal of the land, and of inner transformation.

NOTES

1. For a careful attempt to reconstruct the original shape of these chapters see the discussion in Zimmerli, *Ezekiel,* 1:230–34.

2. Holistic studies of these chapters have been published by H. Van Dyke Parunak, "The Literary Architecture of Ezekiel's Mar'ôt 'Elōhîm," and Greenberg, "The Vision of Jerusalem in Ezekiel 8–11: A Holistic Interpretation."

3. Two of the other three visions in Ezekiel are also assigned a specific date, and the date for the third, 37:1–14, may have been lost in the course of textual transmission. See Zimmerli, *Ezekiel*, 2:253.

4. Read 'îš, man, in v. 2 for MT's 'ēš, fire, following the LXX. Zimmerli, who also recognizes the similarities between the description of this "man" and the divine figure in ch. 1, interprets the figure as a heavenly messenger rather than the deity himself (*Ezekiel*, 1:236). Cf. John Wevers, *Ezekiel*, 79.

5. The book also does not explain how the prophet could be picked up by a lock of hair when his hair had been shaved off with a sword, according to 5:1–3. Perhaps this is a warning against assuming a chronological sequence in the book or attempting to reconstruct the life of the prophet from a literal understanding of the symbolic acts.

6. Walther Eichrodt, *Ezekiel*, 105; Greenberg, *Ezekiel, 1–20*, 168; Zimmerli, *Ezekiel*, 1:237. The word *inner* (v. 3), is not attested in the LXX. Zimmerli's identification of this gate with the city gate depends on Jer. 37:13 and on his understanding of the sin involved. See n. 8 below.

7. Note the stress on the "north" in vv. 3 and 5. Mt. North (Zaphon) was the Canaanite Olympus. Might these references to the north indicate the Canaanite character of this cultic offense?

8. Zimmerli, *Ezekiel*, 1: 239, following W. F. Albright, understands the "image of passion" as a carving on the orthostats of the city gate, but he finds the real offense in an altar built outside the main temple area in violation of the centralization law in Deuteronomy (cf. Jer. 11:13). This identification depends on the deletion of a definite article from the word for altar in v. 5 (see *BHS*; Eichrodt, *Ezekiel*, 108), for which there is no warrant in Hebrew manuscripts or the ancient versions. Unfortunately, the English translation of Zimmerli's commentary is misleading here—and often elsewhere.

9. The MT further identifies them in v. 10 as "creeping things and cattle," but the words are lacking in the LXX and may be a theological gloss on the basis of Deut. 4:17–18. W. F. Albright found in this scene elements of the Egyptian cult of Osiris (*Archaeology and the Religion of Israel*, 166–67). See also James B. Pritchard, *The Ancient Near East in Pictures*, 181 fig. 537 (Assyrian gods standing on animals), 191 fig. 573 (Egyptian theriomorphic deities), and 237 fig. 760 (the Ishtar Gate from Babylon).

10. Greenberg, *Ezekiel, 1–20*, 171, finds it difficult to identify the gate precisely, while Zimmerli, *Ezekiel*, 1:242, and Eichrodt, *Ezekiel*, 125, equate it with the gate leading into the inner temple court from the north.

11. See Thorkild Jacobsen, *The Treasures of Darkness: A History of Mesopotamian Religion*, esp. 47–63.

12. This is the place, according to Joel 2:17, where the priests would recite a lament during a famine.

13. While the MT reads "their," rabbinic notes cited in *BHS* indicate that this is one of the "corrections of the scribes" (*tiqqûnê sōpherîm*), whereby an offensive reading ("my nose") has been changed in the standard text to "their nose."

14. H. W. F. Saggs, "The Branch to the Nose"; M. Gruber, "Akkadian *laban appi* in the Light of Art and Literature."

15. See Greenberg, *Ezekiel, 1–20*, 202. C. C. Torrey, *Pseudo-Ezekiel and the Original Prophecy*, xiv, 64, concluded that the original prophecy was set in Jerusalem in the time of Manasseh.

16. Is this detail meant as an ironic contrast to 8:11, where each of the elders has an incense pot in his hand?

17. *Taw,* the last letter of the Hebrew alphabet, resembled an "x" in this stage of the Hebrew script.

18. For a contemporary interpretation of sighing and groaning, see Walter Brueggemann, "A Cosmic Sigh of Relinquishment," 12–13.

19. In Jer. 7:16; 14:7–15:4 God thwarts the prophet's attempt at intercession in a similar fashion.

20. The word for the cherub's hand (*yad*) is different from the Hebrew used for the hands of the man clothed in linen (*hpny*), perhaps to distinguish between degrees of holiness.

21. *b.* Yoma 77a, as quoted in Zimmerli, *Ezekiel,* 1:251.

22. Greenberg, *Ezekiel, 1–20,* 197–98.

23. The MT even adds that their flesh was full of eyes, but the reading is lacking in the LXX and presumably secondary.

24. Zimmerli, *Ezekiel,* 1:255, proposed that the face of the ox was replaced by the face of a cherub because the redactor found the ox offensive due to its Canannite associations. Did a cherub face replace that of the ox because the oxlike creature is now called a cherub? Vv. 14 and 21 suggest that each cherub had four identical faces.

25. David J. Halperin, "The Exegetical Character of Ezekiel X 9–17," sees early evidence here for the angelic beings called Ophanim in Enoch 61:10 and 71:7. Cf. Othmar Keel, *Jahwe-Visionen und Siegel Kunst,* 150–51.

26. In addition to the two disputation speeches in this chapter, see 12:21–25, 26–28; 18:1–20; 20:32–44; 33:10–20, 23–29; and 37:11b–13. This genre has been recently described by Adrian Graffy, *A Prophet Confronts His People.*

27. This part of the verse is very difficult to translate and interpret. Georg Fohrer, *Ezechiel,* 60, suggested that these are the words of the rich and heartless, who found it unnecessary to build houses quickly for the poor after they had appropriated for themselves the estates left by the more wealthy deportees. According to G. A. Cooke, *The Book of Ezekiel,* 1:122, the people felt that there would be no reason to build houses since the city would never be totally destroyed. Eichrodt, *Ezekiel,* 107, 136, proposed that the speakers were satisfied with their efforts to reconstruct war-torn Jerusalem, and so he translates: "Have not the houses lately been rebuilt?"

28. Zimmerli, *Ezekiel,* 1:229, identifies these verses as secondary and notes their absence from the LXX. The absence of vv. 11–12a from some manuscripts of the LXX, however, results from homoioteleuton (a scribe's eye skipped from the end of one recognition formula to the end of the next). V. 12b appears only in late Hexaplaric manuscripts of the LXX. This is the only recognition formula in Ezekiel where Israel's sins cause them to recognize Yahweh.

29. Eichrodt, *Ezekiel,* 139, attributes Pelatiah's death to the dynamic concept of the word in Hebrew. Cooke, *Ezekiel,* 1:123, sees here an example of "second sight." Ezekiel could see things at a distance and in the future. After discussing eight early solutions to the problem, W. H. Brownlee, *Ezekiel 1–19,* 159–62, opts for the idea that Ezekiel was literally present in Jerusalem. Brownlee is among a minority of scholars who hold that Ezekiel never went to Babylon.

30. Cf. Greenberg, *Ezekiel, 1–20,* 185. In order to be translated as a question, the Hebrew word for "complete end" ought to begin with a *he interrogative.* Since the MT lacks this particle, the accusatory translation seems preferable. Admittedly, the *he* could easily have been lost by haplography.

31. The promise of a new Exodus will be discussed in detail in the interpretation of ch. 20 (chapter 4 below).

32. For a fuller discussion of these promises, see chapter 8 below.

33. See Rudolf Smend, *Die Bundesformel.*

34. The first part of v. 21 is textually corrupt and cannot be translated without conjectural emendation. The consolatory words of 11:14–21 appear in the first half of the book, where we usually find only words of judgment (but see 16:60–62; 17:22–24; 20:33–44). Hence the absence of consolation in the first half of the book is only a general principle, not an absolute rule. Both disputation speeches in ch. 11 indicate that the future lies with the exiles rather than with the unscrupulous new rulers in Jerusalem.

35. Fohrer, *Ezechiel*, 58, proposed that the glory left so that it could appear to Ezekiel by the river Chebar in chs. 1–3; this is correctly rejected by Greenberg, *Ezekiel, 1–20,* 191, since the text in neither place implies this.

FOUR

EZEKIEL THE LITERARY HISTORIAN

(EZEKIEL 16, 20, 23)

The prophet Ezekiel is surely no historian in the modern sense, nor is he to be ranked alongside his biblical colleagues like the Deuteronomistic Historian, the Chronicler, or even the Yahwist, all of whom gave extensive accounts of the history of Israel from a theological perspective. Still, he is a historian in that among his indictments of Jerusalem and Judah he includes three relatively long chapters (16, 20, and 23) that necessitate God's impending acts of judgment by recounting the history of the people's sin.

His history, or his historical preaching if you will, is revisionist: The people's sinning began in Egypt and climaxed in the wilderness; one might even speak of a kind of original sin which later generations inherited from their parents. There is scarcely any reference to the patriarchs—though he does seem to be aware of the theological emphases of the patriarchal narratives—and the bleak story is unrelieved by the goodness of an Abraham, a David, a Hezekiah, or a Josiah. Israel by nature is useless grape wood, and her history of sinning led Yahweh to send the fire of his divine wrath against her. Such miserable wood, now also charred, becomes less than useless (15:5). The Israel portrayed in the historical surveys of chapters 16, 20, and 23 merits inescapable fire (15:7); her faithlessness is the moral cause of the land's future desolation (15:8). She is no noble vine (per contra Ps. 80:8–11).

Chapters 16, 20, and 23 are different from the accounts of Genesis, where originally independent units, probably preserved via oral tradition, have been linked together secondarily by the Yahwist or another redactor. If these chapters in Ezekiel were not written as a complete original composition, it is likely that a basic text drafted by Ezekiel was expanded by one or more supplements. These chapters differ from the books of Kings, not least in that they mention no individual Israelite by name and make no reference to sources or archival material. In fact, without a prior knowledge of Israel's history a person would understand the historical sequence or the allusions to historical events only with great difficulty.

Two main interpretive options present themselves in these historical chapters. One could pay attention to inconsistencies, or changes in perspective and chronology, and draw conclusions from these data about the date or unity of the compositions. In 20:1–31, for example, the setting seems to be before the destruction of Jerusalem in 587, while the setting of 20:32–44 is apparently from the depressing days after the capital's fall. One option, therefore, would be to attribute verses 1–31 to the prophet and the rest to his "school," or at least to a later period in the prophet's life. Such diachronic procedures could also be used on the other two chapters. Chapter 16 focuses primarily on idolatry with foreign gods, while chapter 23 makes the fickle and unfaithful foreign liaisons of Samaria and Jerusalem the center of its indictment. Since both chapters discuss these sins using the metaphor of sexual infidelity or promiscuity, it would not be hard to imagine—according to diachronic analysis—that the emphasis of chapter 16 infiltrated chapter 23 and vice versa.

But does the reader understand the prophet better by eliminating all secondary elements, including the promissory ending to chapter 16 (vv. 53–63), which comes as a major surprise at the end of this longest unit in the book of Ezekiel? And should one also consider 20:1–31 apart from the promise in 20:32–44? The question might also be posed this way: Are we to judge these chapters on purely historical grounds, assigning verses or paragraphs to one author (or decade) or another, in an effort to discover what the prophet really wrote?

A second interpretive option, which will be followed here, suggests that an exegete ought to attempt to interpret as a synchronic literary whole the three historical surveys according to the form given them in the best textual witnesses[1] of the book. The opposite, diachronic approach

and its inherent atomism often hide from us what the redactors were trying to emphasize theologically by the juxtapositions they made.

In this chapter, therefore, we will examine Ezekiel the literary historian. We will note how he arranged and structured his literary accounts of
Israel's history, how he evaluated the history of his people theologically,
and how his accounts compare with Israel's story as we know it from elsewhere in the Bible. We will need to consider not only the theological
implications of his negative accounts, but also the implications of a theology of promise that concludes two of the three accounts. Although there is
no doubt that there have been accretions of both a longer and shorter type
in these chapters, we will approach these chapters with the expectation
that in their present form they make literary and theological sense. In my
judgment, this expectation is not misplaced.

CHAPTER 20: A REQUEST FOR INQUIRY DENIED

The historical summary in this chapter occupies verses 5–29, for
verses 1–4 and 30–31 describe the occasion that called forth this divine
speech mediated through Ezekiel. On 24 August 592, nearly five years
before the temple was burned, the exilic elders gathered at Ezekiel's house
to "inquire" of Yahweh (v. 1). References to this inquiry form a literary
inclusion in verses 3 and 31. We are never told what they wanted to
know,[2] since the chapter is far more concerned about labeling such inquiring of Yahweh as absolutely inappropriate: Yahweh affirms with an oath
that he will not undergo such inquiry because of the abominations of the
ancestral generations. Note, however, that Yahweh invites such inquiry
after the destruction of Jerusalem (36:37).

The prophet's divinely commanded arraignment of Israel explicitly
identifies the abominations of the ancestral generations (v. 4; cf. vv. 18, 24,
27, 30, 36, 42) and divides the nation's history into a series of similar but
increasingly sinful time periods that can be diagrammed as follows.

Historical Periods:	Egypt	Wilderness I	Wilderness II
Divine Favor and Giving of Law	5–7	10–12	17–20
Israel's Rebellion	8a	13a	21a
Yahweh Considers Judgment	8b	13b	21b
Yahweh Acts to Defend his Name	9	14	22
Announcement of Judgment		15–16	23–26

74

In his description of Israel's stay in Egypt, Ezekiel makes his only reference in the whole book to the people's election (v. 5). The threefold reference to an oath in verses 5–6 ("I raised my hand") and the mention of the house of Jacob in verse 5 show his acquaintance with the notion of a patriarchal, or at least pre-Sinaitic, covenant. In addition, both the promise of the Exodus and its connection with the revelation of the divine name link this paragraph to the Priestly call of Moses (Exod. 6:2–9). The promised land in verses 6 and 15 is described as "the land flowing with milk and honey, the most glorious of all lands."

Unique to this presentation of Israel's history is the notion that already in Egypt, Yahweh revealed the substance of the First Commandment: each person ought to throw away the detestable things and not get contaminated with idols. Even more surprising is the idea that Israel rebelled against this commandment in Egypt (but cf. Josh. 24:14 and Ezek. 23:3, 8, 19) and that Yahweh considered bringing his anger to completion against the people already in Egypt (v. 8); that is, even before the Exodus took place. This indictment undercuts any claim to special favors that the exilic elders might raise on the basis of their ancestry. Even the reason for Yahweh not carrying through on this threat had nothing to do with Israel's merits. The deity acted solely to defend his name or reputation, which would have been defiled among the nations if he had not carried out the Exodus (v. 9).[3]

The second phase of Israel's history began with the Exodus and with the revelation of precepts and ordinances to the first generation in the wilderness; that is, with the events connected with Sinai (vv. 10–12). It is through the keeping of these laws, we are told in verses 11 and 13 (cf. 21), that people obtain life. The only specific law mentioned is the sabbath,[4] identified, as in Exodus 31:17, as a sign between God and the people. The ambiguous recognition formula at the end of verse 12 suggests that the gift of the sabbath will enable both Israel and the nations to know that through it Yahweh sanctifies his people (cf. vv. 39–41 and the discussion below). This second phase of Israel's history unfolds like the first, with the house of Israel rebelling and rejecting Yahweh's legal demands (v. 13a). After again weighing the imposition of final judgment in the wilderness (v. 13b), Yahweh decides to act for the sake of his name and so avoid having it defiled in the eyes of the nations (v. 14).

The periods of Israel's history, however, are not an endless repetitive cycle in which rebellion has no consequences. Verse 15 introduces a new element, the announcement of judgment, whose climactic role in the structure is signaled by its beginning with "(and) also I" (wĕgam 'ănî; cf. vv. 23, 25). Yahweh swore in the wilderness that he would not bring the people of the first generation into the land because they had violated his laws. Historically, this incident seems to echo the judgment leveled against all those who murmured at the time of the spies' story (Num. 13–14), leading to the death of all who were twenty years old or older at the time of the Exodus (Num. 14:22–23, 29–30). By this allusion Ezekiel makes the important theological point that a historical link between his contemporaries and those who participated in the great foundational events of Exodus and Sinai offers no basis for the elders of his day to claim to have the right to make inquiry of Yahweh. The announcement of judgment in verses 15–16, therefore, escalates the consequences of rebellion in the second phase of Israel's history.

But the complete end, to which Ezekiel had referred in a lament in his vision of Jerusalem (11:13), did not take place in the wilderness. Instead, Yahweh's eye spared them (per contra 5:11), and he gave the second generation ("the sons," v. 18) strict orders not to walk in the precepts of their fathers or get contaminated with their idols. After a statement affirming his identity ("I am Yahweh, your God"; v. 19; cf. vv. 5, 7), he laid upon them the positive requirement of keeping his precepts and ordinances. This account of a second giving of the law, at the end of the wilderness period, corresponds to the rhetorical setting of the book of Deuteronomy. As in Deuteronomy 5:12, it includes a mandate to sanctify the sabbaths. Ezekiel also repeats here the additional observation, first mentioned in verse 12, that the sabbaths serve as a sign between Yahweh and his people and lead to his recognition as Yahweh.

The second generation in the wilderness also disobeyed the laws and violated the sabbaths, causing Yahweh to consider total destruction in the wilderness (v. 21). Once again only Yahweh's desire to defend his name before the nations that had witnessed the Exodus led him to initiate a reprieve.

At the end of this second wilderness period two additional announcements of judgment are added (vv. 23–26), which make this point in Israel's history even more climactic than the similar, but single, escalation of judgment in verses 15–16. All three of these announcements of judgment begin with the expression "(and) also I," and they undergird the announcements with an oath ("I raised my hand," vv. 15, 23) that gives these judgments the same authority as Yahweh's promise of the land in verses 5–6.

The first additional judgment, in verses 23–24, announces that Yahweh would scatter the people among various lands because they violated the laws, defiled the sabbaths, and clung to the idols of their fathers. In these words we see an astonishing assertion: The history in the land, with its temple, kings, prophets, and all the rest, was an irrelevant exercise. No matter what Israel did during the centuries in the land, it would make no difference. Exile had been determined as the fate of Israel before the ancestors ever crossed the Jordan.

As a further escalation of judgment to the second wilderness generation, Yahweh also gave his people laws that were no good and by which people could *not* live (vv. 25–26). Laws—normally intended for life—now would lead to death and desolation. Through this experience of Yahweh's final judgment the people would discover Yahweh's true identity; that is, they would know that he is Yahweh.

This is, indeed, a hard saying, both because its meaning is not incontrovertibly apparent and because it presents, in anyone's reading, a stark picture of God. It can be compared to the divine hardening of Pharaoh's heart in the book of Exodus or to the command to Isaiah, at the time of his call, to make the heart of the people fat and their ears heavy lest they turn and be healed (Isa. 6:10). Through this process of hardening, God threatens to lead those who anger him into greater sin, for which they will then receive greater punishment (cf. 14:9; Isa. 63:17).

The "no good" laws supposedly required the sacrifice of every firstborn child. Under kings like Ahaz (2 Kgs. 16:3) and Manasseh (2 Kgs. 21:6) child sacrifice was practiced in Israel. The Deuteronomist (Deut. 12:31) and Jeremiah (7:31; 19:5; 32:35) strongly protested this abuse, but the very fervor of these witnesses suggests that those who practiced it believed that such sacrifices were for the benefit of Yahweh. While all firstborn sons were to be dedicated to Yahweh according to Exodus 22:29, other Pentateuchal laws make clear that in the case of human beings, these firstborn were also always to be redeemed (Exod. 13:11–13; 34:19–20).[5] Still, from passages like 2 Kings 3:27 and Micah 6:7, it is clear that people believed it was permissible to circumvent the requirement to redeem male children under extraordinary circumstances. Perhaps such exceptions were justified on the basis of a perverse exegesis of the Pentateuchal texts, or even on the basis of alleged words of Yahweh not preserved for us in the Scriptures. Clearly, Jeremiah and Ezekiel stood aghast at this practice. Ezekiel nevertheless quotes Yahweh in this passage as saying that the law on which people based this practice was, in fact, something which God had given, but that this law (v. 25)—contrary to all other laws (cf. vv. 11, 13, 21)—brought only death and not life.[6]

The land and the law—two of the central tenets of Israel's faith—were thus turned on their heads by Yahweh's judgment on the rebellion of the second wilderness generation. The land that lay before the ancestors was to be only a temporary habitation; their real future was in exile. The precepts and ordinances which Yahweh had given for life to each generation were now "no good" laws, given to bring about their death.

Because of the finality of the announcements of judgment in verses 23–26, many scholars believe that verses 27–29, which briefly summarize Israel's history in the land, were added secondarily by someone who noted that this central part of the history of Israel had been ignored.[7] The very brevity of this paragraph, however, serves to underscore the conclusion reached in verses 23–24; namely, that Yahweh had decided on the inescapability of exile before the ancestors ever reached the land. After the two announcements of judgment in verses 23–26, Israel could only mark time as it continued in its perverse cultic ways until its actual destruction.

The five uses of the adverb *there* in verses 28–29 comprise an important part of the indictment of Israel.[8] What happened "there" (in the land) was a repetition of the unfaithfulness and blasphemy (v. 27) that had characterized their Israelite forebears in the wilderness. Wherever they saw a high hill or a leafy tree, they performed their idolatrous or, at least, illegitimate sacrificial rites. Verse 29 mocks their worship practices in a pun: What is the high place *(habbāmâ)* to which you hie *(habbā'îm)?*[9] As a result of pilgrimages to illegitimate shrines, so the etiology goes, such sanctuaries received the opprobrious name of "high place" (cf. 6:3, 6; 16:16; 36:2; 43:7). Both the worship of idols and the illegitimate worship of Yahweh at multiple sanctuaries are included in the indictment of these verses.

Verses 30–31, which begin with a reference to the house of Israel and a messenger formula, provide a final, categorical no to the request for inquiry. With an astonished question, citing the people's defilement in the idolatrous way of their parents, their "whoring after" detestable images, and their employment of child sacrifice up to the present day,[10] Yahweh affirms on his life that inquiry of him by the house of Israel is out of the question. The sins that so disqualified their forebears, in fact, continue into the present generation ("until today," v. 31).

It is hard to imagine a more devastating response to the request of the elders. At the end of the third phase of Israel's history, exile had been decided on, and God's laws had been transformed to give death and not life. The description of life in the land occupies only three verses, and this phase of the national history offers nothing but a repetition of the sins of the previous generations. What is more, Ezekiel's audience fully participates in the deadly ways of their parents. If the founding fathers of Israel merited punishment, what else could subsequent generations expect, especially since their behavior was no better, and since they were centuries removed from firsthand participation in events like the election in Egypt, the Exodus, and the first and second givings of the law?

Despair Countered by Promise (20:32–44)

Verse 32 presents a despairing response by the elders to the preceding recital of history and to Yahweh's refusal to accept inquiry: "Let us be like the nations, like the tribes of the countries, and worship wood and stone." The words are not defiant,[11] like those of their forebears in the days of Samuel, who expressed their desire for a king in somewhat similar language (1 Sam. 8:20). "Wood" and "stone" are disparaging words for idols, and it is to the worship of such "nothings" that the people feel condemned.[12] Because the words or thoughts of the elders are cited in this verse in order to be debated, verses 32–44 form a typical disputation speech.

It is only with an oath that Yahweh can affirm that he will in fact be their king.[13] This is the only time that either a verb or a noun referring to kingship is used of Yahweh in this book, and this unique usage lends special importance to verse 33. To be the divine king of Israel means to be the savior in the Exodus, as Exodus 15:18 and Ezekiel 20:33–34 make clear. Yahweh's royal actions are military in scope—with a mighty hand, an outstretched arm, and wrath poured out. The first two of these expressions, at least, are used of Yahweh's actions at the first Exodus from Egypt (Deut. 4:34; cf. Exod. 6:6; 2 Kgs. 17:36), but their use in Ezekiel 20, especially in the light of verses 8, 13, and 21, where the pouring out of wrath refers to Yahweh's judgment on Israel, suggests that the military force and the divine anger will be aimed as much against Israel as against any foreign power. Israel had been scattered to distant lands by these demonstrations of divine power, and this power would continue to sift Israel until a group would be found that would obey (vv. 35–39).

A new Exodus will lead to a confrontation between Yahweh and rebellious Israel in the wilderness.[14] Just as Yahweh had destroyed the first generation in the wilderness of the land of Egypt (v. 36; cf. v. 15), so he would purify out the rebels and traitors from exilic Israel before bringing the rest into the bond of the covenant.[15] All exiles will experience the new Exodus, but by no means all will be part of the new Israel in the land. Through this sifting process, too, Israel will learn Yahweh's true identity (v. 38). In their despair they thought that their only option was to turn to idolatry (v. 32). The divine disputation indicates, however, that they will be purified by God's judgment and so will be brought to reject all idolatry.

Exodus and wilderness are to be followed by a procession to Zion, rather than by a new conquest of the land (vv. 39–40; cf. Isa. 51:9–11).[16] The three uses of "there" in verse 40 balance the five uses of "there" in verses 28–29. Back in the land Israel had turned with alacrity to whatever worship was being carried out on every high hill and under every leafy tree. On the return to the temple mountain—the "theres" of verse 40—the whole house of Israel in its entirety is to be obedient or holy. Note that they will no longer defile the *holy* name, but will serve Yahweh on his *holy* mountain in the land. There Yahweh will accept them; there he will require[17] their contributions, their choice offerings, and their *holy* offerings. Through the divine regathering of Israel, Yahweh would show himself *holy* in the eyes of the nations (v. 41). Such holiness would once more prove him to be Yahweh, just as his giving of the sabbaths was to lead to the recognition of him as the one who makes people *holy* (v. 12; cf. v. 20). In bringing them into the land he would fulfill the oath (v. 42) first given in Egypt to their historical parents (vv. 5–6).

The return to Zion would cause Israel to remember "there" their ways and all the deeds by which they had defiled themselves, and they would, therefore, loathe themselves (v. 43; cf. 6:8–10; 16: 61, 63; 36:31–32). A desire to defend his own name, which moved Yahweh to hesitate to carry out his anger in Egypt and in the two wilderness generations (vv. 9, 14, 22), would provide the theological basis for him to restore worship in the land (v. 44). Such saving action, or holiness, displayed before the nations would lead the restored remnant to recognize what it means for God to say, "I am Yahweh" (v. 44).

Conclusion of Ezekiel 20

We have seen that there is a rhetorical unity to chapter 20, regardless of any questions that might be raised about the originality of this or that passage within the chapter.[18] To Ezekiel the lessons of history were plain: neither Israel's forebears (in Egypt, in two generations in the wilderness, and in the land) nor his contemporary audience had any moral basis for making an inquiry of Yahweh (vv. 1–31). But Ezekiel also refused to concede that the only option open to the despairing exiles was idolatry. Yahweh would act as king to liberate his people from their several places of exile and to free them from the rebels and traitors in their midst. This new Exodus would be an improvement over the first Exodus and would be followed by perfect worship on the temple mountain in Jerusalem. Such worship would serve as a positive counterpart to Israel's previous idolatrous history in the land. Throughout the negative past history, as well as in the promissory future, Israel's hope lay in the name of Yahweh (vv. 9, 14, 22, 44) rather than in its own merits or deeds.

Six times in the chapter the recognition formula is used. Twice it is said that the giving or the keeping of the sabbaths will lead to a recognition of Yahweh (vv. 12, 20). Since Israel, furthermore, had defiled itself with idols (vv. 7, 18; cf. vv. 30, 31, 43), Yahweh would defile them through their gifts so that he would have to desolate them and so that they would know his righteous character in judgment (v. 26).[19] Even when he would exercise his promise to the despairing exiles, he would tolerate no disobedience, and this, too, would serve as proof of his consistent character (v. 38). The new Exodus and the new entrance into the land, which brought to completion what had been sworn to the fathers in Egypt, would also lead to recognition of Yahweh's character (v. 42). The last recognition formula, in verse 44, ties both halves of the chapter together. Yahweh's future acts of deliverance for his name's sake (vv. 32–44) would underscore that all his favorable acts toward Israel before 587 stemmed from his fidelity to his name (vv. 1–31, esp. vv. 9, 14, 22). Nowhere in its history—from first Exodus through new Exodus—could the house of Israel place any trust in its own, corrupt deeds.

CHAPTER 16: ABOMINABLE JERUSALEM

In his indictment of Jerusalem, Ezekiel employs allegorical techniques as he compares the city to a faithless prostitute. Throughout chapter 16, which is the longest prophecy in the book, it is clear that the people of Jerusalem stand thinly veiled behind the figurative speech, and the prophet even occasionally moves to a direct, nonfigurative attack on their misdeeds. The motif of sexual infidelity as a metaphor for unfaithfulness appears in the earlier prophets Hosea (chs. 1–3), Isaiah (1:21), and Jeremiah (chs. 2–3).

Unique historical and theological perspectives and the intricacy of the literary composition itself lend great power to this disturbing chapter. It can be outlined as follows:

Indictment of the Harlotrous City (vv.1–34).
> Introduction (vv. 1–2).
> An abandoned woman is "married" by Yahweh and provided with lavish gifts (vv. 3–14).
> The woman trusts in her beauty and turns to idolatry (vv. 15–25).
> The woman has illicit liaisons with foreign lovers and becomes a headstrong whore (vv. 26–30).
> The prostitute pays her lovers (vv. 31–34)

God's Sentence on the City (vv. 35–43)

Comparison of Jerusalem to her Sisters, Sodom and Samaria (vv. 44–58)

The Reestablishment of the Covenant Relationship (vv. 59–63).[20]

The prophet is instructed to make the city know its abominations (v. 2: cf. 20:4). Right from the start of his historical survey Ezekiel addresses the city by the pronoun "you" (contrast ch. 23). Historical events are referred to more ambiguously in this chapter than in chapter 20, and the interpreter cannot always decide whether or not some of the details reported in the allegorical tale of the wayward woman represent events in Israel's history.

Jerusalem's parentage is part of the problem: she hails from the land of Canaan, with an Amorite as father and a Hittite as mother (v. 3). Already in Genesis 9:25 Noah had cursed Canaan, and fear of the dangers of the native Canaanite population pervades much of the Old Testament. According to the table of nations, Canaan numbered among its descendants Heth (the ancestor of the Hittites) and the Amorites (Gen. 10:15–16). Scattered references in the Bible suggest that Ezekiel's identification of Jerusalem's ancestry may be reflecting contemporary knowledge about the city's history,[21] but the moral overtones that he sees in this pagan ancestry were probably uppermost in his mind (see vv. 44–45). In contrast to the biblical patriarchal account, no hint is given of any unique honor due to Jerusalem's forebears. Jerusalem's parents, in fact, neglected the kind of infant care that was practiced in ancient times and abandoned their child to become a foundling (vv. 4–5). No eye pitied her or had mercy on her, a fate that seemed destined for repetition in the prophet's own day (cf. 5:11; 7:4, 9; 8:18; 9:5, 10).

The foundling Jerusalem survived because Yahweh passed her way twice, saw her, and acted on her behalf (vv. 6, 8). The first time the child was still sullied with the blood of afterbirth, and Yahweh saved her with a simple command or invitation: "Live." Under divine blessing the infant grew into a sexually mature young woman, though she was still naked and bare (v. 7). It is hard to tell whether the time between the first and the second divine visitation is a subtle allusion to Israel's stay in Egypt. In any case, Yahweh covered the young woman with his skirt on their second meeting (a metaphor for marriage or betrothal; cf. Ruth 3:9), swore his faithfulness to her, and entered into a covenant with her. This covenant could refer either to a marriage contract (cf. Mal. 2:14) or to the Sinai covenant made with Israel. The Bible nowhere else refers to a divine covenant with the city of Jerusalem. The important point is that through these unmotivated actions of Yahweh "she became his" (v. 8; cf. 23:4).

Yahweh washed her, dressed her with the finest clothes and with elaborate jewelry, and even supplied her with food. The result was an exceedingly beautiful woman fit to be a member of royalty (v. 13). This latter reference and a note in verse 14 about her reputation (name) going out among the nations may be subtle references to the rise of kingship in Israel (Jerusalem) and to Solomon's fame (cf. 1 Kgs. 10:1). Her beauty, in any case, was the result of her divine endowment: "It was perfect because of my splendor which I had put upon you."

The city soon confused the gift with the divine giver and put her trust in the former. She played the harlot with her reputation and extended her sexual favors to every passer-by. In other words, she worshipped other gods instead of or alongside of Yahweh, who had been the first to visit her, when no one else cared. She built illegitimate and/or idolatrous platforms or "heights" and—the indictment proves almost to be vulgar!—spread her legs to every passer-by (vv. 24–25). Words formed from *znh*, "to be a prostitute," appear 21 times in this chapter and an additional 21 times in chapter 23.

A repeated use of the verb *take* in verses 16–20 shows how she perverted the divine gifts of verses 9–14 to idolatrous uses: her clothes were used to decorate her illegitimate high places (v. 16; cf. 6:3, 6); glorious articles of gold and silver, given by Yahweh himself, were transformed into male idols (v. 17); embroidered clothes were placed on these statues,

83

and oil, incense, and various foodstuffs, evidence of divine generosity, were set out before them (vv. 18–19); worst of all, the children produced by the marriage were used for child sacrifices (vv. 20–21). She took the divine gifts and misused them. These abominations and harlotries were epitomized by her failure to remember where she had come from—a naked and bare young woman, spattered with blood, whose life Yahweh had spared and whom he had married when she had nothing (v. 22; cf. v. 43).

According to verses 26–29 her unfaithfulness manifested itself in relationships with various foreign powers: Egypt, Philistia, Assyria, and Chaldea. Dalliance with Egypt was Israel's perpetual temptation and a constant irritant to the prophets. In Ezekiel's days, too, that proved to be a problem, and the contemporaneity of the issue may account for his harsh invective: Egyptians are "oversexed" and have giant penises (v. 26; 23:20). The Philistine women, who hated her, were embarrassed by her promiscuity (v. 27). Affiliation with Assyria and the Chaldeans in a kind of nymphomaniacal frenzy led to no satisfaction (vv. 28–29). All this, in Ezekiel's telling, was the work of a headstrong whore—Jerusalem (v. 30).

With caustic irony the prophet argues that the accused differs from all other prostitutes (vv. 31–34). While they at least get paid for their efforts, Jerusalem pays fees *to* her lovers, apparently a reference to the tribute she had shipped to foreign powers from time to time (e.g., 2 Kgs. 15:19–20; 17:3; Hos. 12:1). Jerusalem, Ezekiel concludes, you surely are "different"!

God's Sentence

Before stating the divine sentence, Ezekiel summed up once more the indictment: sexual liaisons with other gods,[22] idolatry, and child sacrifice (v. 36). Because of these sins, Yahweh announced that he would gather together all Jerusalem's "lovers" against her—that is, the foreign powers to whom she had related, regardless of whether they loved her or hated her (v. 37). Yahweh would then strip Jerusalem, a punishment which he had also threatened against the adulterous mother in Hosea (2:3), and the nations would be eyewitnesses of her naked humiliation (cf. Nah. 3:5). Jerusalem stood condemned by the laws dealing with adultery and with criminal violence (child sacrifice); she would herself suffer violence from those who were angry or passionately outraged by her behavior (v. 38).

Yahweh also threatened to hand her over to these same foreign powers, who would tear down her cultic installations, strip her of the clothes
Yahweh had given her, and leave her naked and bare—just as she was at
the beginning before Yahweh married her (v. 39; cf. v. 7). The nations in
turn would bring up a crowd (v. 40; an invading army?) to stone her (Lev.
20:10; Deut. 22:23–24), hack her to pieces with swords, and burn down
her houses—a reference more suitable to the impending fate of a city than
to the punishment due an adulteress. Other women would witness these
punishments (v. 41; cf. v. 27), and Yahweh would end her sex-for-profit
schemes, including her outrageous payment of fees to her lovers. Only
through such fierce judgments would Yahweh's anger and passion be
sated, so that he could again find peace (v. 42). While modern readers are
profoundly disturbed by the violence of this approach, especially since it is
directed against a woman, we can still recognize through the unfortunate
metaphor the prophet's theological conclusion: Ezekiel sees no way for
Jerusalem to escape the full force of the divine fury.

Like Mother, like Daughter

At this point Ezekiel returns to the original metaphor dealing with
Jerusalem's ancestry, with which he had begun in verse 3. Everyone will
repeat a damning proverb: "Like mother, like daughter." Her mother,
too, had spurned her husband and her children, as did Jerusalem's sisters,
Sodom and Samaria, who have previously not been mentioned in this
chapter. All three daughters are addressed in the final words of verse 45:
"Your [plural] mother was a Hittite and your father an Amorite"—the
whole family is rotten to the core.

The prophet refers to Samaria, the capital of the northern kingdom,
and Sodom, a city of proverbial evil, in order to claim that Jerusalem has
outdone her sisters in evil. Hence, she is not just the sister of her sisters (v.
45), but she actually is worse than they are (vv. 47–48). While Sodom's
sin elsewhere in the Bible is linked to homosexual rape and/or the violation of the laws of hospitality (Gen. 19:4–11), here she is indicted for manifesting the arrogant insensitivity of the rich: she was proud and did not
grasp the hand of the poor and the needy (v. 49). Are we to imagine that
Ezekiel had access to an alternate historical tradition about Sodom? Or
has he merely rephrased the sin of this archetypically evil city in order to
bring it into line with the prophetic charge of social oppression that had

previously been leveled against Israel, Judah, and Jerusalem? The social injustices of Jerusalem and Sodom were abominations, just as much as were the idolatrous cults. The injustices perpetrated in Sodom necessitated divine annihilation, of which Jerusalem itself was a witness (v. 50).

No specific sins are identified for Samaria, but this city, whose fall almost 150 years earlier the prophets had foretold, had not committed half the sins of her southern counterpart, according to Ezekiel (v. 51). Sodom and Samaria were righteous or innocent in comparison with Jerusalem. Jerusalem's many sins served as a kind of intercession with God that led to a declaration of innocence for her northern and southern rivals and to shame and disgrace for herself (v. 52). Even a restoration of Jerusalem would be preceded by the prior restoration of Sodom and Samaria; Jerusalem would be restored as one city among the three (v. 53). Her wickedness would serve as reassuring comfort to her sisters. Just as Sodom had been despised by Jerusalem before the latter's own wickedness had been disclosed, so contemporary women like the Edomites[23] and the Philistines despise the "holy city." The comparison with Samaria and Sodom is anything but kind. Jerusalem has no possibility to escape the guilt of her depraved abominations (v. 58).

Divine and Human Memory in the Restoration

The final paragraph in the chapter, verses 59–63, talks of life after the fall of Jerusalem, but even its promissory character is coordinated with the city's sinful history. First of all, Yahweh will act toward Jerusalem in a way appropriate to her violation of the divine oath and covenant of which she was a part. Anyone who knows Israel's tradition of covenant curses could not mistake the intention of this threat. Judgment is coming.

While Jerusalem had been forgetful of the moral obligations stemming from her transformation from rags to riches (vv. 22, 43), Yahweh promised to act in memory of the (wedding) covenant made with her in her early days and to reestablish an everlasting covenant.[24] Jerusalem had not remembered, but Yahweh would remember, and his remembering and consequent restoration of Jerusalem would lead the city in turn to remember its evil ways and to experience disgrace when she would receive her older and younger sisters[25] as her own daughters (v. 61)—though not as part of her covenant. The latter phrase is quite ambiguous. It might mean that the restored cities would not be part of the covenant community, or it might mean that such a restoration would go beyond anything ever envisioned in the covenant tradition, or it might even mean that the restoration would not be the result of Jerusalem's covenant fidelity.

Reestablishment of the covenant in any case would lead to Jerusalem's recognition of Yahweh's true identity. Through the divine work of atonement she would come to know her God, and she would also discover that there was no justification for any kind of boasting on her own part (v. 63). How her heart would burn within her when she recognized that the only reason why there had to be a restoration at all was because of her wanton sinfulness!

Conclusion to Chapter 16

This chapter is not for the theologically squeamish. Ezekiel's review of Jerusalem's history never lets the reader forget that the city was of questionable lineage and that it was the worst of a notoriously wicked family. Once the prophet had settled on the metaphor of a prostitute to characterize the city's character, he exploited it with almost maniacal fury. So vivid is his indictment that it occasionally borders on vulgarity; so comprehensive is his critique that it not only includes worship of other deities, but it also mentions child sacrifice and even fickle foreign policy as extensions of the root sin.

The figure is skewed toward the end of the chapter in that Jerusalem is compared unfavorably, not only to other prostitutes (vv. 31–34), but even to cities like Samaria and Sodom, to whom she no doubt usually felt quite superior, even in her most introspective moments. The prophet's indictment is not limited to his own or to any other identifiable age. Specific eras in Jerusalem's history, in fact, are only vaguely mentioned—her Amorite or Hittite connections before the time of David; her election in and deliverance from Egypt; the gift of the covenant; her resorting to child sacrifice (perhaps in the time of Ahaz and Manasseh); her consorting with foreign powers like Egypt, Assyria, and Babylon on many different occasions; and her subjugation to the Philistines, perhaps at the time of Sennacherib.[26] From beginning to end, Ezekiel depicted a history of idolatry—repeated, persistent, beyond all limits or alibis.

Jerusalem trusted in her beauty (v. 15) and made it abominable (v. 25). The divine benefactions, therefore, were rejected and turned into idols. She worshiped the gift instead of the giver. There is no release from this scathing indictment, no mitigating circumstances, no high points or reforms. The whole history of Jerusalem was that of a headstrong whore.

Whoever gave the chapter its final form believed that there would have to be a better future after Yahweh himself and the nations had vented their wrath on the city. Any future depended on God's remembering his earlier favors to a helpless, abandoned woman and on his acting consistently with such grace once more. Jerusalem would be restored as one city among other restored evil cities, and God's remembering would reawaken her own memory. A restored Jerusalem would know that she had once been naked and bare, and that because of her infidelity she had returned at the end of her history to her naked and bare condition. Still, a covenant would be (re)established that would be everlasting in its effect, and the reticence and disgrace she would experience would be triggered by the atonement offered by Yahweh. While there would be no escape from the implications of her sordid history, one thing she would learn from this history: Yahweh had met her twice in her early life, calling her to life and to fellowship with him. Yahweh's remembering and his desire to atone were the bases for her restoration. His divine word—"oracle of Lord Yahweh"—in judgment (vv. 19, 23, 30, 43, 48, 58, 63) and in grace (vv. 8, 14, 63) was sure. Jerusalem's history proved that Yahweh was faithful to himself.

CHAPTER 23: FAITHLESS OHOLAH AND OHOLIBAH

Chapter 23, like chapter 16, uses the theme of sexual unfaithfulness to indict Jerusalem and Samaria, though no mention is made here of Sodom. Unlike chapter 16, however, Israel is faithless in chapter 23 right from the start, with no period when she grows and flourishes under God's care and blessing. Unlike both chapters 16 and 20, chapter 23 is not concluded with a promissory paragraph. As in chapter 20, Israel is accused of apostasy already in Egypt. The chapter can be outlined as follows:

Oholah and Oholibah introduced; their sin in Egypt (vv. 1–4)
Oholah's sins with the Assyrians and the Egyptians; her punishment (vv. 5–10).
Oholibah's sins with the Assyrians, Babylonians, and the Egyptians (vv. 11–21).
Announcements of judgment (vv. 22–35).

Yahweh hands Oholibah into the hands of her enemies (vv. 22–30).
Oholibah to drink "cup" of her sister (vv. 31–35).
Indictment of both sisters (vv. 31–44).
Announcement of judgment on both sisters (vv. 45–49).[27]

The youth of Oholah and Oholibah was a period of rampant infidelity (vv. 3, 8, 19, 21) rather than the period when Yahweh loved and cared for his people (16:22, 43, 60). Their involvement with other gods already in Egypt becomes clear through a reference to the fondling of their virginal breasts. Jeremiah had already referred to the northern and southern kingdoms as sexually faithless sisters, naming them "faithless Israel" *(mĕšûbâ yiśrā'ēl)* and "false Judah" *(bōgēdâ yĕhûdâ)* respectively. Ezekiel coins his own names and gives them to the capitals of the two kingdoms, Samaria and Jerusalem (cf. ch. 16). Surprisingly, no clear allegorical meaning can be discerned in the names Oholah (Samaria) and Oholibah (Jerusalem). The latter ("my tent is in her") might allude to the tent of meeting whose successor was Solomon's temple.[28] In this first period the sisters were joined to Yahweh (they became mine, v. 4), a possible reference to the events of Exodus and covenant, and they experienced a growth in population (Exod. 1:7). This chapter lacks any reference to the patriarchal period and ignores the phases of Israel's history after the stay in Egypt, except for the treaty politics that began approximately in the ninth century.

The wicked history of Oholah (Samaria) is reviewed first, beginning with her liaisons with the Assyrian empire. She lusted (v. 5; cf. vv. 7, 9, 11, 12, 16, 20) after various lovers from the Assyrian military and the government (vv. 5–6) and defiled herself with their idols (v. 7; cf. v. 30 and 2 Kgs. 16:10; 21:5; 23:4–5, 11–12). Even this was no monogamous relationship, for she continued her treaty politics with the Egyptians (cf. Hos. 7:11; 8:9; 12:1; 2 Kgs. 17:4), with whose gods she had fornicated in her youth. This fickle foreign policy, widely condemned by previous prophets, persuaded Yahweh to hand her over into the hands of her lovers (cf. 16:37, 39), who stripped her as an adulteress, exiled her children, and killed her (v. 10). The last two judgments are more appropriate to the historical fate of the north than the punishment of an unfaithful woman. Her reputation became famous among foreign women (cf. 16:41, 57), who also executed punishments on her.

One can imagine that Ezekiel's indictment to this point would have found agreement in his audience (cf. Amos 1:3–2:3), but he goes on to indicate that Oholibah (Jerusalem) was worse than her sister (cf. 16:47; Jer. 3:7). Her foreign alliances began with Assyria (v. 12), but her lust was soon aroused by pictures of Chaldean and Babylonian soldiers that were drawn on the wall (cf. 8:10). This charge may refer to contacts between Judah and the Babylonians during the reign of Josiah, when the Assyrian empire was breaking up. When Jerualem dispatched messengers to Chaldea, the Babylonian forces came to her, resulting in an association which was defiling (v. 17). Her loyalty to her new allies, however, was fickle, despite the intimacies involved, and she turned away from them. In divine punishment appropriate to such a crime Yahweh turned away from her in the same way that he had turned away from her sister Oholah (v. 18). Note the undercutting of any pretensions to superiority in Jerusalem. Jerusalem recalled the days of her youth by allying herself with the Egyptians, a reference to the revolts against Babylonian hegemony under Jehoiakim or Zedekiah (v. 19). Thus Jerusalem found it easy to remember and repeat the sins of her youth, though she seemed incapable in 16:22 of remembering Yahweh's early kindnesses. The prophetic anger at these developments is indicated by crude references to the sexual capabilities of the Egyptians (v. 20; cf. 16:26).[29] With verse 21 the prophet addresses Jerusalem directly for the first time, charging her with longing for the infidelities of her youth in Egypt.

Announcements of Judgment

This direct, second-person address continues in the first announcement of judgment against Oholibah (v. 22). Yahweh plans to hand her over into the power of her lovers whom she has jilted, just as he had done with Oholah (v. 9; cf. 16:39). The Babylonians, the Chaldeans, various Aramaic tribes, and even the Assyrians[30] will march against her, and Yahweh will convey to them authority to exercise his own judgment on Oholibah (v. 24). Yahweh's passion will be matched by the anger of these enemies (v. 25), who will mutilate Oholibah by cutting off her nose and ears, destroying with a sword those of her people who are not exiled, and burning up the remaining property. Clearly Ezekiel has in mind the realities of the forthcoming Babylonian invasion. The outraged lovers, however, will also strip her, and through them Yahweh will put an end to her infidelities, which have persisted since the beginning in Egypt (v. 27; cf. v.

48). Never again will she look up to Egyptian gods, nor will she even remember Egypt.[31]

A new messenger formula in verse 28 introduces a further development of this judgment. In handing her over to her lovers, Yahweh is in fact giving her to those who now hate her (cf. 16:27, 37), who will act toward her out of their hatred, deprive her of all her profits from her harlotry, and abandon her naked and bare (cf. 16:7, 39).

Because Oholibah has followed the way of her sister, she is condemned to drink the same cup of judgment that Oholah drained. Verses 32–34, beginning with a messenger formula, poetically describe that large and stupifying cup, which must be drunk to the very last drop.[32] Oholibah has forgotten Yahweh (cf. 22:12) and thrown him behind her back (cf. 1 Kgs. 14:9; Neh. 9:26), and so she must bear the consequences of her depraved abominations (v. 35).

Indictment and Judgment of Both Sisters

Verses 36–44 recapitulate the charges against the two sister cities, and begin with a question ("Will you [Ezekiel] arraign them?") that we have seen before (20:4). Their abominations consist of adulterous relationships with idols, compounded with child sacrifice (v. 37; cf. v. 45; 16:20–21). Additionally, they have defiled the sanctuary (cf. ch. 8) and desecrated the sabbaths (v. 38; cf. 20:13, 16, 21). Child sacrifice to idols was followed on the same day by frequenting Yahweh's own sanctuary, thereby defiling it. When foreign emissaries arrived, the women washed, put on makeup, and sat alluringly on their beds, sharing with the foreigners incense and oil which belonged to Yahweh. These charges are made all the more cutting since they are cast in the form of second-person, direct address in verses 40b–41.[33] The final summation of the charges comes in verse 44: "They [the foreigners] came to her [or to them][34] as one comes to a whore. That is the way they came to Oholah and Oholibah, women of depravity."

On the basis of this indictment the foreign powers who will administer the punishment are considered innocent—at least by comparison (v. 45; cf. 16:37–38). Yahweh urges these powers to call up a crowd (v. 46; cf. 16:40), who will stone the adulteresses and hack them to pieces with their swords, and then murder their children and burn their houses with fire. By so stopping their depraved ways, Yahweh offers a moralistic lesson to all women, who are warned not to mimic the depravity of Oholah and Oholibah. When the foreign powers have punished the two sisters for their depravity and their sins with idols, the whole community (of the exiles?) will come to recognize Yahweh (v. 49).

Conclusion to Chapter 23

This final historical survey begins with the sins of the ancestors of the two kingdoms in Egypt, traces their sins and their punishments independently in the land, and concludes with a recapitulation of the sins of both and the judgments which their sins necessitate. Both sisters were guilty from the very start; and both sisters in their maturity, when they became unfaithful by relating to foreign powers, also returned to the sins of their youth, to the original sins with the Egyptians. Oholah's sins were outdone by her sister Oholibah, whose name may mean "my tent is in her," an ironic sign of her special favor in being home to the temple in Jerusalem.

Their sins result in punishment administered on Yahweh's authority (v. 24), but by the hands of the very lovers with whom they have consorted and to whom they have proved unfaithful. These lovers act in hatred because they have been spurned (vv. 28–29), but the lovers are in the final analysis innocent (righteous), at least by comparison with the two sisters. Trusting in foreign powers leads inevitably to trusting in their gods, to child sacrifice, and to desecration of the sabbath (vv. 37–38). The sisters' infidelity to Yahweh is matched by their infidelity to each of their foreign mates.

The sisters used the gifts of Yahweh for the service of idols, and in all their history they forgot him. Their association with other powers has defiled themselves (vv. 7, 13, 17, 30). The punishment of Oholibah by her aggrieved lovers anticipates that to be delivered by Babylonian invaders, as it resembles the vicious justice of an aggrieved and jealous husband. Only Yahweh is found to be true to others and to himself during all this sad history. When the lovers will have carried out their just punishment, as they surely must, the community in exile will understand that Yahweh is true to his name: "You will know that I am Yahweh" (v. 49).

Ezekiel's one-sided historical surveys in chapters 16, 20, and 23 are major elements in his indictment of Israel. His literary histories are designed to express his total rejection of Israel's behavior even if this results in departures from the usual progression of events as recounted elsewhere in the Old Testament. His tough love foresees a future history for Israel and Jerusalem on the other side of judgment, but never unscathed by this judgment. Israel on its return to Zion would remember its defiled ways and loathe its earlier behavior. Restored Jerusalem would remember that she had started out naked and bare before Yahweh visited her, and she would recognize that her recent naked and bare history resulted from her own infidelity. The divine word about her history, both in past judgment as well as in future promise, was sure.

NOTES

1. When a reading in the MT is lacking in the LXX, however, and text critical criteria suggest that the Greek preserves a shorter and more original form of the text, I will treat such a reading as secondary and not part of the text to be interpreted.

2. A. Menes, "Tempel und Synagoge," 272–73, and J. A. Bewer, "Beiträge zur Exegese des Buches Ezechiel," 195–97, proposed that the elders asked if they could establish a sacrificial cult of their own in Babylon, while Georg Fohrer, *Ezechiel*, 108, thought they wanted to set up an image of Yahweh made of wood and stone. Zimmerli, *Ezechiel*, 1:406, points out how improbable it would have been to come to a stern prophet like Ezekiel with such a request. Zimmerli himself conjectures that the elders here, and in 8:1 and 14:1, wanted to know if the exile of 597 was about to end.

3. A similar concern that the destruction of Israel in the wilderness would lead to Yahweh's losing face with the nations appears in Exod. 32:12; Num. 14:15–16; Deut. 9:28.

4. "Sabbaths" are referred to in Ezekiel also in 22:8, 26; 23:38; 44:24; 45:17; 46:3. The singular noun appears in 46:1, 4, 12. J. Lust, "Ez., XX, 4–26, une parodie de l'histoire religieuse d'Israel," 144, suggests that the plural form of the noun might refer to the observance of sabbath years rather than to the weekly sabbath day (see Lev. 26; 2 Chr. 36:21). Walter Eichrodt's excision of all references to the sabbath in Ezekiel has not proved convincing; see "Der Sabbat bei Hesekiel," 65–74.

5. Some have suggested that the redemption provisions are secondary accretions since these are lacking in what they consider to be the oldest law, Exod. 22:28b–29 (cf. Num. 3:11–13, 40–51; 8:17–18; 18:15–16). Surely by the time of Ezekiel, however, these provisions were fully part of the biblical law. See George C. Heider, *The Cult of Molek: A Reassessment*, 252–58.

6. Hartmut Gese, "Ezechiel 20,25f. und die Erstgeburtsopfer," 149–50, proposed that sacrifices of firstborn animals, which could not be considered mere slaughter, would have taken place at a sanctuary other than the temple before the time of Solomon and at the high places thereafter. From Ezekiel's perspective, after the Deuteronomic reform they were by definition sinful; cf. Bernhard Lang, *Ezechiel*, 83. Jörg Garscha, *Studien zum Ezechielbuch*, 119–20, on the other hand, believes that the laws about the firstborn were no good, not because they prescribed child sacrifice, but because they could not be carried out in certain circumstances, such as if one were in exile or a foreign land, or if the temple had been destroyed. Unfortunately, this opinion, like many others by him, depends on his radical literary critical judgments. Heider, *The Cult*, 372, concludes: "If Israel would not obey God's good laws for life, they would obey his bad laws for death, but they *would* obey."

7. Zimmerli, *Ezekiel*, 1: 412, denies this passage to Ezekiel because of its resemblance to 6:13–14 and because he believes the original author was following the outline of the so-called "historical credo." Zimmerli also calls attention to vocabulary usually at home in Deuteronomistic works. While the word *therefore* often begins the announcements of judgment in Ezekiel and elsewhere, its use in v. 27 to introduce additional reasons for judgment is not without parallel in Ezekiel (cf. 5:7). Eichrodt, *Ezekiel*, 259, radically rearranges this section of the text: vv. 22, 28, (29), 23, (24), 25–27, (30a), 30b–31 (less: "when you make your sons pass through the fire"). The parentheses in this list represent secondary material to him.

8. There is an echo of these adverbs in the second half of the chapter, particularly v. 40.

9. High places were apparently legitimate at some stages in Israel's history (1 Sam. 9:12), but later they came under strong condemnation. See Num. 33:52 and throughout the Deuteronomistic History (Deut. 12:2–3; 1 Kgs. 12:31–32; 14:23; 2 Kgs. 21:3).

10. Heider, *The Cult*, 374, suggests that a cult dedicated to Molek had resumed in Tophet, near Jerusalem, after the time of Josiah.

11. See Adrian Graffy, *A Prophet Confronts His People*, 66. Greenberg, *Ezekiel 1 –20*, 371, interprets their statement as defiance and Yahweh's response as indignation. He believes that vv. 32–44 are denunciatory throughout and that all allusions to restoration are ancillary to God's rebuke (cf. p. 388).

12. All speeches attributed to the exiles are despairing (12:27; 33:10; 37:11), while those of the people in Jerusalem are confident or even arrogant (11:3, 15; 12:22; 18:2; 33:24). See Graffy, *A Prophet Confronts His People*, 66–67.

13. An oath also begins the refutation of a disputation speech in 18:3–4 and 33:11. Zimmerli has made an extensive comparison between Ezekiel and Second Isaiah on the new Exodus theme; see "Der 'neue Exodus' in der Verkündigung der beiden grossen Exilspropheten." He points out that the figure of the shepherd here in Ezekiel is judgmental, whereas it is "motherly" in Isa. 40:11, 49:10. The kingship of Yahweh in Ezekiel must be affirmed by oath, but in Second Isaiah it is shouted in praise by the redeemed (Isa. 52:7). The notion of Yahweh as judge of the exiles (Ezek. 20:35) is totally absent from Second Isaiah.

14. The expression "wilderness of the peoples" (v. 35) may have been chosen because this indefinite designation would have been appropriate for a people experiencing a new Exodus from a number of lands. No place as definite as the Sinai peninsula or even the Syro-Arabian desert could be chosen. Greenberg, *Ezekiel 1 –20*, 372, notes that the Syro-Arabian desert was surrounded by many peoples and so could be accurately called the "wilderness of the peoples."

15. This is the reading in the MT (see Greenberg, *Ezekiel, 1 –20*, 372–73, for an analysis of the rare word *bond*, or *obligation*). The LXX reads: "I will bring you in by number [*bmspr*]." It lacks an equivalent for the word *covenant*, which some would see as a dittograph of the first word of the next verse. Greenberg argues that the LXX reading is not appropriate in the context. Its omission of the word *covenant* could easily be explained as due to haplography.

16. The first half of v. 39 is very difficult and possibly corrupt. Graffy, *A Prophet Confronts His People*, 71, points out that the MT suggests that Yahweh invites the people to continue in the service of idols. It is hard to believe that Ezekiel would use such an ironic ploy in an attempt to bring about a change of heart.

17. Note that the word *require (drš)* is the same verbal stem that is used for *inquiry* in vv. 1, 3, and 31. While Yahweh categorically rejected any inquiry of him, he would not hesitate to make "requests" of Israel after it had been restored to its land.

18. Zimmerli, *Ezekiel*, 1: 412–14, considers vv. 27–29 and 32–44 secondary to vv. 1–26, though vv. 32–34, which may have been formulated in stages, were written by Ezekiel himself after the fall of Jerusalem.

19. This recognition formula is absent from the LXX and may be secondary. While the linguistic terminology in this verse differs from recognition formulas elsewhere in Ezekiel, the theology is perfectly consistent with that of the prophet.

20. In contrast with this interpretation of this chapter as a literary whole, see the discussion in Zimmerli, *Ezekiel*, 1: 347–48. He omits, in addition to single words, phrases, or parts of verses, all of vv. 14, 16–23, 26–34, 38, 42–63.

21. Hittite connections with Jerusalem are evidenced by Abdihepa, a King mentioned in the Amarna letters, whose name indicates that he was a worshiper of a Hittite or Hurrian goddess, and by Uriah the Hittite, the first husband of Bathsheba. Adonizedak, King of Jerusalem in the thirteenth century, is identified in the Bible as an Amorite (Josh. 10:3–5).

22. The word translated "shame" *(nĕhūštēk)* by the RSV in v. 36 is interpreted by Greenberg, *Ezekiel 1 –20*, 285–86, as a reference to the secretions produced in women by sexual arousal. This is another example of the graphic, almost vulgar depiction of Jerusalem's unfaithfulness.

23. Many Hebrew manuscripts and editions read "Edomites"; codex Leningradensis and the ancient versions read "Arameans." The words are very similar in the Hebrew script and are often confused. "Edomites" seems far more appropriate in this context.

24. It is not clear in v. 60 whether Yahweh plans to establish the former covenant as an everlasting covenant, or whether the text speaks of his establishing a new covenant as an everlasting covenant. For references to a new covenant in Ezekiel see 34:25 and 37:26.

25. Samaria and Sodom are each referred to as sisters (plural) because the prophet addresses both them and their "daughters" (dependent cities).

26. This may refer to Sennacherib's joining parts of Judah to the Philistine territory in the aftermath of the battle of 701. See the discussion in Zimmerli, *Ezekiel*, 1: 345. Unfortunately, the English translation in his commentary is incorrect at this point and says the opposite of what Zimmerli's German text intended.

27. Zimmerli, *Ezekiel*, 1: 480–81, again considers large portions of this chapter to be secondary. He omits vv. 4b, 7b, 8, 9b, 10b, 12–14a, 18, 21, 23abb, 25b, 26, and 27–49, nearly two-thirds of the chapter.

28. The word *tent*, which is central in these names, has been seen as a reference to idolatrous high places (Fohrer, *Ezechiel*, 132) or to the desert origins of Israel (Zimmerli, *Ezekiel*, 1: 483–84). If the latter interpretation is true, the point of view is decidedly different from ch. 16 with its focus on the city of Jerusalem. Eichrodt, *Ezekiel*, 322, understands both names as referring to the sanctuary of Yahweh (Oholah = [She who has] her own tent; Oholibah = My tent is in her), for which the term *tent* is found in the Pentateuch. John Wevers, *Ezekiel*, 180, rejects all of these solutions and finds the names obscure.

29. The Egyptian penises are compared with those of donkeys; their ejaculations with those of horses.

30. The reference to the Assyrians as punishers of Jerusalem is historically inaccurate and is deleted by some scholars. From a literary perspective, however, it seems appropriate that the Assyrians, to whom Oholibah had been unfaithful, are included among her final destroyers. Note that the references to the Assyrians in vv. 12 and 23 are followed by a listing of governmental and military personnel similar to that of vv. 5–6.

31. According to this chapter the sisters remembered the sins of their youth and returned to them (vv. 8, 19), though, thanks to the divine judgment, they will no longer remember Egypt in the future (v. 27). In ch. 16 Jerusalem did not remember Yahweh's gracious actions toward her when she was a foundling (vv. 22, 43), but Yahweh remembered his covenant with her in her youth (v. 60), and his gracious actions toward her in the future would lead to her remembering her former sins with shame (v. 63).

32. As a final punishment, the poem adds that Oholibah will tear off her breasts, which had been fondled in the course of her sinning in Egypt (vv. 3, 21). These words, however, are lacking in the LXX and are probably secondary.

33. Vv. 42–43 are obscure and nearly untranslatable. For a discussion of the philological difficulties, see Zimmerli, *Ezekiel*, 1: 478–79.

34. Because both sisters are mentioned at the end of this verse and throughout vv. 36–44, one would expect the pronoun *them*, though this is found only in the Syriac. The MT and LXX read "her." Note that the verb *came* is also in the singular in the vast majority of Hebrew manuscripts, though not in the ancient versions.

FIVE

DISPUTED DOCTRINES: RETRIBUTION AND REPENTANCE

(EZEKIEL 14, 18, 33)

Retribution is a prominent, though often disputed, theological idea in the Bible. Modern readers have sought to discover whether the connection between an act and its consequence is automatic and inherent, or whether the bridge between the two is something effected externally—that is, by God himself.[1] The nexus between act and consequence forms a particular problem in discussing prophetic speech.[2] The book of Job poses the problem of retribution in an especially dramatic way as it ponders the relationship between suffering and the moral character of an individual. Divine retribution in the Old Testament seems sometimes to be contradicted by the suffering love of God (Hos. 11:1–11), just as divine retribution in the New Testament is given a whole new meaning by some understandings of the significance of the cross.

Ezekiel enters this discussion at a somewhat different position. He denies the notion of vicarious retribution (i.e., that the merits of righteous people benefit their descendants or others; 14:12–23) and of intergenerational retribution (i.e., that the moral behavior of one generation determines the moral options for the following generation; 18:1–20). He also denies that retribution for a person's past behavior limits his or her ability to repent (18:21–32). Yet because he recognizes that sins like idolatry and murder have serious retributive consequences, he denies claims to land possession based simply on the promises made to Abraham (33:23–29): "Abraham was only one man, yet he got possession of the land; but we are many; the land is surely given us to possess." In most of these cases he openly disputes a saying attributed to his opponents, but in every case it is clear that his interpretation of the effect of retribution is not the only one held in his day.

Controversy about repentance in the Bible is usually not, as with retribution, about its theoretical value. One finds rather that people deny their need for it, or doubt that repentance is possible or that it will make any real difference. The need for repentance is broached by Ezekiel in 14:1–11 (cf. 33:23–29); the possibility of repentance is discussed in 18:21–32; and the worthwhile effects of repentance are treated in 33:10–20. In 18:21–32 and 33:10–20 the prophet disputes a word attributed to his opponents; in 14:1–11 he disputes the theological attitudes that are implicit in their actions.

Ezekiel's responsibility to call for repentance is made most clear in the discussion of his watchman role. As watchman he was to warn the wicked to repent, and his performance of this duty or his failure to perform it would seal his own fate (3:18–19; 33:8–9). Similarly, as watchman he was required to warn the righteous not to backslide or turn away from Yahweh in a kind of negative repentance. His faithfulness or faithlessness in this duty would also determine his own future (3:20–21).

Ezekiel's attack on contemporary false prophets criticizes them for their attitudes and actions toward retribution and repentance. Those prophets who say "Peace, peace, when there is no peace" deny at once the retributory consequences of the people's evil behavior and the desperate need of these same people to repent (13:10). The prophet Ezekiel criticizes certain female prophets for discouraging the righteous, who might have expected favorable retribution from Yahweh, and for encouraging the wicked not to repent (13:22).

The twin issues of repentance and retribution are prominent in Ezekiel 14, 18, and 33. Our discussion will explore the details of these controversies according to the order of the present book of Ezekiel. We will note that most of these accounts can be dated at or after the fall of Jerusalem, and that the canonical juxtaposition of these issues justifies the discussion of retribution and repentance in the same chapter. The prophet's use of irony is also especially prominent in these passages.

14:1–11: THE NEED FOR REPENTANCE

The geographical setting of this passage is among the exiles in Babylon, though it is not clear if the passage is to be dated before or after the fall of Jerusalem.[3] The elders (cf. 8:1; 20:1) once more appeared before Ezekiel, apparently to inquire of Yahweh through him, but their intention was met with strong divine criticism. Their pious demeanor in requesting an answer from Yahweh through his prophet was contradicted by their "dedicating themselves to idols" and putting the "stumbling block of their iniquity" before their eyes (vv. 3–4). Greenberg takes these descriptions of sin metaphorically, as indications of an unregenerate state of mind that presumed all was well between God and Israel, and not as indications that the exiles were themselves idol worshipers. In his view the elders regarded themselves as true devotees of Yahweh, who therefore had a right to approach the prophet for inquiry.[4] Zimmerli suggests various sins that might be implied by the terms *idols* and *iniquity*—idol worship itself, use of magic and amulets, or the institution of a sacrificial cult during the Exile, though he too is not inclined to see syncretism here.[5] The fact is that the passage is not specific enough for us to be certain of the exact nature of the offense, though a double allegiance to Yahweh and to (Babylonian) idols does not seem implausible. Syncretism, after all, was practiced by Judean exiles in Egypt (cf. Jer. 44). In any case, the attitude of the elders clearly denied the necessity for repentance, and therefore it evoked a negative response to their inquiry (v. 3).

In the name of Yahweh and under his instruction, the prophet delivered a most ironic message. Though disturbed by their double-mindedness, Yahweh let himself be forced to "answer" them (vv. 4, 7). This answer was bad news and not good, however, since Yahweh thereby set his face against them, turning them into a sign and a byword, and cutting them off from the community of the faithful (v. 8). Such an answer was really a denial of their attempt at inquiry. Hence there is no real contradiction between the rhetorical question of verse 3 (Will I be inquired of by them?) and his "answer" of verse 4.

What is the goal of this passage? Does the prophet announce judgment against the exiles (vv. 5, 7–11) and at the same time call them to repentance (v. 6), leaving mysteriously unresolved the relationship between these two messages?[6] Or is the goal throughout the passage to call the exiles to repentance and to motivate them for it?[7] The issue involves not only details of exegesis, but also the continuity—or lack of it—between the prophet's present addressees and the future people of Yahweh.

A decision about these alternate interpretations must come through an exegesis of the statements in verse 4 ("Any one of the house of Israel who raises his idols into his heart and puts the stumbling block of his iniquity before his face, I, Yahweh, will provide him with an answer") and especially in verses 7–8 ("Any one of the house of Israel or of the sojourners who sojourn in Israel who separates himself from me and raises his idols into his heart and sets the stumbling block of his iniquity before his face, and comes to the prophet to make inquiry of me by him, I, Yahweh, will by myself provide him with an answer"). Both statements are clearly dependent on casuistic priestly laws dealing with individual behavior. Zimmerli argues that Ezekiel has used these old individualistic laws and applied them as prophetic words of judgment to the nation as a whole.[8] The result is that the prophet gives a double message of total judgment and a call for repentance without indicating how these contradictory messages are to be resolved.

Mosis proposes that the casuistic laws in verses 4, 7–8 are cited for legal instruction or education. Thus, they are examples of how given offenses could be treated, but are not necessarily realistic announcements of judgment against exilic Israel.[9] A double-minded people that inquires of Yahweh (v. 4) and a prophet who would provide an answer to such an inquiry (v. 9) stand equally under the threat of condemnation.[10] The "statement of legal education," which forms the devastating "answer" to the request of the elders, was intended to confront the hearts of the house of Israel, now devoted to idols and alienated from Yahweh (v. 5), and to lead them to repent (v. 6).

The command for the prophet to speak to the house of Israel and his call for repentance have as their goal that the house of Israel will no longer wander away from Yahweh and no longer defile themselves with their rebellions (v. 11). Yahweh hopes, instead, that this repentant people will once more stand in a good covenant relationship: "They will be my people and I will be their God" (cf. 11:20, 36:28; 37:23). In the usual understanding of this passage the relationship between the announcement of judgment and the call to repentance is left unresolved, and it is implied that some unspecified divine action will be necessary to restore the covenant. But by reading the casuistic laws as legal education, we discover that exilic Israel is viewed as fully capable of being restored to full covenantal relationship with Yahweh by turning away from those things that made them "double-minded." Survival in Babylon is in itself no guarantee of divine favor, and the Israelite community in Babylon cannot hope to continue without a drastic change of direction. But neither are they a community under a sentence of death with no hope for internal renewal.

14:12–23: IRONIC COMFORT

This passage, addressed by the prophet to his fellow exiles shortly after the final fall of Jerusalem, has a double focus: a rejection of the idea of vicarious retribution, and an ironic and critical interpretation of the significance of any survivors who might arrive in Babylon from Jerusalem.

"Vicarious retribution" refers to the idea that one person's righteousness could positively affect the wider community or even his or her own descendants by providing a reason for Yahweh to refrain from carrying out his judgment. While this point of view is not put into the mouth of any opponent in this passage, it is easy to see that Ezekiel is disputing contemporary theological opinion. A proverb cited in 18:2 affirms a belief in such intergenerational retribution in a negative sense—parents' sins lead to children being punished—even if the opponents clearly viewed this alleged effect of retribution as unfair.

The famous conversation between Yahweh and Abraham in Genesis 18 could have provided theological justification for the idea that the righteousness of some could provide deliverance for the many. As a result of the patriarch's intercession Yahweh promised that he would not destroy Sodom if fifty—and, finally, even if ten!—righeous persons were found in it (vv. 22–23). This divine concession becomes academic in Genesis 19 when the righteous do not amount to more than the members of Lot's immediate family, and even this small band is diminished when Lot's wife is turned into a pillar of salt for faithlessly looking back at the doomed city. The emphasis in the Genesis account, nevertheless, is actually on the intercessory role of the patriarch and on the generosity of Yahweh, who was willing to spare a proverbially wicked city for the sake of a few righteous people.

Ezekiel's negative view toward vicarious retribution finds a partial parallel in a lament and subsequent divine response preserved in the book of Jeremiah (Jer. 14:19–15:4). An exilic group in that passage offered petitions to God not to spurn or dishonor them. While this group acknowledged their own and their parents' iniquity, they appealed to God's name as reason enough for him not to break his covenant with them. Yahweh responded to this intercession by saying that even if such outstanding early prophets as Moses and Samuel were to intercede for the people, he would not accept them. The sins of such exemplary sinners as Manasseh precluded the effectiveness of even high-placed intercessors.

Ezekiel deals with the effect of exemplary righteousness itself, rather than explicitly with intercession, but he concludes with Jeremiah that the piety of others cannot make up for the impiety of the citizens of Jerusalem. His carefully crafted argument begins with a series of four casuistic statements about a hypothetical wicked city. First, he states that if Yahweh could send famine against a wicked city and wipe out its population and its livestock, the presence in it of three proverbially righteous people—Noah, Daniel, and Job—would only result in the deliverance of these three men, not of the whole city (14:13–14). Elsewhere in the Bible, of course, Noah's righteousness had led to the deliverance of himself plus his family from the flood (Gen. 6:9; 7:1). Job's righteousness, too, led to the divine restoration of his fortune and even of his family (Job 42:10–13). The Daniel mentioned here seems not to be the wise figure who supposedly lived during the exilic period and whose faithful deeds and visions were used in the second century to frame a response to the persecution of Antiochus Epiphanes.[11] Rather, recent scholars have focused on the figure of Danel in the Ugaritic texts, whose social justice and wisdom were widely hailed: "He judged the cases of widows, presided over orphans' hearings."[12] In any case, Noah, Daniel, and Job—ancient and even pre-Israelite righteous men—would save no more than themselves in a city experiencing famine sent by Yahweh.[13]

In a second hypothetical case dealing with this wicked city, Yahweh affirms with an oath ("As I live") that these three righteous people would save only themselves, not their sons or daughters, if he were to send wild animals against the land (vv. 15–16). With only slight variations in wording this principle of inescapable retribution is reasserted in a third case about a divinely sent sword (vv. 17–18), and in a fourth case about pestilence (vv. 19–20). Although tradition taught that vicarious retribution was possible (Gen. 18), and that at least two of the three righteous people

(Noah and Job) had positively affected the fate of their children, such "deliverance" was not to be expected by a city that had merited any of the four proverbial agents of divine assault—famine, wild animals, sword, and pestilence. The anonymity of the city in question may mean that vicarious retribution is being rejected in principle and not just because of the extreme nature of the sin in Jerusalem.[14]

In the final verses of this pericope, however, the argument takes a surprising turn and deals with additional issues. The oracle in verse 21 applies the discussion of the fate of a hypothetical wicked city to Yahweh's recent attack on Jerusalem by sword, famine, wild animals, and plague. While three of the previous cases had explicitly denied that sons and daughters would be saved,[15] Ezekiel announced that the sons and daughters of Jerusalem would in fact "come out"[16] as refugees. The arrival of these refugees in Babylon, with their manifestly evil record, would demonstrate for the exilic audience that Yahweh's destruction of Jerusalem was totally righteous. These refugees would offer ironic comfort to the exiles. Such comfort would not consist in the news of Jerusalem's escape from destruction, nor even in the presence of a partial remnant, but only in the assurance that the evil that had befallen Jerusalem was in accord with Yahweh's righteousness: "You shall know that I have not done without cause all that I have done in it" (14:23).

According to 16:54, the restoration of Jerusalem in the midst of Samaria and Sodom would offer similar modest comfort to her proverbially wicked sisters. Though the sins of Samaria and Sodom had been great, Jerusalem's had been even greater, and Jerusalem was restored only as one among the three sisters. Ezekiel's ironic interpretation of the word *comfort* is a far cry from that of Second Isaiah, whose book opens with an announcement of divine comfort (Isa. 40:1), by which he meant the full restoration and rebuilding of the city of Jerusalem (52:9).

Ezekiel's more severe approach may result from his historical position at the beginning of exile, when a demonstration of guilt rather than a remedy for despair was the top theological imperative. For him wholeness or salvation did not mean the preservation of some kind of material goods or benefits, however small. Rather, it was enough for his audience to know of the continuing existence of Yahweh's righteousness. Such a faith could only be dared by someone who knew that the final goal of Yahweh's righteousness was always life and not death (cf. 18:23, 32; 33:11). If Yahweh is absolutely righteous in his judgment, there is reason to hope that he will also be faithful to his covenant promise.[17]

18:1–20: IS GOD'S RETRIBUTION FAIR?

While the previous passage denied that the righteousness of one generation could benefit subsequent generations, the question of how the sins of one generation affect following generations was not necessarily thereby resolved. The accounts of the Decalogue in the Pentateuch report that the iniquity of parents is "visited" upon the children to the third and fourth generations (Exod. 20:5; 34:7; Deut. 5:9; cf. Num. 14:18). This may mean no more than that the head of the family is responsible for the ethical behavior of all his descendants during his lifetime, and that they, through family solidarity ("the third and fourth generation of those who hate me"), also reap the effects of his wickedness. It is not hard to see, however, that these words might be taken to mean that the sins of one generation automatically bring subsequent generations under the threat of judgment.

In one of his confessions (Jer. 18:21), Jeremiah uttered an imprecation against those who had been plotting against him, asking that the children and the wives of his tormentors would experience famine, the sword, and childlessness because of the sins of their fathers and/or husbands. The book of Job states that the wicked will find that their children, even if many and therefore apparently a blessing, will eventually fall to the sword or famine (27:13–14).[18]

It is not surprising, therefore, that intergenerational retribution would be used in explanations of the fall of Jerusalem. The final lament in the book of Lamentations apparently accepts this doctrine with equanimity:

Our fathers sinned, and are no more;
and we bear their iniquities (5:7).

This is part of a complaint leading up to a petition for Yahweh to restore his people, but we detect in it no accusation of divine unfairness. On the contrary, the speakers admit that they too are sinners.

In a (Deuteronomistic) hope oracle in Jeremiah, however, it is announced that in days to come people will no longer say: "The parents have eaten sour grapes, and the children's teeth are set on edge,"[19] but each person will die for his or her own sins (Jer. 31:29–30). Yahweh's determination to build and plant will be just as sure as his former determination to pluck up and break down. The book of Jeremiah, therefore, implicitly concedes the contemporary validity of the charge inherent in this slogan—that the sins of one generation have consequence for the next—but affirms that in the coming new age this slogan will no longer be true.

Ezekiel, however, contests the validity of the saying about parents eating sour grapes and children's teeth being thereby set on edge (18:2; cf. vv. 19, 25, 29) and makes this critique part of an extended discussion of the need for and the possibility of repentance.[20] After denying with an oath the people's right to repeat the proverb about sour grapes and children's teeth, Yahweh offers a summary or programmatic refutation of it in 18:4. Since the life of both generations, that of the parents and that of the children, is under divine control, only the person (or the generation?) that sins shall die.[21] God's unlimited power should lead one to expect fairness and justice, not arbitrariness in his judging.[22]

A detailed refutation of the proverb follows in verses 5–18 and is built on a consideration of the behavior of three successive generations. In the first generation (vv. 5–8) the good deeds of the righteous person are described.[23] They consist of 1) not eating idolatrous sacrifices on the mountains; 2) not looking to idols for help; 3) not defiling the wife of the neighbor; 4) not having sexual intercourse with a woman during her menstrual period; 5) not wrongfully doing a person out of property; 6) restoring a pledge after the payment of a debt; 7) not robbing; 8) giving one's bread to the hungry; 9) covering the naked with clothing; 10) not exacting interest on a loan; 11) keeping clear of injustice in court; and 12) arbitrating between people.[24] While this list is not as comprehensive as the Decalogue itself, it does include concerns about idolatry and ritual purity as well as about personal and social ethics. Seven of the statements are negative and five are positive; they seem to be cited for their illustrative value.

With regard to the second generation (vv. 10–13) only seven of these concerns appear, in a slightly different order and with minor variations in terminology (Nos. 1, 3, 5,[25] 7, 6, 2, 10). The third paragraph (vv. 14–17) repeats ten of the twelve issues of the first paragraph[26] as it describes the righteousness of the third generation. The fuller listing of ethical examples in verses 5–9 and 14–17, detailing righteous behavior, is appropriate to the emphasis throughout the pericope that the righteous person will always receive life regardless of the behavior of the previous generation. The description of the judgment due to the wicked (vv. 10–13) can be shorter since it is really not in dispute in this chapter.

In any case, a person who conforms himself or herself to the twelve concerns in verses 5–8 is defined as righteous and entitled to life. Since there is no mention of this person's parents, this example does not seem immediately relevant to the question about intergenerational retribution. Within the wider context, of course, it fits in well with the logic of the argument.

Suppose, however, that this righteous person engenders a wicked child, defined as "violent and a shedder of blood" (v. 10; cf. 22:3–6; 23:45; 33:25). This child is not entitled to life because of his or her abominable behavior, nor is this person benefitted by the behavior of the parental generation. Rather, such a person should be put to death, with no blame accruing to the executioners—"his blood shall be upon him" (cf. Lev. 20:9, 11, 12, 13, 16). This case does not directly apply to the proverb in dispute (v. 2) since here a wicked child of a righteous parent is described in verses 10–13, and not vice versa as in the proverb. These verses do make clear, however, that the law of retribution can be applied only within one generation, and that the righteousness of a previous generation is no guarantee of one's own righteousness, let alone a guarantee that one will be blessed.

In verses 14–18 Ezekiel proposes a case that is, finally, a direct refutation of the meaning of the disputed proverb. Suppose that the wicked person of the second generation has a child, who, after reflection on the sins of his or her parents, decides not to follow their example. He or she will not die because of the parental sins, but will surely live. Just as surely, the sinful parent must die.

The disputation word concludes with a rejoinder by the people (v. 19a) and a reply by the prophet (vv. 19b–20). The rejoinder to the prophet's argument about the possibility of repentance (vv. 14–18) has the people defend the very notion they had once protested in verse 2. They now ask: "Why does not the son suffer for the iniquity of the father?" If they had admitted the force of the prophet's argument in verses 5–18, of course, they would have had to draw a different conclusion: Their own sins had led to their own teeth being set on edge, that is, to the punishment of the fall of Jerusalem. If intergenerational retribution is inoperative, the people would have to admit their blame for the current situation.

The prophet's reply to the rejoinder repeats the normal doctrine of retribution ("If the son does justice and righteousness and keeps all my statutes by doing them, he shall surely live," and "The righteousness of the righteous shall be upon him, and the wickedness of the wicked will be upon him") and the programmatic refutation first cited in verse 4: "The person who sins shall die." But the prophet also adds that children do not suffer for the iniquity of parents, and that parents do not suffer for the iniquity of children. Deuteronomy 24:16 had ruled out capital punishment for parents on the basis of what their children had done, as well as capital punishment for children on the basis of what their parents had done. Ezekiel extends this principle to divine retribution as well.

18:21–32: THE CONSTANT POSSIBILITY FOR REPENTANCE

The discussion of intergenerational retribution, of course, is no academic exercise with Ezekiel. But before he announces the goal of this disputation word, the call to repentance in verses 30–32, another question must first be addressed: Does a person's earlier wicked behavior limit the possibilities for repentance?

Verses 21–24 spell out the positive principles involved, as Ezekiel understood them. 1) A wicked person who turns from his sin and does right will not die but live. 2) A righteous person who turns away, or backslides, from his previous righteousness will not live but die. Between these two statements is a sentence providing motivation for the first principle: Yahweh has no pleasure in the death of the wicked, but that the wicked turn from his ways and live. This statement in the present context indicates that verses 4 and 20, which stated that the soul that sins will die, are not to be understood as ruthless or cold statements. Rather, righteous though he is, Yahweh has a bias toward repentance.

The following paragraph (verses 25–29) is framed by a quotation attributed to the house of Israel. It is often understood as a frontal attack on Yahweh: "The way of the Lord is not just." Graffy argues persuasively, however, that the verb in this sentence means "to be fathomed." What the people affirm, therefore, is that the Lord's ways cannot be fathomed or understood[27] (see the discussion of 33:10–20 below). The prophet in turn responds that the people's ways are the ones really beyond comprehension. When backsliding to death and repenting to life are the alternatives, the house of Israel's failure to repent is hard to fathom. They ought not claim that their present status has been determined by the behavior of the previous generations (vv. 5–20), nor ought they argue that their own sinful past makes repentance impossible (vv. 21–29). Above all, the claim to innocence inherent in the proverb cited in verse 2 must be given up.

Verses 30–32 draw a conclusion based on 1) the preceding arguments (vv. 5–20, 21–29); 2) Ezekiel's understanding of the doctrine of retribution ("I will judge you each according to his ways," v. 30); and 3) Yahweh's lack of pleasure in the death of the wicked (vv. 23, 32): "Turn away from your rebellions and no longer let them be a stumbling block that leads to iniquity." Because repentance is the goal of this chapter, the new heart and spirit are described as human achievements. Elsewhere, where the emphasis is more theocentric, the new heart and spirit are identified as gifts of Yahweh (11:19; 36:26).

Ezekiel 18 has often been understood as the beginning of individualism within biblical theology. Individual responsibility, indeed, is present in Ezekiel. The marks placed on those who sigh and grieve over the abominations done in Jerusalem guarantee the deliverance only of those who bear such marks (9:4). As we saw in our discussion of 14:12–23, righteous people such as Noah, Daniel, and Job could also save only themselves by their righteousness. In the course of his account of the new Exodus, Ezekiel announces that the rebels will be purged from Israel; not everyone who goes through the Exodus will reenter the land (20:38). In this latter case, however, the rebels are purged only so that the community as a whole can be pure. What chapter 18 insists upon, therefore, is really not individualism, but the moral independence of the house of Israel. They are not limited by the deeds of previous generations or even by the sinful past of their own generation. Chapter 18 calls them to do what they can in fact do: to turn and to live.[28]

33:10–20: OPEN DESPAIR

Chapter 33 begins with a restatement of the prophet's role as watchman (vv. 1–9; see the discussion of watchman in chapter 1 above). In normal circumstances the person who ignores the warning of the watchman and is overtaken by an invading army has only himself to blame ("his blood will be on his head," v. 4). But if the watchman failed to warn the city and an army subsequently overtook it, Yahweh would lay the responsibility on the head of the watchman himself (v. 6).

Now it is Yahweh who has appointed Ezekiel as a watchman to warn the wicked to repent. If Ezekiel fails in this assignment, the wicked will perish, but Yahweh will seek their blood from the prophet's hand (v. 8). If the prophet, however, has given a warning—even if his admonition is unheeded—he will be excused from any responsibility for the wicked's destruction. The astonishing thing is that Yahweh sends a watchman to warn against his own invasion. This shows how much he wants the wicked to turn from their evil ways.

The disputation word in verses 10–20 continues this line of thought.[29] The house of Israel now laments that they are burdened down by their rebellions and sins, in which they are wasting away and because of which they cannot live (v. 10). Verse 11 offers a programmatic refutation of this saying, followed by a detailed refutation in verses 12–16. The programmatic refutation consists of a divine oath affirming that Yahweh has no pleasure in the death of the wicked (cf. 18:23, 32) and a question challenging the need of the house of Israel to die (cf. 18:31). The detailed refutation begins in verse 12 with two theses: 1) the righteousness of a person will not save a person if he or she rebels, and 2) the wickedness of a person will not cause that person to stumble when he or she repents. Verse 13 states that righteous persons who trust in their own righteousness and do evil will die, with no benefit from their erstwhile righteousness, but verses 14–16 state that wicked persons who are warned and subsequently turn will live, with no negative repercussions from their previous evildoing. The emphasis is clearly on the second case—the wicked person who repents.[30]

The rejoinder of the people in verse 17 fits coherently into the flow of this passage (per contra 18:25–29). It reports that people who felt they were wasting away in their own sins (v. 10) also could not fathom a God who was passionate for the sinner to repent (vv. 11, 13–16). What is truly unfathomable from the prophet's point of view, however, is a people who know that the way to life lies in repentance, but who do not repent. Their complaint about wasting away in transgressions and sins is not an inevitable fate; instead, it is now up to the complainers to do what needs to be ⁻ʲone—that is, to turn and to live.

33:23–29: RETRIBUTION AND THE PROMISE OF THE LAND

After a report about the messenger who came to tell Ezekiel of the fall of Jerusalem (33:21–22), we find an additional disputation word that once more shows the ongoing validity of the doctrine of retribution. Those living in the ruins of Jerusalem (v. 24) appealed to the fact that their ancestor Abraham was only one person and yet gained possession of the land. Since they were numerous—and thus the promise of numerous progeny made to the patriarchs (Gen. 16:10) had come true in their lives—they fully expected that the land would be given to them (see 11:15 for a similar claim of the Jerusalemites before the final fall in 587).

This claim of those living in Jerusalem is refuted in a direct, second-person address which maintains that renewed possession of the land is impossible because of their sins, which are similar to those cataloged in chapter 18. Twice the prophet asks rhetorically, "And will you claim possession of the land?" (vv. 25–26). In a subsequent third-person refutation the prophet announces[31] that those in the ruins of Jerusalem will fall by the sword, those in the open field will be turned over to wild animals, and those in the strongholds and caves will be sought out by the plague (vv. 27–28).

Thus, no advantage is held by those dwelling amidst the ruins of Jerusalem. In fact, their demonstrable sins contradict the validity of their claim to possess the land and necessitate instead an additional round of judgments. As Ezekiel has made clear throughout this chapter, life is offered only to the house of Israel with him in exile (cf. 11:16, 18), and to them only on the basis of prior repentance.

CONCLUSION

It may be helpful to summarize some of the theological propositions which Ezekiel explicates in chapters 14, 18, and 33.

1. It is possible for the exiles to repent, and this possibility is not restricted by the behavior of previous generations or even by the conduct of the present generation in earlier stages of its life.

2. One person's righteousness cannot reverse the retribution faced by others in the community who are wicked or even the retribution faced by that person's own wicked descendants.

3. People cannot interpret their punishment as retribution for the sins of a previous generation.

4. Those who live righteously will always receive life regardless of the behavior of previous generations. No one can say that repentance is impossible.

5. The righteousness of a previous generation is no guarantee of one's own righteousness.

6. Yahweh has no pleasure in the death of the wicked, but wants them to turn and live; he also sends warnings about his own impending judgmental invasion so that it may not have to take place.

7. The righteousness of a person will not prove beneficial to anyone if he or she later rebels against Yahweh.

8. Without repentance the laws of retribution inevitably bring about their destructive effects. Unrepented evil behavior makes null and void the self-serving and seemingly pious appeal to the blessings inherent in Yahweh's promises.

In short, Ezekiel is capable of mounting a sophisticated theological argument on extremely complicated issues. At the center of his theology is Yahweh, a partisan in favor of all those who repent.

NOTES

1. Klaus Koch, "Is There a Doctrine of Retribution in the Old Testament?" 57–87.

2. Patrick D. Miller, Jr., *Sin and Judgment in the Prophets: A Stylistic and Theological Analysis.*

3. See Zimmerli, *Ezekiel,* 1: 306.

4. Greenberg, *Ezekiel, 1–20,* 253.

5. Zimmerli, *Ezekiel,* 1: 307.

6. Zimmerli, *Ezekiel,* 1: 309.

7. Rudolf Mosis, "Ez 14, 1–11–Ein Ruf zur Umkehr," 162.

8. Zimmerli, *Ezekiel,* 1: 40, 302–05.

9. Mosis, "Umkehr," 181–82.

10. V. 9 is often understood to mean that the prophet who is seduced into giving an answer to an improper inquiry has himself been previously seduced by Yahweh (cf. 1 Kgs. 22:19–23). It is more likely that a punishment appropriate to the sin is being announced. Just as the prophet lets himself be made a fool by the iniquitous inquiry, so Yahweh will turn such a prophet into a fool.

11. For a modern understanding of Daniel see John J. Collins, *The Apocalyptic Vision of Daniel,* or P. R. Davies, *Daniel.*

12. Michael David Coogan, *Stories from Ancient Canaan,* 27, 35. In Ezek. 28:3 the prince of Tyre is compared to the same ancient figure: "You are indeed wiser than Daniel; no secret is hidden from you."

13. In Ezek. 21:3–4 Ezekiel asserts that not even the righteous would be spared at Jerusalem's fall.

14. David Daube, *Studies in Biblical Law,* 155–58, proposed that if the nation had been less wicked, the unrighteous might have been spared for the sake of the righteous on the basis of "communal merit."

15. The prophet thus offers bad news about the exiles' relatives back in Jerusalem, who were no doubt an object of great concern; cf. 24:21: "Your sons and your daughters whom you left behind will fall by the sword."

16. It is no accident that their escape is not described with the word meaning "to be saved" (cf. vv. 14, 16, 18, 20), but only with a neutral verb meaning "come out" (yōṣĕʾîm) which indicates their simple departure from the doomed city.

17. Zimmerli, Ezekiel, 1: 316.

18. This passage is ascribed to Job in the canonical form of the book, but many scholars believe it is really a speech of Zophar or one of the other "friends."

19. Nelson Kilpp, "Eine frühe Interpretation der Katastrophe von 587," suggested that the proverb was not originally directed against Yahweh, but was an accusation spoken by the exilic generation against the pro-Babylonian and foolish political leadership that had been exerted by the likes of Manasseh. Whatever the merits of this hypothetical original meaning, this is clearly not the intention of the passage in Ezek. 18:2 or in Jer. 31:29–30.

20. To Zimmerli, Ezekiel, 1: 377, the proverb presupposes the fall of Jerusalem, whereas Greenberg, Ezekiel 1 –20, 342, argues that the misfortunes before 587 are sufficient to account for the bitterness of this passage. Chs. 17 and 19 describe judgment on a succession of kings, while ch. 18 deals with—and denies—judgment on a succession of generations.

21. The exact connotation of death and life in this chapter is not clear and is therefore in some dispute. Zimmerli, Ezekiel, 1: 384, argues that "life" means access to God's presence or help. Granting life in exile resembles the granting of access to the temple in the "entrance liturgies" which are thought to have been used in preexilic Israel. He apparently takes the sentences of death (vv. 4, 13, 17, 21, 24, 28) more literally and does not understand them as imitations of the entrance liturgies. Greenberg, Ezekiel, 1 –20, 345, understands "life" as "this-worldly enjoyment of good things," and he understands the lists of virtues and vices in ch. 18 as pedagogic in setting, rather than as part of a temple entrance liturgy. G. A. Cooke, The Book of Ezekiel, 1: 197, assigns a "mystical" sense to living and dying: "The physical event of death comes to godly and ungodly alike; but only the former live to enjoy the future restoration; the latter die, they have no share in it."

22. Zimmerli, Ezekiel, 1: 378; cf. Num. 16:22; Gen. 9:1–7.

23. These deeds are summarized as the doing of justice and righteousness, a requirement expected of Israel's kings (2 Sam. 8:15; 1 Kgs. 10:9; Jer. 22:3, 15–17; 23:5; 33:15), but also expected of the whole people according to Gen. 18:19 and Amos 5:24. See Greenberg, Ezekiel 1 –20, 343–44.

24. For commentary on these ethical standards and biblical parallels to them, see Greenberg, Ezekiel, 1 –20, 328–30, and Zimmerli, Ezekiel, 1: 380–81.

25. The oppression is identified as being explicitly against the poor and the needy.

26. Concerns 4 and 12 are absent, and concern 11 is listed before concern 10.

27. Adrian Graffy, A Prophet Confronts His People, 76–77.

28. See P. M. Joyce, "Individual Responsibility in Ezekiel 18?"

29. Graffy, A Prophet Confronts His People, 58–59, argues that this paragraph is original here and secondary in ch. 18; whereas Zimmerli, Ezekiel, 1: 386, asserts that 18:21–32 is prior to 33:10–20. Graffy seems correct in pointing to the more coherent argument now preserved in ch. 33, but errs, in my judgment, by limiting the rhetorical unit in ch. 18 to the first 20 verses.

30. Note that the second case is given a more extensive statement and the climactic position. The person called to repent is also addressed in the second-person singular. In the parallel passage, 18:21–24, both the righteous and the wicked are described in the third person, and the case of the wicked who converts (18:21–22) is described before the case of the righteous one who falls away (18:24).

31. Note that the divine oracle is supported by an oath formula, as are the refutations in 18:3; 20:33; and 33:11.

SIX

FAILED KINGS AND THEIR
COUNTERPARTS

(EZEKIEL 17, 19, 34)

Confrontation and interaction characterize the history of kingship
and prophecy in Israel. Samuel, a prophet of the eleventh century, was
remembered as an early opponent of kingship (1 Sam. 8; 10:19), but also
as the one who anointed Israel's first king, Saul, in the name of Yahweh (1
Sam. 9:1–10:16; cf. 8:7, 22). Samuel broke off his relationship with Saul
because of the latter's misdeeds (1 Sam. 13, 15) and eventually announced
to him the end of his reign and the end of any hope for dynastic succession.
Even Saul's death was accompanied by a posthumous prophetic word
from Samuel (1 Sam. 28).[1] Similarly, the prophet Elijah's struggle with
the royal couple Ahab and Jezebel forms a major part of the book of 1
Kings. Mention the prophets Amos, Isaiah, or Jeremiah, and one thinks
immediately of their royal counterparts—Jeroboam II, Ahaz and
Hezekiah, Jehoiakim and Zedekiah. It has even been argued that prophecy in the strict sense came to an end with the cessation of monarchy in
Israel.

Up until this point in our discussion of the prophet Ezekiel, however,
kings have played almost no role,[2] and perhaps that should come as no
great surprise. Ezekiel spent his entire prophetic ministry in exile and held
out no hope for the remnant left in Jerusalem after the first deportation,

let alone for the pretensions of the royal house. By dating his oracles to the reign of exiled king Jehoiachin he seems to undercut implicitly the credibility of Zedekiah, the puppet king installed by Nebuchadrezzar in Jerusalem. Ezekiel was preoccupied with syncretistic and idolatrous worship (ch. 8), with Israel's liaisons with foreign gods and foreign nations (chs. 16, 23), and with cultic, moral, and social offenses of the people (ch. 18). Life in God's presence and in the temple was at the heart of his positive theological agenda.

But Ezekiel also had something to say about Israel's kings—present, past, and future. His highly metaphorical speeches about the kings in chapters 17, 19, and 34 discuss the failures of the kings from a variety of perspectives. He also identifies a series of counterparts to the kings—in their Babylonian enemies, in the parallel behavior of Israel, in the judgmental and restorative actions of Yahweh, and in the future kings and restored dynasty promised by Yahweh. If we want to understand the person of the prophet Ezekiel and his theology, we dare not ignore his reactions to kings and kingship.

CHAPTER 17: AN ALLEGORICAL RIDDLE

In chapter 17 Yahweh instructed Ezekiel to pass on to the people a riddle and a parable. Since the characters in the parable are plants and birds, this pericope might also be called a fable;[3] or, since the characters from the plant and animal kingdoms in the fable also symbolically represent well-known and specific figures from Israel's past and present history, we might even designate it as an allegory.[4] Chapter 17 embodies, in fact, all of these genres—a riddle to be solved,[5] a parable or figurative saying, a fable, and an allegory.

The chapter opens with the narration of a figurative tale (vv. 3–10), in which a large, heavily feathered and multicolored eagle came to Lebanon,[6] plucked off the top, or prime, part of a cedar tree, and brought it back to the land of "Canaan."[7] To replace the cedar the eagle set out a native slip in a well-watered spot, and it became a sprawling vine of modest height. With its branches around it and its roots beneath it, this vine produced boughs, but when another splendidly endowed eagle appeared, the vine inclined its roots and branches toward him in a quest for water and nourishment. Though its original seedbed should have been enough to produce fruit and to help the slip become a noble vine, the vine twined its roots and branches toward the second eagle. In short, the vine broke its relationship to the first eagle by traitorously turning to the second.

Just as the reasons for judgment in the previous paragraph were introduced by a messenger formula, "Thus says Lord Yahweh" (v. 3), so the announcement of judgment in verses 9–10 begins in the same way. "Will such a vine succeed?" the prophet is instructed to ask. "Of course not" is the unstated but clear reply to Yahweh's rhetorical question. Someone will come to uproot the vine and cause its fruit to rot, a task for which very little effort is required—"not with great strength or with a numerous army" (v. 9). Again Yahweh asks, "Will it succeed?" No, as soon as the east wind touches it, it will wither right in the bed where it is planted.

The canonical interpretation of this figurative tale consists of an identification of the counterparts to the plants and birds (vv. 11–15) and an identification of the crimes committed against the human (vv. 16–18) and divine (vv. 19–21) treaty partners. The allegorical counterparts to the symbols of verses 3–10 can be listed as follows (allegorical counterparts are listed first):

Judah = cedar
king of Babylon (Nebuchadrezzar) = first eagle
Jerusalem = Lebanon
the king (Jehoiachin) and the princes of Judah = top part of a cedar tree
deportation to Babylon = taking the top of the cedar to the land of "Canaan"
royal seed (Zedekiah) with whom covenant is made = planting the slip from the seed of the land
lowly kingdom = sprawling vine
Pharaoh (Psammetichus II) = second eagle
dispatching of emissaries to Egypt = twining of roots and branches toward second eagle

While Nebuchadrezzar, Jehoiachin, and Zedekiah are not mentioned by name in verses 11–15, their identification is clear to the ancient and modern reader alike. As far as the Egyptian king is concerned, the majority opinion today inclines toward Psammetichus II, who won a victory in Nubia in 593 BCE with the help of Judean troops and visited Palestine and

Phoenicia in the next year.[8] The only real alternative is his successor, Hophra, whose later intervention in Palestinian politics helped to relieve the siege of Jerusalem for a short while. In verse 13 the reference to covenant and oath apparently signifies the treaty obligations imposed on Zedekiah by Nebuchadrezzar and the oath of fealty that the Israelite king swore.[9] Verse 15 repeats the questions of verses 9–10, "Will he [Zekediah] succeed?" The rebel king is then identified as the one "who has done these things," that is, who sought cavalry and troop support from Egypt and violated the treaty arrangements.

In verses 16–18 Ezekiel further defines the crimes committed by Zedekiah against the king of Babylon and states their sure theological consequences. Nebuchadrezzar had made the one born as Mattaniah into a king and renamed him Zedekiah (2 Kgs. 24:17). This puppet Judean king, however, who had violated both his oath and the treaty obligations that had been sealed with a handshake, would have to die in his sovereign's land, in Babylon; there would be no escape.[10] Because capital punishment would have been one of the sanctions written in the treaty itself, it is not necessary to hold that the notice of Zedekiah's death could only be written after the fact.[11] In any case, Nebuchadrezzar's "uprooting" or exiling of Zedekiah would require only a relatively small military force (vv. 9, 17).[12]

With a second oath formula (cf. v. 16) and a messenger formula, Ezekiel identifies Zedekiah's acts of rebellion as a crime against Yahweh ("he despised *my* oath and frustrated *my* covenant," v. 19)[13] requiring divine retribution (v. 20). Nebuchadrezzar's acts of capturing and exiling Zedekiah are only the earthly counterparts to Yahweh's own judgmental actions. The allegorical narrative itself had alluded to divine punishment by its mention of the east wind in verse 10. Naturally, the sanctions executed on the king would also have negative consequences for the people of Judah (v. 21).

Except for minor details, therefore, the correlations between the riddle/allegory and the facts of contemporary history are quite clear. The plants under condemnation represent Jehoiachin and Zedekiah, and the distinction between a lofty cedar and a sprawling vine expresses Ezekiel's evaluation of the two kings respectively. The two eagles in verses 3–5 and 7–9 have their counterparts in the kings of Babylon and Egypt, and the wrath of the first eagle corresponds to the retaliatory invasion of Judah by Nebuchadrezzar, whose quest for justice has divine wrath as its appropriate counterpart.

A final paragraph, verses 22–24, moves beyond the riddle/allegory and its interpretation to an announcement of salvation that will take place in future times.[14] The principal actor, as in verses 19–21, is Yahweh, though other characters appear as plants and birds, just as in the riddle/allegory itself. Greenberg notes that verses 1–10 have nonhuman characters and take place on an earthly plane; verses 11–18, the first interpretation, have human characters and take place on an earthly plane; verses 19–21, the second interpretation, have human characters and take place on a divine plane; and verses 22–24, the coda, have nonhuman characters and take place on the divine plane.[15]

The final paragraph in chapter 17 promises that Yahweh will once again plant the peak of a cedar tree on the mountains of Israel, where it will sprout branches and bear fruit. Since the plant to be set out comes from the cedar and not the vine, we may conclude that the prophet expected a future monarch from the descendants of Jehoiachin in exile (cf. Jer. 24) and not from the discredited line of Zedekiah—though his polemic against the latter king here is less severe than in 21:25–27.[16] This noble cedar will serve, appropriately, as a roost for all kinds of birds. Thanks to what Yahweh will do for Israel, all the trees of the forest—that is, all nations (cf. 20:41, 48; 36:23)—will recognize his ability to raise and lower the status of countries or their rulers, regardless of their inherent strength or weakness (cf. 1 Sam. 2:7; Pss. 18:28; 75:8; 147:6; Isa. 2:12–17; 57:15).[17]

Thus, according to verses 22–24, Yahweh does have a plan for Israel's future, though Ezekiel does not make clear how that plan can be coordinated with the present divine decision to punish Israel, except that the promissory plan will go into effect after the punishment. Yahweh's actions for Israel stand in sharp tension with Israel's present plans to succeed by revolting against Babylon. The deity's actions on behalf of Israel—taking a sprig from a cedar, setting it out, etc.—are a positive, symbolic counterpart to Nebuchadrezzar's actions that brought Zedekiah to the throne.

The primary theological focus of this chapter is its polemic against the idea that any kind of revolt in Israel would provide a means to escape the coming divine and human judgment. While limited by the figure of speech to the actions of the king, this critique has its counterpart in Ezekiel's consistent message that the house of Israel will find no way to escape the coming catastrophe. The royal infidelity resembles Israel's unfaithfulness to its God and its illegitimate alliances with foreign gods and nations in chapters 16 and 23. Violations of human commitments, even those with nations like Babylon, are at the same time violations of the obligations to the deity.

The secondary, if climactic, focus of this chapter is the promise that in the end Yahweh will preserve his people. This promise offers no escape from the consequences of sin, but indicates that God's no to Israel is not his final word. What future there will be, however, will result from divine initiative and not from human efforts. Yahweh's saving action will be the graceful counterpart to his own and Nebuchadrezzar's act of judgment. The Deuteronomistic History and Deuteronomistic portions of Jeremiah show a similar theological logic. On the one hand, they assert that God's word of judgment is just as sure as his word of promise (Deut. 28:63; Josh. 23:15), but they also assert, on the other hand, that God's word of salvation is also sure to happen. In fact, the word promising salvation is as sure as the divine word that brought about Jerusalem's destruction in the first place (Jer. 31:28; 32:42).[18]

CHAPTER 19: A DIRGE

In a lament or dirge a person mourns ceremonially for one who is dead. While such dirges can be said or sung after a person dies, they were also used in Israel's prophetic literature in anticipation of death. Amos hailed the coming destruction of Israel as if it were an accomplished fact:

Fallen, no more to rise, is the virgin Israel;
   forsaken on her land, with none to raise her up (Amos 5:2).

Ezekiel himself said a dirge over Tyre that was not fulfilled during his lifetime (28:12–19).[19] The dirge in chapter 19, therefore, may date to either before or after the end of the monarchs it laments.

Israelite dirges display a characteristic poetic meter (3 + 2), and often contrast the former state of the deceased with his or her present condition.[20] In this chapter we see a contrast between the king's former roaring and his present silent voice (vv. 7, 9), between a bough that once soared to the heights but that now has ceased to exist (vv. 11, 14), and between the well-watered vine and its current location in the wilderness (vv. 10, 13). The dirge in chapter 19 has been combined with a narrative, thus providing also a metaphorical account of the fall of the one being lamented.[21]

In the first stanza (vv. 2–4) the poet tells how the addressee's mother was a lioness which chose one of her cubs to be a lion, that is, a king. This king behaved like a violent lion, but he was caught in the snares of the nations and led in shackles to the land of Egypt. The king referred to is Jehoahaz, son of Josiah, who was deposed by king Neco and taken by him to Egypt (2 Kgs. 23:30–34). The identification of the mother is less certain, though she probably stands for a collective entity such as Israel, Judah, Jerusalem, or the dynastic house.[22]

The narrative dirge continues in a second stanza (vv. 5–9), according to which the mother lioness chose another of her cubs to replace the first exiled king. He too behaved like a violent lion, making the land appalled by his roaring.[23] The nations threw a net over him and brought him to the king of Babylon so that his roaring voice would no longer be heard on the mountains of Israel.

Two candidates fit this second lion cub king. He may represent Jehoiachin, deported at the same time as Ezekiel, though his short three-month reign would not have provided much opportunity for his violent character to express itself. Of course, this would be true also for Jehoahaz, who likewise ruled three months, though he is the nearly unanimous choice of scholars as the first violent lion cub king. The other possibility is Zedekiah, the last king of Judah. Four factors lead me to choose Jehoiachin as the king referred to in verses 5–9. First, it is difficult to imagine that Ezekiel would have ignored Jehoiachin in talking about kings who were deported. Second, the text notes that the lion cub was brought to the king of Babylon (v. 9)—not just to Babylon—and this fate corresponds to what we know about the actual exiling of Jehoiachin, who was kept in custody in the royal palace. Third, the king referred to in the next stanza (vv. 10–14) is definitely Zedekiah, and it is unlikely that the second and third stanzas discuss the same king while attributing to him different offenses (violence and pride respectively). Fourth, the exiling of Jehoahaz (v. 4) and Jehoiachin (v. 9)—to western and eastern sites respectively—is paralleled in Jeremiah 22: 11–12, 24–30, where Jeremiah also laments for Jehoahaz and Jehoiachin. If this identification of the second lion cub as Jehoiachin is correct, Ezekiel seems to imply that neither Jehoahaz nor Jehoiachin would ever occupy the throne of Judah again.

In the third stanza of the dirge (vv. 10–14) the mother is now described as a vine planted by water, which produced fruit and many branches.[24] While her mighty boughs were fit for rulers' staffs, one of her boughs exalted itself among the clouds and was conspicuous because of its height (cf. 31:10–11, a similar condemnation of Egypt). Since this bough is clearly the last king of Judah, he is to be identified with Zedekiah. His arrogant ascent into the clouds may refer to his foolish revolt against his Babylonian overlords.

Because of the sin of the pretentious bough, the vine itself—and not just its royal offspring—underwent severe punishment. The fire that comes from the bough and burns up the fruit of the vine suggests that the people (or the dynasty) will be destroyed because of the sin of the king.[25] Note also that the vine is uprooted, cast to the ground, smitten by the east wind, planted in the parched wilderness, and consumed by a fire. The multiple references to the vine's destruction, a type of "overkill," represent the finality of its situation. The mother herself, or the vine (i.e., the dynasty or the people), is the focus of the punishment, not primarily the ruler as in verses 2–4 and 5–9. She whose strong boughs were appropriate for rulers' staffs will no longer have a strong staff to serve as a ruling scepter.

The last line of the chapter may also say something about the history of the composition. "This is a dirge," the poet notes (cf. 32:16), confirming the identification of the genre given in the opening line: "Lift up a dirge about the princes of Israel."[26] This dirge, which the prophet had been commanded to speak in advance of the death of the lamented ones, became an actual dirge in response to the death of the lamented ones in the course of Ezekiel's career. We might paraphrase verse 14b as follows: This is a dirge, employed by the prophet to announce judgment on the monarch himself and on the dynasty or people of Judah, but it became a real dirge when the death-dealing events it announced took place.

This plausible reading of chapter 19[27] makes violence (oppression) and pride the cardinal faults of the monarchy rather than treaty infidelity (ch. 17; see above) or self-aggrandizement and failure to protect the people (ch. 34; see below). The lion imagery is not positive but thoroughly violent.[28] The cubs take booty from their citizens and do not shrink from violent acts. In 11:6 Ezekiel made similar accusations against the house of Israel: "You have multiplied your slain in this city, and have filled its streets with the slain." In chapter 22 he compared the kings to wild animals: "Her princes[29] in the midst of her are like a roaring lion tearing the prey; they have devoured human lives; they have taken treasure and precious things; they have made many widows in the midst of her (v. 25; cf.

vv. 23–31 and Zeph. 3:3). The punishment visited on the vine/mother and her bough (the dynasty and its last king)[30] is an expression of wrath (v. 12), first of all the wrath of the nations and finally also the wrath of Yahweh (cf. 7:8–9; 23:24–25). The dead end of the people/dynasty confirms that there is no hope for the future, at least from a human perspective. Even in chapter 17 the future of the monarchy beyond the judgment depended entirely on divine intervention (vv. 22–24). The dirge spoken about the kings in chapter 19, however, is not a taunt. It occurs in a context that affirms that Yahweh has no pleasure in the death of the wicked (18:32).

CHAPTER 34: A WOE ORACLE

Chapter 34, the third metaphorical saying about the kings, consists of a woe oracle (cf. 13:3–16, 18–23),[31] introduced by a messenger formula and directed against the shepherds of Israel. The term *shepherds* in the ancient Near East, as well as in Israel, was used to denote the royal rulers of a country or even to describe divine rulership. By the broad term *shepherds of Israel*, Ezekiel seems to include all rulers of Israel, throughout its entire history, perhaps even the contemporary leaders of the community in exile. But the principal focus would appear to be on Israel's kings. The prophet seems to depend here in a variety of ways on a similar oracle in Jeremiah 23:1–8.[32] There too the leaders are referred to as shepherds, and the sheep are said to be lost, driven away, and scattered. Yahweh is identified as the one who judges the flock because of the wicked shepherds, but also as the one who restores the flock, and whose restorative role has a counterpart in an earthly messianic institution.

In an indictment introduced by a messenger formula (v. 2), the shepherds are criticized for failing to care for (act as shepherd toward) the sheep. They did not hesitate to profit from the products of the flock—their fat or milk,[33] their wool, and their meat—but there was no reciprocal concern for the welfare of the sheep. Verse 4 notes the shepherds' inattention to those who are weak, sick, broken, driven away, or lost, while those who are strong were ruled violently. Lacking shepherds who might look out for and seek for those entrusted to them, the sheep were scattered and fell prey to predatory animals. Lurking behind these metaphors is Israel's exilic situation, whose moral cause is attributed to the failed political leadership. The counterpart to and consequence of evil shepherds, therefore, are a judged people.

Verses 7–8 begin as if they were going to announce judgment on the shepherds for this, but the judgment speech breaks off in verse 8, and the prophet instead repeats the charges against the political shepherds already raised in verses 2–6: The flock became a prey to wild animals because the shepherds did not look out for the sheep, though they took very good care of themselves.

The consequence of this behavior is spelled out in an announcement of judgment against the shepherds (vv. 9–10), introduced by a messenger formula. While the shepherds had not looked out for *(drš)* the flock, their divine counterpart Yahweh would in fact fulfill this role (note that *drš* is used in vv. 10–11) and would deprive the shepherds of the right to exercise their office and to profit from it ("They shall no longer care for themselves"). Yahweh's action for his sheep means that he will deliver them from the mouths of the shepherds, just as he earlier promised to deliver his people from the mouths of the false prophetesses (13:21, 23). While Ezekiel had noted the flock's falling prey to animals in verses 5 and 7, he now attributes the devastation of the flock to the mouths of the shepherds themselves.

This move of Yahweh *against* the shepherds is balanced by Yahweh's move *for* the sheep as their good shepherd in verses 11–16, again introduced by a messenger formula. Now the language refers more concretely to historical realities: The sheep were scattered on a day of clouds and thick darkness (a transparent reference to the fall of Jerusalem in the language of the proverbial "day of Yahweh"), but their future will be brought about by a divinely wrought new Exodus and a new gift of the land (vv. 12–13). The effects of Yahweh seeking the flock in this way are threefold: he will remove the bad shepherds from their office, free the sheep from the control of these shepherds, and, finally, liberate the sheep from exile. He promises to shepherd them with good pasturage on the mountains of Israel, a responsibility not carried out at all by Israel's political shepherds (vv. 2, 3, 8, 10). Verse 16 makes the contrast between Yahweh and the earthly shepherds crystal clear, for Yahweh promises to perform precisely those functions in which Israel's shepherds had proven faithless (v. 4): seeking the lost, bringing back those driven away, binding up the broken, and strengthening the sick. Whereas the royal shepherds had oppressed even the strong with violence, Yahweh promises to keep[34] even the strong within his just rule.

In verses 1–16, therefore, Yahweh announces judgment against the shepherds for their failure to help the sheep, but he also reveals to Israel his own saving acts as shepherd. Such a combined oracle—reasons for judgment plus an announcement of judgment and salvation—is repeated in verses 17–24, but now the accused are the sheep themselves, whose misdeeds form a counterpart to those of the evil shepherds. For the fourth time in this chapter a major unit is introduced by the messenger formula (v. 17).

The sheep were not content to enjoy their good lot, but messed up their food and their drink with their feet, so that it could not be used by others. Their greed is compared with animals who push with their side and shoulder, or who gore the weak with their horns. Such actions lead Yahweh to act as judge between members of the community (v. 20, a sentence again marked with a messenger formula), and they cause the scattering of the sheep, just as the misrule of the shepherds themselves had also caused the scattering of the sheep/Israel (vv. 5, 6). In his saving action Yahweh will distinguish within the flock between those who oppress and those who have become a prey. This paragraph makes clear that the sin of the rulers is mirrored by the sin of at least some of the people, and that the coming divine salvation will also make a distinction between good and evil in the people (cf. 20:35–38).

Though Yahweh promises to be the good shepherd in the place of the former faithless shepherds, he also promises to raise up an ideal earthly counterpart shepherd to rule with him (cf. Isa. 9:5–6; Jer. 23:5–6; Zech. 3:8; 6:12). This future messianic figure will be "one"; that is, the kingdom of Israel will not be divided into two as it was after the death of Solomon (cf. 37:15–22). This "prince" will also be the servant of Yahweh, and he will rule *among* (v. 24), rather than over, the people. The oppressive shepherds, of course, had ruled *over* the people. Twice it is said of the messiah that he will be "David." This does not seem to represent a hope for the resurrection or return of the first dynastic ruler. Rather, it expresses the view that the coming king, or series of kings, will form a counterpart or parallel to that great king of Israel's early history (cf. Hos. 3:5; Jer. 30:9–10). The promise of the divine and human rule of Israel is then summed up in a modified covenant formula: "I, Yahweh, will be their God, and my servant David will be a prince in their midst" (cf. 37:23–24). Covenant formulas appear earlier in 11:20 and 14:11, as well as later in 36:28. This gracious reversal of the bad performance of former evil shepherds is guaranteed by the word or promise of Yahweh: "I, Yahweh, have promised." (cf. 5:15).

A subsequent paragraph in chapter 34 spells out some of the details of this renewed covenant existence (vv. 25–30; cf. 16:60). People would live in a condition of peace or wholeness; people would live securely (cf. 28:26; 38:8, 11, 14; 39:26), and without threat from rapacious animals (cf. 5:17; 14:15, 21; 33:27, where wild beasts assist Yahweh in judgment). According to Leviticus 26:3–6 such security results from human obedience, but in Ezekiel 34 it is identified as a gift of God. Those living around Yahweh's holy hill would be turned into a blessing, and the divinely sent blessing of rain would make for agricultural productivity. By liberating them from their oppressors, identified here as the nations who had enslaved them,[35] Yahweh will help the people recognize who he is: "They will know that I am Yahweh." No one would terrorize them (v. 28; cf. Jer. 30:10; Mic. 4:4). Neither hunger (cf. 5:12, 16–17; 6:11–12; 7:15; 12:16; 14:13, 21) nor the ridicule and gibes of the nations will afflict them again. This paragraph is concluded with a combination of a covenant formula (v. 30; cf. v. 24) and a recognition formula. The people of the restored Israel will recognize that "I, Yahweh their God, am with them, and they are my people, the house of Israel."

A final covenant formula in verse 31 relates the detailed promises of verses 25–30 to the flock imagery, which dominated the first 24 verses of the chapter:[36] "You are the sheep, the sheep of my pasture [cf. Jer. 23:1]; I am your God."

In this third metaphorical treatment of Israel's political leadership Ezekiel makes telling use of his "counterpart" theme. The selfish and careless behavior of the royal shepherds led to the punishment of the flock, but such royal misbehavior did not allow the people to blame all their problems only on others, for the sheep themselves had acted as mirror images of their leaders (vv. 2–9, 17–21). In contrast to the failed shepherds and the oppressive sheep, Yahweh will act as the good shepherd, a righteous counterpart to those who had exercised wicked leadership in the past. The rapaciousness of the uncaring rulers and the aggressive sheep has its analogue in the nations, who also make Israel into slaves, a prey for their appetites (v. 28). Yahweh the faithful shepherd is to have an earthly counterpart in a restored Davidide, who will shepherd a united Israel. Israel will recognize Yahweh in the future through his deliverance of them from the yoke of foreign and domestic oppression (v. 27) and his presence with them in his temple (my hill, v. 26) and in his words of assurance: "I am with them"; "I am your God"(vv. 30–31).

CONCLUSION

The three metaphorical speeches discussed in this chapter clarify the prophet's indictment of his contemporaries. Kings like Jehoiachin and Zedekiah are accused of infidelity to their treaty obligations in chapter 17, while Jehoahaz and Jehoiachin are criticized for their violence and Zedekiah for his pride in chapter 19. The whole royal establishment is cited for its self-aggrandizement and failure to care for its responsibilities in chapter 34. The sins of the kings are mirrored by the sins of the people, especially in chapters 17 and 34, but the destruction of the vine, which stands for the people or the dynasty in chapter 19, also suggests their culpability. The people are counterparts to the kings in their sins.

Judgment is exercised by foreign kings and foreign nations in these chapters, but behind judges like Nebuchadrezzar, the Babylonians, and other nations stands a divine counterpart: Yahweh, who brings the house of Israel to a final and inescapable destruction. This theological perspective, of course, signals the real depth of the destruction faced by the kings and house of Israel.

For the time after this judgment, however, Ezekiel announces a day of salvation, in which Yahweh and his messianic counterparts will rule the people justly. These words of hope in chapters 17 and 34 depend totally on Yahweh, the ultimate indictor and judge, and the only savior. His no to Israel is not his final word; it has a positive counterpart. Even in bringing salvation beyond judgment, he makes a distinction between those who oppressed and those who were merely the prey.

Yahweh and his messianic counterparts will bring about the ideals of divine and human rulership—unity of the people, nonhierarchical rule, security, blessing, the abolition of hunger and the derision of the nations. Through Yahweh's deliverance of his people and his presence with them in the temple, he will enable these erstwhile counterparts of the failed kings to recognize his true identity.

NOTES

1. For a detailed explanation of my understanding of these passages see Ralph W. Klein, I Samuel.
2. But see the symbolic action in 12:1–16, dealing with Zedekiah, discussed in chapter 2 above.

3. George W. Coats, *Genesis, with an Introduction to Narrative Literature*, 318, defines a fable as follows: "Depicts a world of fantasy with the principal figures drawn from both human and subhuman creatures. Describes a static situation. Typically, a presumptuous character has an overblown ego pricked by a pointed moral."

4. Bernhard Lang, *Kein Aufstand in Jerusalem*, 48. Zimmerli, *Ezekiel*, 1: 360, calls it a fable with allegorizing features.

5. For a thorough discussion of riddles in the Old Testament, see James L. Crenshaw, *Samson*, 99–120.

6. Within the allergory the name Lebanon may connote the high status of the king who has been elected by Yahweh (Zimmerli, *Ezekiel*, 1: 361); or, since Jerusalem was on a mountain and one of its royal buildings were called "the house of the forest of Lebanon" (1 Kgs. 7:2), the dynastic capital could also be called Lebanon (Greenberg, *Ezekiel, 1 –20*, 310).

7. "Canaan" should be understood as the common noun for merchant and as a cryptic reference to Babylon; see W. H. Brownlee, *Ezekiel 1 –19*, 263–64. Note the reference to the "city of traders" later in v. 4, and the parallel expression "merchant land" (literally, land of Canaan) in 16:29.

8. Greenberg, "Ezekiel 17 and the Policy of Psammetichus II."

9. The "nobles of the land," v. 13, are not easily identified. Zimmerli, *Ezekiel*, 1: 364–65, sees them as hostages held in Babylon to ensure Zedekiah's faithfulness. If so, Zedekiah's rebellion would have had dire consequences for them, making them permanent exiles. Greenberg, *Ezekiel, 1 –20*, 314, believes the nobles of the land belong among those who were exiled in v. 12. Lang, *Kein Aufstand*, 55-56, argues that the treaty made with Zedekiah would also have been made with these nobles of the land.

10. See Jer. 39:7 (Zedekiah was blinded and taken to Babylon); Jer. 52:11 (Zedekiah was imprisoned in Babylon until his death). It is not clear whether Zedekiah was executed or whether he died of natural causes or of hardships stemming from his capture and deportation.

11. Contra Zimmerli, *Ezekiel*, 1: 364.

12. Greenberg, *Ezekiel, 1 –20*, 315; Lang, *Kein Aufstand*, 50–52. The mention of Pharaoh (Hophra) in v. 17 is identified as a gloss by Greenberg and Lang. Greenberg suggests that the original prophecy proved untrue; i.e., it took Nebuchadrezzar a larger than expected army to capture Jerusalem, and this led to the insertion of the word *Pharaoh*. The result is that the small military force mentioned in v. 17 comes to refer not to the attacking Babylonian army, but to the relief forces sent by Egypt (cf. Jer. 37:5–11).

13. Lang, *Kein Aufstand*, 57, suggests that the oath and covenant are identified as Yahweh's because Zedekiah would have invoked Yahweh as a witness to his treaty with Nebuchadrezzar. It is likely that Nebuchadrezzar left both the monarchy and Judah's religion intact, since he did not turn Judah into a Babylonian province at this time. Greenburg, *Ezekiel, 1 –20*, 322, proposes, unconvincingly in my judgment, that the convenant violated is the general one Yahweh had with Israel (cf. 16:59), which the king was bound to uphold. Note that in this reading the covenant and oath of v. 19 are different from the ones referred to in vv. 16-18.

14. Zimmerli, *Ezekiel*, 1: 366–68, argues that this paragraph is secondary. Lang, *Kein Aufstand*, 65, 84, holds to its originality and notes that Ezekiel figured on an end to the exile in the foreseeable future, though not nearly as quickly as the false prophets imagined in 13:9. See also Greenberg, *Ezekiel, 1 –20*, 324.

15. See the excellent diagram in Greenberg, *Ezekiel, 1 –20*, 320.

16. In v. 25 Zedekiah is called an "unhallowed wicked one" whose time of final punishment has come. According to my understanding of ch. 19 (see below), Ezekiel did not expect that Jehoiachin himself would return from exile.

17. As Lang, *Kein Aufstand*, 77, correctly points out, this recognition of the greatness of Yahweh among the nations does not suggest their conversion to the faith of Israel. Cf. 29:13–

16, where Egypt is promised restoration to its land forty years after its exile. In its lowly restored condition it will recognize the power of Yahweh.

18. See Ralph W. Klein, *Israel in Exile*, 63.

19. Other dirges in Ezekiel include 26:17–18; 27:3–36; 32:2–15. See also 2:10.

20. For other characteristics of the dirge form see Lang, *Kein Aufstand*, 92.

21. Zimmerli, *Ezekiel*, 1:392.

22. Greenberg, *Ezekiel, 1–20*, 357. Another commonly proposed candidate is Hamutal, wife of Josiah and mother of both Jehoahaz (2 Kgs. 23:31) and Zedekiah (2 Kgs. 24:18). But there is no evidence that she played any role in the coming to power of either of her two sons, and the emphasis placed on the lioness in vv. 10-14 seems inappropriate for the relatively obscure Hamutal.

23. V. 7a gives details about his violent behavior but is textually uncertain and obscure. Greenberg, *Ezekiel, 1–20*, 348, translates: "He knew his widows and desolated their cities"; Zimmerli, *Ezekiel*, 1: 389, emends the text to read: "And he did evil to their palaces, and made ruins of their cities." Brownlee, *Ezekiel 1–19*, 294–95, also emends the text and proposes the following: "He lay in wait near dwellings and frightened their towns."

24. Depending on one's identification of the mother, the branches could refer to the citizens of Judah or the multitude of its kings. Because a dirge may be spoken before the death occurs, it is not necessary to date these verses after the actual collapse of Jerusalem (per contra Zimmerli, *Ezekiel*, 1: 393).

25. Greenberg, *Ezekiel*, 1–20, 354.

26. The term *prince* is used frequently in Ezekiel (e.g., 12:10, 12) to designate one whom we would call the king. This term has roots in Israel's early history, and it is also used of the coming messianic figure in Ezekiel (e.g., 34:23–24; 37:25). The LXX in v. 1 translates the noun *princes* in the singular, but this seems to be contradicted by the content of the poem, in which we see three "princes" being discussed. The Greek reading may have arisen in the Hebrew *Vorlage*, where the *yod* of the construct plural was lost by haplography before the initial *yod* in the word Israel.

27. Lang, *Kein Aufstand*, 102–03, identifies the king in both the second and third stanzas as Zedekiah. His claim that Zedekiah's rebellion is being criticized in the second stanza is contrary to the specific violent offenses listed in vv. 6–7, which distinguish this stanza from the third stanza and from ch. 17. Zimmerli, *Ezekiel*, 1: 390–91, 397–98, sees the references to Zedekiah in vv. 11 and 14 as secondary and dates the basic form of the third stanza to a period *after* the fall of Jerusalem. Greenberg, *Ezekiel*, 1–20, 356–57, hesitates to identify any of the "kings" except Jehoahaz in stanza 1 and finds in the other stanzas stereotypical descriptions of Israel's kings.

28. Lang, *Kein Aufstand*, 105. Cf. the charge of violence leveled by an earlier prophet against Nineveh: "Where is the lions' den, the cave of the young lions, where the lion brought his prey, where his cubs were, with none to disturb? The lion tore enough for his whelps and strangled prey for his lionesses; he filled his caves with prey and his dens with torn flesh" (Nah. 2:11–12).

29. Read *'ăšer nešî 'ehā* instead of *qešer něbî' ehā*. See the apparatus of *BHS*.

30. Vine and bough are organically connected, and one punishment befalls both. In the figure of a lioness and her cubs, vv. 2–4, 5–9, only the cubs, and not the mother, experience judgment.

31. Zimmerli, *Ezekiel*, 1: 290. For bibliography on modern study of the woe oracles, see J. J. M. Roberts, "Amos 6.1–7," 162–63 nn. 5, 7.

32. For this relationship see J. W. Miller, 106. For an exegesis of Jer. 23:1–8, see Ralph W. Klein, "Expository Article on Jeremiah 23:1–8."

33. The vocalization in the MT *(haḥēleb)* suggests fat, but many substitute vowels that lead to the reading "milk" (or "cheese"; *heḥālāb*).

34. Emend *'šmyd* of the MT to *'šmr* on the basis of the LXX. Cf. *BHS*.

35. V. 28 promises that in the future Israel will not be a prey to the nations, nor will wild animals eat them. V. 8 states that the people became a prey to the animals because of the evil shepherds. V. 22 notes that the weak sheep had become a prey to the ruthlessly strong sheep.

36. The word *ṣō'n* (sheep) is used in vv. 2, 3, 6, 8, 10, 11, 12, 13, 17, 19, 22.

S E V E N

I WILL GLORIFY MYSELF IN
THE MIDST OF YOU:

THE NATIONS IN THE BOOK OF EZEKIEL

Each of the three longest prophetic books in the Old Testament has a major section devoted to oracles against foreign nations (Isa. 13–23; Jer. 46–51; Ezek. 25–32; cf. Amos 1:3–2:16).[1] In the case of Ezekiel, an oracle against Edom (ch. 35) is also included within the promissory section of the book. This pericope, therefore, and the response to it in 36:1–15 need to be included in any discussion of Ezekiel's attitude toward the nations.

Seven nations or city-states are given special attention in Ezekiel: Ammon (25:1–7), Moab (25:8–11), Edom (25:12–14; 35:1–36:15), Philistia (25:15–17), Tyre (26:1–28:19; 29:17–21), Sidon (28:20–23), and Egypt (29:1–32:32). Conspicuous by its absence is Babylon.[2] The reason for this silence, of course, can only be conjectured. In Ezekiel's early years he had steadfastly hailed Babylon, to which he had been exiled in 597, as the agent through which Yahweh would bring the final destruction of Jerusalem. The nearly contemporary prophet Habakkuk also announced judgment through Babylon (the Chaldeans, Hab. 1:5–11), but then protested that the situation under Babylon was more unjust than the previous unrequited wrongs of Jerusalem (1:12–17). Though such a protest is absent from Ezekiel, he too surely believed in the finite character of Babylon's hegemony, since he frequently spoke of Yahweh gathering the exiles from Babylon, as well as from other countries, and taking them home to Jerusalem. Was he silent about Babylon's fate out of political expediency? Or is his silence to be explained by his chronological position at the beginning of the exilic period when higher priority might be given to the fate of the nations surrounding Israel, all of whom outlasted her, than to the great world power Babylon itself? As we will see, the oracles against the nations in Ezekiel can be dated either just before or a short time after the fall of Jerusalem. The prophet at the end of the exilic period, Second Isaiah, spoke much more openly about the defeat of Babylon and about the Persian Cyrus, under whom the Jews would be allowed to return home (e.g., Isa. 41:25; 45:1–7, 13, 46:11).

A theological key to Ezekiel's oracles against the nations can be found in a word of Yahweh against Sidon, introduced by a messenger formula: "Thus says Yahweh, 'See, I am against you, O Sidon, and I will glorify myself in the midst of you,[3] and they shall know that I am Yahweh when I sit in judgment over her and reveal myself as holy in her' " (28:22).[4] In the following pages I will argue that an attempt to vindicate Yahweh—that is, to defend his glory and his holiness—is the central theological theme that unites Ezekiel's treatment of the nations in his oracles against foreign nations.

THE INDICTMENT OF THE NATIONS

The Nations' Rebellion

Yahweh's honor and holiness can be maintained to the extent that the nations are proven to be sinful. A survey of the oracles against the foreign nations demonstrates their culpability from a variety of perspectives. Five of the seven nations—Ammon, Moab, Edom, Tyre, and Sidon—participated in the rebellious convocation in Jerusalem in 594/593, which Jeremiah viewed as a rebellion against Yahweh (Jer. 27:3). While Ezekiel does not discuss this conspiracy in so many words, it is not insignificant that he was called to the prophetic office at approximately the same time as this conspiracy and that his message from then until the fall of Jerusalem stands totally opposed to any effort to resist the Babylonian power. In his mind Nebuchadrezzar's destruction of Jerusalem was both justified and inevitable; therefore, it was not to be resisted. Still, his oracles against these five nations do not deal explicitly with their rebellion against Babylon.[5]

The oracles against Egypt, however, do refer to its efforts to aid Judah against Babylon. Three of the oracles are explicitly dated to the very last years of Jerusalem (29:1–16: 17 January, 588; 30:20–26: 10 April, 588; 31:1–18: 2 June, 588), when Jerusalem looked to Egypt for last-minute military support.[6] We know from Jeremiah that the final siege against Jerusalem was temporarily lifted, probably in 588, because of an invading Egyptian army under Pharaoh Apries (Hophra; Jer. 37:5–15). The hiatus in the siege even led the Jerusalemites to renege on a promised manumission of slaves (Jer. 34:8–22), but, as Jeremiah warned (37:9), the Babylonians did not stay away for long.

This incident—or another like it—appears to be represented by the events reported in Ezekiel 30:20–26. In a word directed to the prophet, Yahweh announces that he has broken the arm of the king of Egypt; aye, that he will shatter both of Pharaoh's arms and cause the sword to drop from his hand. At the same time Yahweh will strengthen the arm of the king of Babylon and put his own sword in his hand. The broken arm of Pharaoh would seem to represent the defeat of the Egyptian force that came to the aid of Jerusalem.

Compounding Judah's sin of rebellion against Babylon was Egypt's tempting Judah to consider such a course of action. Both Jeremiah (2:16–19) and Ezekiel (17:7–10) warned about reliance on Egypt. One problem with this strategy was that Egypt was so undependable, or, as Ezekiel puts it, such "a reed staff" (29:6). When grasped by the hand, the Egyptians split apart; when leaned on, they made Israel's loins to shake (29:7). The king of Assyria had enunciated a similar theological and political opinion of Egypt in the days of Hezekiah: "You [Hezekiah] are trusting in Egypt, that broken reed of a staff, which will pierce the hand of any man who leans on it. Such is Pharaoh king of Egypt to all who trust in him" (Isa. 36:6; 2 Kgs. 18:21). The same opinion was voiced by the prophet Isaiah himself (Isa. 30:2–3; 31:1). The worst thing about relying on Egypt, however, was not the latter's weaknesses or unreliability, but that Israel thereby negated any claim they might make about trusting in Yahweh. When Yahweh promised through Ezekiel that Egypt would one day be restored, he said Egypt would be only a lowly country so that it could not again entice Israel into false trust (29:16).

The Nations' Pride

One of Ezekiel's principal charges against the foreign nations is their pride. In addition to the instances cited below, pride may also have been a contributing factor in their rebellion against Babylon, although Ezekiel never explicitly makes this connection.

He scores Tyre, on the contrary, for bragging about its perfect beauty (27:3; see 28:7, 12, 17) and Egypt, portrayed as an unrivaled cedar tree with incomparable beauty (31:8), for becoming proud of its height (31:10). One of the most stinging indictments of pride comes in a judgment oracle against the prince of Tyre, whose proud heart led him to Promethean heights: "I am a god [El], I sit in the seat of the gods" (28:2)—just as the god El had his dwelling in the heart of the seas. Through his wisdom, which exceeded that of the legendary Canaanite Daniel, this prince skillfully carried on trade and accumulated wealth for himself, wealth that only increased his pride (28:3–5). Although he regarded his wisdom as divine, the prince's mere humanity would be fully revealed though his ignominious and violent death (28:9).

The lament over the king of Tyre contrasts his claim to wisdom and beauty with his forthcoming demise (28:11–19).[7] The king is presented as a resident in the garden of Eden, sharing the innocence of an Adam and functioning as a priest of the divine sanctuary on the mountain of God.[8] A number of words suggest a connection to the primeval situation: the day of creation (v. 13), the stationing of a guardian cherub (v. 14; cf. Gen. 3:23–24),[9] and the king's original state of innocence (v. 15), which was destroyed by his arrogant heart (v. 17). One effect of these motifs is to portray the fall of the king of Tyre as a repetition of the story of a primeval human being. Hence what is said about the king grasping selfishly for something that was really a divine gift is actually understood to be everyone's story.

In any case, the king of Tyre's iniquity would eventually be discovered and appropriately punished. Through the abundance of trade—a fitting charge against the commercial empire of Phoenicia—the King had perpetrated violence (28:16). By the unrighteousness of his trade he also had profaned his sanctuaries (28:18). Goods forcibly seized from people may have found their way into Phoenician temples.[10]

In addition to, and perhaps related to, Egypt's support of Israel's rebellion is the charge of pride that Ezekiel lays at its door. Clutching at its property, the great dragon Pharaoh disowns the creator: "My Nile is my own, since I made it for myself" (29:3). The pomp of Pharaoh (31:2, 18; 32:31, 32) and of Egypt itself (32:12, 16, 18, 20) is repeatedly scored in the oracles against foreign nations.[11] Other nations display similar pomp, namely, Elam (32:24) and Meshech (32:26). Edom's reviling of Israel is explicitly related to its arrogance: "You [thereby] magnified yourselves against me with your mouth, and multiplied your words against me; I heard it" (35:1–13).

The Contempt of the Nations

Proud rebellion against Yahweh led to contempt for Israel and a concomitant questioning of Yahweh's honor. Tyre, which hoped to profit from Jerusalem's fall, shouted "Aha!" when the holy city's gate was broken (26:2), and Ammon used the same mocking word over the sanctuary, the land of Israel, and the house of Judah (25:3). The enemy castigated in 36:2 (Edom?) joins its "Aha" to a claim of ownership of the promised land. The Ammonites, Philistines, Edomites, and all the nations round about Israel had rejoiced and showed contempt *(šʾṭ)* at the land's misery (25:6, 15; 28:24, 26; 36:5). Yet God had not pronounced his judgment against his own people in order that the scornful of this world would have the last word.[12] His honor and his holiness had to be defended.

Moab despised Judah by saying that it was like all other nations (25:8). That is, Moab held that the judgment imposed by God was a refutation of God's special relationship with his people. The prophet speaks of Edom's anger and envy; he charges Edom with hatred and abuse of Israel (35:11–12). This southern neighbor of Israel rejoiced when the inheritance of Yahweh's people was laid waste (35:15). Other unidentified nations made Israel the subject of gossip, calumny, and derision (36:3–4). They reproached the mountains of Israel and the land because they devoured men and women and made the people childless (36:13).[13] Yahweh's mercy extended to Israel precisely because she had been reproached by the nations and had suffered disgrace from the peoples (36:15; cf. vv. 6–7). Such challenges to Yahweh's honor would not be permitted in the future (28:24–26; 36:15), and the nations who had uttered them would suffer the consequences of their hostile attitude (36:7).[14]

The Violence of the Nations

The final indictment against the nations deals with their violence (cf. the discussion of the effects of Tyre's trading policies, 28:16, 18). A number of texts from the exilic period indicate that Edom took advantage of Jerusalem's defeat to loot the city (Ps. 137:7; Obad. 11, 13–14). Ezekiel added his voice to this chorus by accusing Edom of acting revengefully (25:12), a charge he also makes against the Philistines (25:15). The Philistines had not been among the rebellious ambassadors to Jerusalem, according to Jeremiah 27:3, but they may have profited from the Babylonian hegemony by taking over some of the territory of Judah, just as an earlier generation of Philistines seems to have done after the defeat of Hezekiah by Sennacherib.[15] Both Edom (35:5) and Philistia (25:15) are also accused of "eternal hatred." Edom delivered Israel to the sword at the time of its final punishment (35:5), showing anger, envy, and hatred (35:11). The Edomites tried to take possession of land belonging to both kingdoms (35:10), and they were ready to eat them up: "[These two nations] are laid desolate, they are given us to devour" (35:12; cf. 36:2, 4, 5).

THE PUNISHMENTS OF THE NATIONS

Yahweh's defense of his honor and the revelation of his holiness in the face of such sins required him to execute punishment against these nations. This theological understanding of the harsh words about the nations in Ezekiel sets them off from the desire for personal vindication often expressed by the speaker in the imprecatory psalms, and it indicates that these chapters are not incidental to a total understanding of the prophet.

Ezekiel announced to both the Ammonites and Moab that they would be handed over to the peoples of the East, an undefined group, probably Aramaic-speaking desert hordes (25:4, 10). Yahweh's anger and wrath against Edom would be exercised by Israel itself, who, appropriately enough in view of Edom's revengeful attitude, would implement Yahweh's own vengeance against them (25:14). Yahweh promises to exercise such vengeance himself on the Philistines (25:17).

In a judgment oracle against Tyre the prophet uses the metaphor of the city's confident security in its location on an island to portray its devastating defeat at the hand of many nations (26:3–5).[16] Tyre, etymologically the (protecting) rock, will become Tyre the bare, eroded rock. It will be a place for fishermen to spread their nets, not a refuge in the midst of the sea. The sword sent by Yahweh will seek out Tyre's "daughter" cities on the mainland (RSV), or it will ravage its women in the open field (26:6).[17]

Yahweh also promises to punish Tyre by a fierce king from the north, Nebuchadrezzar, king of Babylon and king of kings (26:7). His siege and devastating attack on the city are vividly described in 26:7–14. The Babylonian troops are elsewhere characterized as brutal foreigners (28:10; 30:12), the most terrible of nations (28:7; 30:11; 31:12). According to Josephus, Nebuchadrezzar undertook a thirteen-year siege of Tyre (roughly 585–573 BCE) after his victory in Jerusalem.[18] This Phoenician city, which was not connected to the mainland before the time of Alexander, held out more or less successfully under Nebuchadrezzar's attack. The failure of the judgments announced in 26:7–14 to be completely fulfilled forced Ezekiel to update his announcement against Tyre in the latest dated oracle in the book, 29:17–21. There, on 8 April, 572, Ezekiel reported that Yahweh planned to reward the Babylonian king for his tireless, if unsuccessful, efforts in attacking Tyre by giving him the land of Egypt—instead of Tyre—as his wages for working for Yahweh.

This remarkable revision of an earlier word of Yahweh is significant for a theological understanding of Ezekiel. The prophet believed that Yahweh was always faithful to such words of judgment or, for that matter, to his words of promise. Yet he also believed that Yahweh was free to adapt himself to changing historical conditions. In this paradoxical affirmation of the faithfulness and freedom of Yahweh, Ezekiel enunciated a hermeneutic that enabled him to apply the word of Yahweh to a new generation. In the process he supplies the modern reader with an appropriate way to apply the canonical Scriptures to his or her situation. From Ezekiel's point of view, Yahweh's word was a success if God would at some time and in some similar way exercise judgment; a literalistic, one-to-one fulfillment was not required.[19]

Even this revised prophecy was not fulfilled in a literal manner. While Nebuchadrezzar did invade Egypt in 568, the final result of his campaign was indecisive, and Egypt did not fall to a foreign conqueror until the time of Cambyses in 525 (see the discussion of Egypt's exile below).

Another description of Tyre's punishment suggests that Yahweh's glory would be manifested in the midst of Tyre through the death of the personified city: "Will not the coastlands shake at the sound of your fall, when the wounded groan, when slaughter is made in the midst of you?" (26:15). The princes of the sea will utter a poignant lament over the city

(26:17–18) and carry out appropriate mourning rites—stepping down from their thrones, removing their robes, trembling, and sitting on the ground.[20] Tyre will be forced to descend to the netherworld, never to return:[21] "that you may reign no more and that you spread no longer your glory over the land of the living" (26:20).[22] The final verse of the chapter states Tyre's doom in a formulaic way: "I will bring you to a dreadful end, and you shall be no more; though you be sought for, you will never be found again" (cf. 27:36; 28:19).

Proclamations of judgment in the oracles against the nations in Ezekiel are often followed by laments, which graphically contrast the present exalted state of a king or nation with its future humiliating destruction.[23] In the lament of chapter 27 the prophet depicts Tyre as a ship, staffed by rowers, navigators, and caulkers from the surrounding cities (vv. 8–11), and laden with products from the various countries with which the island city traded (vv. 12–25).[24] After slowly describing the building and staffing of the ship, the poet sinks it in a single verse: "The east wind has wrecked you in the heart of the sea." While the poem never explicitly identifies Yahweh as the agent of destruction, this is clearly implied by the fact that Yahweh orders the lament to be said (vv. 2–3).

The godlike prince of Tyre is threatened by ignominious death[25] at the hand of the invading Babylonians (28:7), who are sent by Yahweh, and who are the most terrible of the nations. In the lament over the Adamic king of Tyre (28:11–19), it is Yahweh himself[26] who casts him off the mountain of God and brings out fire to consume him. Yahweh makes him go down to Sheol, where he will experience the scorn of the kings already there (vv. 16–17).

In chapter 35 Yahweh threatens to turn Edom into a wilderness and to hand its people over to the power of the sword because of their eternal hatred. Blood will always pursue them, and their cities will remain uninhabited. Many of these punishments seem to be particularly appropriate responses to the violent and vengeful crimes with which Edom is charged. Yahweh promises to deal with it in accord with its anger and to rejoice over its desolation, just as Edom had once rejoiced over the desolation of Israel's inheritance.[27]

For Yahweh to manifest his true glory in the sight of the nations requires him to visit upon them their sins of rebellion, pride, unreliability, tempting Israel to false trust, contempt for Israel, and taking vengeance on her. This is also brought out in twenty-one recognition formulas which are sprinkled throughout these chapters.[28] In some cases the nation that experiences the judgment will be the one to recognize Yahweh in his act of judgment; at other times Israel or the nations in general are said to be the ones who will make this recognition.[29] But in either case the recognition of Yahweh means that he has succeeded, through acts of judgment against the nations, in manifesting his glory and holiness among them.

The Punishment of Egypt

The pharaoh, portrayed as a great dragon in 29:1–6, receives punishment appropriate to his metaphorical identity: Yahweh drags him out of the Nile and hurls him into the desert. Yahweh even threatens Egypt with exile among the nations (v. 12; also 30:23; 32:9). Its homeland will remain unpopulated for forty years (v. 11), until Israel's God would perform for them a new Exodus (vv. 13–14). The divine threats against Egypt were never carried out, and the country was not even captured until after the end of the Babylonian period. What chapter 29 states about the fate of Egypt, however, is what the honor of Yahweh requires—despite the way in which the history of Egypt turns out.

Most unusual is the promise to Egypt that it will be restored after its destruction and deportation (29:13–16). Such a sequence of destruction and restoration for Egypt is not unknown elsewhere in the Bible. In one of his oracles against foreign nations Isaiah spoke of the erection of an altar and a pillar to Yahweh in Egypt (Isa. 19:19) and of an eschatological highway between Israel's two great enemies, Egypt and Assyria, that would permit their joint worship of Yahweh and their becoming, with a restored Israel between them, a blessing in the world (19:23–24). Jeremiah, too, spoke of the repopulation of Egypt after the Babylonian destruction (Jer. 46:25–26). Greenberg suggests that the special treatment for Egypt results from the fact that it at least tried to help Jerusalem when it was under siege.[30] This is nowhere stated in the text, however, and in my judgment is somewhat unlikely. Both Jeremiah and Ezekiel viewed the ongoing resistance of Jerusalem to Babylon as contrary to the will of Yahweh and saw Egypt's assistance as incompetent meddling at best and as open rebellion against Yahweh at worst. More likely is Zimmerli's view that any future world was inconceivable without an Egypt, just as any future Israel was inconceivable without a restored monarchy. In both cases Ezekiel predicted restoration of a limited sort: a king, or prince, would be present in Israel, with few identifiable duties outside of preeminence in worship, and Egypt would be restored as a nation lower than others, unable to rule them (29:15). In this reduced capacity Egypt would not serve as a temptation for nations to trust in anyone or anything other than Yahweh, but rather as a reminder of the evil Israel had committed in turning to it (29:16).

The ancient idea of the day of Yahweh (ch. 7; Amos 5:18) is invoked in the punishments against Egypt in chapter 30. The holy war that will be waged on the day of Yahweh will be executed through the hands of Nebuchadrezzar and other "strangers," the most violent of nations (30:10–12). Yahweh himself will dry up the Nile. His sword will be entrusted to the hands of the Babylonian king, who will use it to scatter Egypt among the nations in retaliation for its seditious support of Jerusalem in her final rebellion (30:20–26).

Foreign brigands will cut down the arrogant cypress that Pharaoh has become (31:11–12). This lofty tree and all the other trees of Eden will be forced to go to the underworld (31:14–16), and the specific fate of Pharaoh is extended to include all world powers in general in verses 17–18. Proud Pharaoh is condemned to go to the most undesirable parts of the underworld, among those "uncircumcised" and "slain by the sword."

Chapter 32 repeats and develops earlier themes from the oracles against the foreign nations. The dragon Pharaoh, who considered himself a lion among the nations, will be caught by the fisherman Yahweh and thrown into the open field so that animals can feed on him (vv. 2–4; cf. 29:3). This death will have worldwide, even cosmic consequences. Other nations and kings will be shocked at it (vv. 9–10), and the heavenly bodies will grow dark in sympathetic horror (vv. 7–8).

The oracles against Egypt end with a devastating lament depicting the descent of the country to the underworld, to lie with the dishonored dead, who are frequently referred to in these verses as the "uncircumcised" or the "slain" (32:17–32). The precise connotations of these terms are not totally clear, though they are unmistakably pejorative. "Uncircumcised" might refer to those who were relegated to unfavored parts in the land of the dead because their parents failed to carry out the rites of the eighth day, or to those infants who died before the eighth day.[31] Since Egypt's major enemy at this time was Babylon, and the Babylonians did not circumcise, it would have been an especially galling prospect for the Egyptians to face being buried with the likes of the uncircumcised Babylonians. Others find in the designation "uncircumcised" overtones of castration.[32]

138

The term "slain" or "slain by the sword" has similar negative connotations. Otto Eissfeldt proposed that it referred to people who had been executed or murdered,[33] while Boadt associates the slain with those fallen in battle, perhaps a reference to unburied soldiers.[34]

In any case, the inhabitants of the dishonorable areas in the underworld include Assyria and its whole company, who were all slain by the sword though they had once spread terror in the land of the living (vv. 22–23), plus Elam and Meshech, fallen by the sword, who had gone down to the pit uncircumcised though they too had spread terror in the land of the living (vv. 24, 26). The fate of these nations that lived by violence prefigures Egypt's end. Egypt will not lie with the ancient heroes of war, who had been given honorable burial (v. 27), but with Assyria, Elam, Meshech, Edom, and the commanders of the north (vv. 29, 30)—all ranked with the uncircumcised and those slain by the sword, bearers of shame with those who descended into the pit (vv. 24, 25, 30).

SALVATION WITHIN THE ORACLES AGAINST FOREIGN NATIONS

Three of the recognition formulas in these chapters come at the end of words of promise directed to Israel. In 28:24 it is promised that the house of Israel is to be delivered from the nations' briers, thorns, and contempt—references to the derogatory and violent actions of the nations against Israel—and thereby it will come to recognize Yahweh's true identity (cf. 29:21; 36:11). This positive note is really not surprising since the oracles against the foreign nations are usually seen as a kind of middle ground between words of judgment toward Israel and words of hope toward Israel. Many believe that the arrangements of books like Isaiah and Ezekiel (and the LXX of Jeremiah) follow a sequential pattern: first words of judgment against Israel (Isa. 1–12; Ezek. 1–24); then words of judgment against the nations (Isa. 13–23; Ezek. 25–32); then words of hope for Israel (Isa. 24–39 [24–66]; Ezek. 33–48).[35]

The eventual restoration of Israel is also presupposed in several of the oracles against the nations. Divine vengeance on Edom, for example, will take place through the hand of Israel, who will act toward Edom in accord with Yahweh's own anger and wrath (25:14). The strong Israel that will implement Yahweh's vengeance is clearly quite different from the defeated exiles among whom Ezekiel lived. It represents Israel after its restoration.

After the word of Yahweh in 28:24 promises Israel release from the briers, thorns, and contempt of the nations, the next two verses add that Yahweh will continue to manifest his holiness through Israel in the sight of the nations by gathering them from among the peoples and making them dwell in the land. Their life will become secure when Yahweh will execute his judgments on all their neighbors who treated them with contempt.

Ezekiel 29:16 affirms that Egypt, when it is restored from its exile to a position of lowliness, will never be a source of temptation for Israel. This passage, too, presupposes that Israel, like Egypt, will have been restored to its land. The following pericope, 29:17–21, the latest of all of Ezekiel's oracles, states that at the time when Egypt will fall to the Babylonians, the horn of the house of Israel will rise (29:21),[36] and the prophet will speak with cheerful confidence.

The balance between judgment on the nations and consequent deliverance for Israel comes out most clearly through a comparison of chapter 35, a declaration of judgment for Mount Seir, and 36:1–15, a declaration of salvation for the mountains of Israel.[37] The wickedness of Edom and other nations provides the motivation for Yahweh to save Israel. Yahweh speaks against the remaining nations and against Edom, which had taken possession of the land (36:5). Because these nations have reproached Israel, they shall themselves suffer reproach. But the nation Israel will soon come home, and the mountains will yield abundant fruit. Israel's land will be tilled and sown, and her population will be increased in her cities and in her rebuilt waste places. Yahweh will do more good to Israel than ever before. The mountains of Israel will be freed from the reproach of the nations.

CONCLUSION

The nations in their pride sought to capitalize on Yahweh's judgment. They derided Israel for its recent losses and even took advantage of its weakened position to aggrandize themselves. But God, according to Ezekiel, would not allow the nations to liquidate Israel even though the latter presently stood condemned. The other nations, even if they had so far outlasted Israel, would one day have to reckon with Yahweh's anger against them and his justice in exercising judgment. Although Yahweh had indeed pronounced a sentence of death against his own people, he did not thereby abandon them, nor would he allow his own name to be dishonored. The proud, insulting nations were no doubt a source of grief to Israel and a grievous threat to her self-esteem, but Ezekiel argues that they were also a problem to God. The solution: Yahweh would demonstrate his glory and his holiness through Israel and in the eyes of the nations. Yahweh's glory and holiness could be maintained only if the nations were judged, and if Israel, beyond its present judgment, were finally saved.

NOTES

1. For a recent study of the early oracles against the nations, see Duane L. Christensen, *Transformations of the War Oracle in Old Testament Prophecy*. John B. Geyer, "Mythology and Culture in the Oracles Against the Nations," has claimed a sharp form-critical distinction between Ezekiel 25 and chs. 26–32. This claim and the consequent identification of ch. 25 as secondary are not persuasive.

2. Zimmerli, *Ezekiel*, 1: 448–51, finds in 21:28–32 a paragraph he considers secondary, words against Ammon and Babylon. In this view, vv. 30–32 announce that Yahweh will bring judgment on Babylon, the instrument by which he destroyed Jerusalem (cf. Isa. 10:12–19). See also Greenberg, "Ezekiel," *Encyclopedia Judaica* 6.

3. The only other occurrence of *kbd* in the niphal in Ezekiel is in 39:13.

4. Cf. 20:41; 36:23; 38:16; 39:27. Zimmerli, *Ezekiel*, 2:99, recognizes the theological significance of 28:22 for understanding the oracles against the nations, but he judges it and the entire oracle against Sidon, of which it is a part, to be secondary.

5. Ammon seems to have been a center of anti-Babylonian feeling. In 21:18–23 Ammon is identified as a possible target of Nebuchadrezzar's attack. The murderers of Gedaliah, the governor installed by the Babylonians, had Ammonite connections (Jer. 40:14; 41:1–2). Sidon participated in the rebellious gathering in Jerusalem according to Jeremiah (27:3), but, strangely, no reason for its punishment is provided in Ezekiel.

6. Other oracles against Egypt come after the fall of Jerusalem (32:1: 15 Mar. 586; 32:17: 29 Mar. 586). Also from after the final destruction of Jerusalem come 26:1 (13 Feb. or 15 Mar. 586) and the undated oracles in chs. 25, 27–28.

7. Anthony J. Williams, "The Mythological Background of Ezekiel 28:12–19?" 60–61, finds here a castigation of the Tyrian ruler on the basis of his commercial activities and his participation in the sanctuary rites of sacral kingship. He therefore denies the importance of the "mythological" ties to Gen. 2–3. Claus Westermann, *Genesis 1–11*, 246, however, finds the biggest difference between Ezek. 28 and Gen. 2–3 in that the central figure in Ezekiel is a divine or semidivine being.

8. H. J. Van Dijk, *Ezekiel's Prophecy on Tyre (Ez. 26, 1–28, 19): A New Approach*, 116–17, argues that the word translated "covering" in v. 13 of the RSV *(mesūkātekā)* is better construed as a defense wall around a sanctuary, protecting it from profanation. The list of precious gems comprising this wall is drawn from the high priest's breastplate in Exod.

28:17–20. See Carol A. Newsom, "A Maker of Metaphors—Ezekiel's Oracles Against Tyre," 160–63.

9. Van Dijk, *Tyre*, 93, 119–21, thinks that the king himself was designated as a cherub. Cf. the discussion of v. 16 in Zimmerli, *Ezekiel*, 2: 86.

10. Zimmerli, *Ezekiel*, 2: 94. Van Dijk, *Tyre*, 122, suggests that the plural "sanctuaries" refers in fact to a single shrine. Hence the sanctuary the king profanes is the one on the mountain of God that is surrounded by the wall of gems.

11. Lawrence Boadt, *Ezekiel's Oracles Against Egypt: A Literary and Philological Study of Ezekiel 29–32*, 90–92, 124–27, translates the word *pomp (hāmôn)* as "horde" on all these occasions. But Zimmerli, *Ezekiel*, 2: 131, prefers the connotations that go along with pride and finds here a mild polemic.

12. Zimmerli, *Ezekiel*, 2: 20.

13. See the discussion of the textual problems in Zimmerli, *Ezekiel*, 2: 231. Childlessness in Israel was traditionally regarded by women as a reproach (cf. Gen. 30:23).

14. As Zimmerli, *Ezekiel*, 2: 19, notes, the mocking words of Israel's neighbors are spoken by people who took advantage of the judgment of God against others in order to give free rein to the hatred in their own hearts.

15. James B. Pritchard, ed., *Ancient Near Eastern Texts Relating to the Old Testament*, 288.

16. See Newsom, "Maker of Metaphors," 154–56.

17. The latter understanding is defended by Van Dijk, *Tyre*, 12–14.

18. *Antiquities* 10. 11. 1 and *Contra Apionem* 1. 21. Ernst Kutsch, *Die chronologischen Daten des Ezechielbuches*, 69, finds it impossible to assign exact dates to the siege of Tyre.

19. See Boadt, *Oracles Against Egypt*, 53.

20. See Van Dijk, *Tyre*, 31.

21. On Sheol as the land of no return, see Job 7:9, 10; 10:21; 16:22: Ps. 78:39.

22. The translation follows Van Dijk, *Tyre*, 2.

23. Cf. ch. 26 with ch. 27; 28:1–10 with 28:11–19; chs. 29–31 with ch. 32. See also 2:10; 19:1, 14.

24. E. M. Good, "Ezekiel's Ship: Some Extended Metaphors in the Old Testament."

25. In 28:8 we read about "the death of the slain," and in v. 10 about "the death of the uncircumcised." See the discussion of ch. 32 below.

26. And/or the guardian cherub. See n. 9 above.

27. Ch. 35 appears to be later than ch. 25, where Ammon was threatened because of its enmity to Israel. In ch. 35 Edom is charged with laying claim to the entire land (cf. 33:24). Since the time of the return of Israel from the Exile had not yet arrived (36:8), chs. 35–36 must be dated before 539.

28. 25:5, 7, 11, 14, 17; 26:6; 28:22, 23, 26; 29:6, 9, 16; 30:8, 19, 25, 26; 32:15; 35:4, 9, 12, 15.

29. Some uncertainty about who is to make this recognition results from the ambiguity of the pronouns and their antecedents in Hebrew. For example, in 25:5, 7, it is clear that the Ammonites themselves are to make this recognition, but in 25:14, it is not clear whether Edom, Israel, or the nations in general are to "know Yahweh."

30. Moshe Greenberg, "Ezekiel," 1086.

31. Zimmerli, *Ezekiel*, 2: 173, refers to the *limbus infantium*, the place of repose for unbaptized infants in Roman Catholic tradition.

32. Van Dijk, *Tyre*, 113.

33. Otto Eissfeldt, "Schwerterschlagene bei Hesekiel," 73–81.

34. Boadt, *Oracles Against Egypt*, 120–121.

35. The LXX of Jeremiah places the oracles against foreign nations in the middle of the book, after 25:13, although in the Hebrew Bible they appear near the end of the book, in chs. 46–51.

36. The "horn" here is a description of the nation's power, not a reference to a member of the Davidic line, as in Ps. 132:17.

37. The declaration of salvation for the mountains of Israel forms a parallel to ch. 6, which speaks a word of judgment against the mountains of Israel.

EIGHT

FORMULAS FOR THE FUTURE

(EZEKIEL 36–37)

In four major pericopes of chapters 36–37 Ezekiel sketches out Israel's future as Yahweh's people. Despite the fact that these passages are expressed in a variety of genres and that they were probably spoken or written in a variety of circumstances and at a variety of times, the reader is aware of a theologically unified scenario, enunciated in the typical phraseology of the prophet/priest Ezekiel. Well-known formulas abound. Two of the pericopes open with the word-experience formula ("The word of Yahweh came to me"; 36:16; 37:15), and eight messenger formulas appear at strategic places throughout these chapters ("Thus says Lord Yahweh"; 36:22, 33, 37; 37:5, 9, 12, 19, 21). Seven times the prophet employs the recognition formula ("You/They shall know that I am Yahweh"; 36:23, 36, 38; 37:6, 13, 14, 28), and three times he cites the covenant formula ("I will be their God; they will be my people"; 36:28; 37:23, 27).

While repetitive language abounds throughout the book, the formulaic character stands out boldly here, partly because Yahweh's promises for the future are given so little theological justification. Twice Ezekiel grounds hope in the future solely on the reliability of the divine word—"I have spoken and I will do it" (36:36; 37:14), underscored the second time with the formula, "an oracle of Yahweh" (the formula also appears in 36:23 and 32). Most of the promises strike the reader as mere formulas, not as the expressions of the gracious heart of God. Missing from Ezekiel's descriptions of Yahweh are such standard Old Testament terms as steadfast love, mercy, faithfulness, salvation, and love. The prophet's lean theological vocabulary leaves the positive actions of Yahweh hard to explain, and it also reveals something of the personality, or at least the theology, of the prophet, who finds it unnecessary to provide further justification for his future hopes. He explicitly denies that Yahweh's promises come for Israel's sake (36:22, 32)—either because of its merits or because of Yahweh's pity for it. Instead, the promissory future results primarily from Yahweh's desire to defend his own reputation.

Even the rhetorical unity of these chapters, in which the first and fourth pericopes serve as an inclusion (both referring to Yahweh's sanctifying actions), can be expressed formulaically: Yahweh sanctifies his name (36:16–38); Yahweh enlivens Israel (37:1–14); Yahweh unifies Israel (37:15–24a); Yahweh sanctifies Israel (37:24b–28). Such formulaic rhetoric, however, should not blind us to the real creativity of Ezekiel's response to the defeat of exile, nor to the fine balance between gift and demand in his future program. Israel's future, according to Ezekiel, is to be both theocentric and worship-centered. For such a strong affirmation of Israel's promising tradition, we should not begrudge Ezekiel his use of formulas.

36:16–38: YAHWEH SANCTIFIES HIS NAME

Israel's residence in Palestine had made the whole land unclean (v. 17) according to the prophet, and its wicked deeds seemed to him as unclean as menstruation. While Ezekiel abhorred the idea of sexual congress with a woman during her menstrual period (18:6; 22:10; cf. Lev. 15:19–24), he also used references to menstruation to express general feelings of repugnance toward actions or things: "Their gold is like a menstruous substance.... I will make [their beautiful ornament] a menstruous thing for them" (7:19–20). According to the Holiness Code, a land made unclean by any of a variety of sexual offenses would have to vomit out its inhabitants (Lev. 18:28). Because of the uncleanness[1] of the house of Israel, Yahweh had been forced to pour out his wrath on Israel (v. 18; cf. 7:8; 9:8; 14:19; 20:8, 13, 21; 22:22; 30:15).

145

Expelled by Yahweh from the land, the exiles had brought defilement to Yahweh's name by their mere presence among the nations, who said, "These are the people of Yahweh, and [yet] they have gone out of his land." Though Yahweh had shown no pity for persistent sinners (5:11; 7:4, 9; 8:18; 9:5, 10; cf. 16:5), he grieved with pity over his holy name that had been defiled in the nations' eyes (36:21). The foreigners gloated over the fact that the people of Yahweh had been separated from the land of Yahweh.

The prophet, as Yahweh's messenger, told that people that the actions promised in the future would not happen for their sakes, but in order to defend Yahweh's name or reputation (v. 22).[2] The nations would come to recognize Yahweh when he would display his holiness through what he did for Israel and what he did before the nations (v. 23; cf. 20:41; 28:26; 39:27; Isa. 45:14).

The first way in which Yahweh would display his holiness would be by leading Israel in a new Exodus from the foreign lands to which they had been deported and by bringing them back into the promised land (v. 24; cf. 34:13). In a related gesture Yahweh promised to purify them from uncleanness (v. 25; cf. v. 29) and from idols, lest the land be forced to vomit them out again after their return. These promised purification rites recall purifications for the ritual defilement of death (Num. 19:9–22), and they anticipate the purifying effects of baptism in Judaism and Christianity. More positively, Yahweh promised the people a new heart and a new spirit (v. 26; cf. 11:19; 18:31). This new heart would be responsive (a heart of flesh) in the place of their old stubborn sinfulness (a heart of stone; cf. 3:7).[3] The spirit placed within them would be "my" spirit, the spirit of Yahweh, designated by the name and power of its giver, and it would guarantee that the restored people would obey Yahweh's legal requirements (v. 27). Verse 28 sums up both sides of this first proof of divine holiness: Israel would live in the land first given to their forebears, and the relationship between the people and the deity would be whole, with each living up to the obligations of the relationship, according to the covenant formula: "You will be my people, and I will be your God."[4] Thus, Yahweh's acting for the sake of his name has far greater consequences than in chapter 20, where such acting only meant that Yahweh would not execute punishment for sins committed in Israel's earlier history (20:9, 14, 22).

A second promised manifestation of Yahweh's holiness would come in his gift of abundant grain,[5] fruit, and field crops (vv. 29–30; cf. 34:27). Such providential generosity would spare the people from the reproach that resulted when Yahweh placed them among the nations in a condition of famine (v. 30; cf. v. 15; 22:4). Presently, the land ate its inhabitants instead of giving them food (v. 13).

In demonstrating his holiness Yahweh would also, thirdly, repopulate Israel's abandoned cities, rebuild their ruins, and cause their land to be tilled (vv. 33–34; cf. v. 9). While passersby currently considered the land to be desolate (cf. vv. 20, 23), they would be forced to confess in the future that the land had been made as fruitful as the garden of Eden by Yahweh (v. 35; cf. 28:13; 31:9, 13, 16), and that its devastated cities had been repopulated and fitted out with appropriate fortifications. Such renewal and rebuilding would force any neighboring nations that might survive Yahweh's punishment (cf. vv. 3–5) to acknowledge that Yahweh was the one who could build and plant (v. 36).[6]

The fourth proof of Yahweh's holiness would be his renewed openness to Israel's making inquiries of him (v. 37; per contra his refusal to be inquired of in the period before the final fall of Jerusalem; 14:7, 10; 20:3, 31). Specifically, he promised to provide whole "flocks" of human beings, similar to the flocks of sacrificial animals at Jerusalem. A covenant relationship is often associated with increase of population in the Bible, and it was, of course, a particularly welcome idea in Israel's exilic period (cf. Gen. 17:2; Lev. 26:9; Isa. 49:19; 54:1–3; Jer. 23:3; Zech. 2:4). This final demonstration of holiness would lead Israel rather than the nations to recognize Yahweh (v. 38).

In response to these benefactions Israel would remember its evil ways and loathe itself on account of its iniquities and abominations (v. 31; cf. 16:54, 61, 63; 20:43). The people's remorse for their sins, of course, underscores the fact that the future given by Yahweh is not one produced by the merits of Israel—"it is not for your sake that I am doing this" (vv. 22, 32). Elsewhere in Ezekiel the experience of judgment also calls forth shame and regret about past behavior (6:9; 16:52).

37:1–14: YAHWEH ENLIVENS HIS PEOPLE

The vision of the dry bones is one of the best-known pericopes in the entire book of Ezekiel and is an important expression of the prophet's views about the future. It consists of the vision itself (37:1–10) and an interpretation of the vision (vv. 11–14).[7]

In the vision the prophet is brought[8] by the spirit of Yahweh to a valley that is full of bones, presumably representing Israel devastated on a battlefield (cf. v. 11). His tour of the valley emphasizes the impossibility of the situation—the bones are very many and very dry. The hopelessness of the situation is probably also expressed by the divine question ("Can these bones live?") and the prophet's ambiguous reply ("Lord Yahweh, you know").[9]

At the instruction of Yahweh the prophet addresses the bones with the divine promise that will give them breath to live and will connect them with sinews and cover them with flesh and skin. The distinction between reconstituting the bodies themselves and giving them the breath of life recalls the Yahwist's creation story in Genesis 2:7, where the human is formed of dust from the ground before Yahweh breathes into its nostrils the breath of life. Yahweh's action in this vision has creation overtones, an important dimension of the passage. The divine benefactions in any case will cause the revivified bones to recognize the deity in his identity as Yahweh.

The prophet reports his carrying-out of the assignment (cf. 3:2, 23; 8:8, 10; 12:7; 24:18) and its effects: as the bones came together there was a loud sound, perhaps of thunder, and the earth quaked (v. 7). Both of these phenomena are common accompaniments of theophanies in the Old Testament and also in Ezekiel (cf. 1:24, 25; 3:12, 13). So these creative acts, too, resulted solely from the intervention of God. Still, while Ezekiel's prophesying brought about the reassembling of bodies and their being covered with flesh and skin, the restored bodies had not yet received the breath that would give them life. The necessity for a second word of Yahweh through the prophet stresses the enormity of the problem that is being resolved.

The breath or wind that Ezekiel summons in Yahweh's name comes from the four winds simultaneously, emphasizing its mysterious character and the need for Yahweh to enable it to function.[10] Ezekiel begs the wind to enter the "slain," who are so called because the scattered bones of the battlefield have in the meantime been reassembled into recognizable human beings. When Ezekiel carried out this second assignment (v. 10), the wind entered the bodies and enlivened them, and they stood as a great army, or, as the text says literally, a "very, very great army." The very many and very dry bones have been drastically transformed! The fact that the bones have been transformed into an army indicates that the vision deals with the reconstituting of Israel from its death and not with the resurrection of individuals.[11]

148

The interpretation of the vision in verses 11–14 is a disputation word.[12] The communal understanding of the vision is identified in Yahweh's opening comment: "These bones are the whole house of Israel." The complaint of the people—"Our bones are dried up, our hope has perished, and we are cut off"—expresses a feeling of national death. The psalmist, on the verge of death, complained that his bones were disjointed (Ps. 22:14) or were wasting away (Ps. 31:10). The servant in Second Isaiah was said to be cut off from the land of the living (Isa. 53:8), while the psalmist notes that he is cut off from God's hand and therefore is on the brink of the grave (Ps. 88:5–6). The book of Lamentations also makes a connection between "being cut off" and the grave. Zimmerli argues that the complaint ascribed to the people provided the metaphor which was developed so effectively in the vision.

The prophet is instructed to prophesy for a third time (v. 12), and the words of Yahweh he reports serve both to interpret the vision and to rebut the complaint of the people. The imagery shifts from battlefield to graves, thereby setting the stage for the frequent understanding of this passage in both Judaism and Christianity as referring to individual resurrection.[13] The shift seems to have been conditioned by the lament about (the nearness of) death in the previous verse. Now Yahweh promises to open the graves and to "bring the people up" from them before bringing them into the land. The verb *bring up* (*ʿālâ* in the hiphil) may have a double meaning, referring at once to being lifted out of a grave and to the new Exodus from the land(s) of exile. The coming exit from the graves and the entrance into the land will lead the people to acknowledge Yahweh. Both announcements of deliverance from the graves conclude with an address to Israel as "my people" (37:12,13), thus expressing a covenantal relationship with an abbreviated form of the covenant formula.[15]

The final verse of the interpretation gives a new specificity to the imagery of the vision. In the vision itself it was the wind or the breath that was to enter the slain to give them life. Here Yahweh identifies this breath as *my* spirit (cf. 39:29). The gift of "my spirit" according to the previous chapter (36:27) would compel Israel to keep Yahweh's laws. The power of Yahweh's transformative spirit corresponds to the function of the spirit of Yahweh which moves the prophet in 37:1. Just as the spirit of Yahweh empowered the prophet, so the life-giving spirit of Yahweh will empower reconstituted Israel to a life of obedience. The promise of the land is repeated in verse 14 and seems to make concrete the meaning of the term *life* for Ezekiel.

The vision of the dry bones is even more silent than the previous pericope about the motivation for Yahweh's actions. No mention is made of Yahweh's covenant faithfulness or divine mercy, nor even of Yahweh's acting to protect his own reputation. But of the power who is behind Israel's resurrection into a future there can be no mistake. It was the hand of Yahweh that came upon Ezekiel, and it was the spirit of Yahweh who moved him out into the valley of the dry bones. The actions carried out for Israel and the metaphorical images in which they are expressed can only be attributed to Yahweh. Resurrecting dead Israel, whose bones are many and very dry, could only be done by Yahweh. The distinction between re-forming the bodies and giving them the breath of life suggests that it is the power of the creator that stands behind Israel's future. Whatever historical or political factors played into Israel's exodus from Egypt, or whatever political or religious considerations might lead Cyrus to send the exiles home, from Ezekiel's theological perspective the Exodus—new or old—is something only Yahweh can do. The God who alone can resurrect, re-create, and effect an exodus is the one who promises to enliven Israel, and this Israel, according to its own testimony, sees itself locked in the chains of death.

This prophecy is made sure by three divine words addressed to the prophet which he passes on to the bones (37:5), to the life-giving wind itself (37:9), and to the exiles who lamented with disheartening words (37:12). Yahweh's word is enough to evoke faith in the future: "I have spoken and I will do it." All this is reinforced by the final words in the pericope: "an oracle of Yahweh" (37:14).

Divine *power* lies behind the promise, and the promise is made sure by the guarantee of the divine word. Both the divine power and the reliable divine word are typical characteristics of Ezekiel's theocentric message about the future. The majestic God—now present in Babylon (ch. 1)—is the one who will enliven Israel.

37:15–24A: YAHWEH UNIFIES HIS PEOPLE

This pericope is one of the prophet's symbolic actions (see chapter 2 above), and the only one with a primarily positive message. As with many of these other symbolic actions, the pericope consists of an address by Yahweh to the prophet, with no actual completion of the act by the prophet being reported.

The unity of the restored people of God is the theme of this action, signaled by the 11 uses of the word *one*.[16] Yahweh instructs the prophet to take two sticks,[17] writing on one of them "Belonging to Judah and the Israelites his companions" and on the other "Belonging to Joseph, the stick of Ephraim, and all the house of Israel his companions." The sticks thus stand for the citizens of the former southern and northern kingdoms. Ezekiel is instructed to bring them together in his hand as one stick.

In response to a question from the people about the significance of this symbolic action (v. 18; cf. 12:9; 21:7; 24:19), Yahweh instructs the prophet to report to them what Yahweh is doing: He is taking the stick of Joseph and joining it to the stick of Judah so that the two sticks become one in his hand. Thus verse 19 states that Yahweh will act in the same way as the prophet did and offers in itself no real interpretation of the symbolic action.

Verse 20 repeats the essence of the symbolic action—"the two sticks on which you write will be in your hand in their sight"[18]—and it forms a transition to verses 21–24a, which offer an interpretation of the significance of the symbolic action. The interpretation may well be secondary,[19] since the "taking" refers not to the taking of sticks but to taking Israel from the nations in a new Exodus. By taking them from among the nations and bringing them to their land, Yahweh is creating one nation, with one king. Never again will Israel be divided into two nations or two kingdoms. Ezekiel here picks up a tradition of unity in the restored Israel that is also found in Jeremiah (3:18; 31:1, 31). Added to this promise is another announcing freedom from defilement by idols, abominable things and rebellions, and salvation from backslidings. As in 36:15–28, inner renewal of the people will be an essential aspect of their return to the land. This restored and obedient relationship is summarized by a covenant formula: "They will be my people, and I will be their God."

A final verse gives specifics about the king in the new age, showing acquaintance with Ezekiel's vocabulary and concepts elsewhere. The future king will be "my servant David" and "one shepherd for all of them" (see the discussion of 34:23–24 in chapter 6 above). By placing this promise after the covenant formula, the prophet expresses the unity of people, Yahweh, and king: "They will be my people, and I will be their God, and David my servant will be king over them" (cf. 34:24).

The prophets had long held to the unity of the single sanctuary tradition (cf. Amos 1:2) and had criticized the division within Israel that came with Jeroboam I. Ezekiel's idealized picture of the future makes no room for repetition of this schism. In passages thought to be an original part of the prophet's message (4:5 and 27:17 are often thought to be secondary), Ezekiel never uses the term *Israel* in the sense of the northern kingdom as opposed to Judah.[20] The unity Yahweh promises is a gift, not a human achievement. The one king embodies this unity, and Yahweh makes provisions protecting against any dissolution of this unity. The prophet apparently held that involvement with idols, abominations, rebellions, and backslidings were the surest route to schism.

37:24B–28: YAHWEH SANCTIFIES ISRAEL

Though this paragraph forms an appropriate conclusion to chapter 37, there is little that links it directly to the preceding units. It can be classified as an announcement of salvation, climaxing in a recognition formula and held together by the fivefold repetition of the word *forever*. The transitional sentence, verse 24b, could as easily go with the preceding unit as with this final unit, though the concerns emphasized—walking in Yahweh's ordinances and observing and keeping his statutes—were already treated in verse 23.

The first, formulaic promise announces that they [the people Israel] will dwell in the land generation after generation—they, their children, and their grandchildren will live there. The land is also identified as the land given to "my servant Jacob." In one of the few other passages mentioning Jacob in the book of Ezekiel (28:25–26),[21] the themes we have been examining in this chapter are treated in a remarkably similar way. Yahweh promises in 28:25 to gather the house of Israel from the peoples (but see 36:24; 37:21; cf. 11:17; 20:34, 41; 39:27) and to manifest his holiness through them in the sight of the nations (see 36:23). Then they will dwell in their own land, where they will build houses and plant vineyards (see 36:36)—a land where their ancestors dwelled and which was given to "my servant Jacob." Israel's ancestors had lived there in fulfillment of the promises made to them, promises that Ezekiel clearly claims as valid for the future Israel he foresees. But these ancestors—or at least their descendants—lost the land in Ezekiel's lifetime. Possession of the land in the future will be *forever*.

A second formula promises, "And David my servant will be prince over them forever" (v. 25b). David is the only person other than Jacob who is referred to in Ezekiel as "my servant." Like Jacob, he too was the recipient of great promises (2 Sam. 7), but his line came to a dreary end with its final member, Zedekiah. Ezekiel promises the permanent restoration of king and/or dynasty, though in this final pericope in chapter 37[22] this "messiah" is designated only by the title "prince," the ancient and honorable term for a ruling office in Israel, but often also expressing in Ezekiel a limitation on the powers and activities of the Davidic house (see esp. 40–48). This "David my servant" (cf. 34:23, 24) will be prince *forever.*

Unlike the Priestly writer, Ezekiel did not hold to the unbroken covenant with Israel's ancestors as the basis for assurance during the Exile or shortly thereafter.[23] Rather, like Jeremiah, he looked forward to a new, or renewed, covenant representing wholeness, peace, and plenty, a covenant of peace (cf. 34:25–29). This is the third promise in this paragraph. This covenant relationship would be accompanied by a great population increase (v. 26; cf. 36:10–11, 33, 37–38), and, of course, it would last *forever.*

In a fourth promise, Yahweh declares that he would put his own sanctuary (*mqdš*) in the midst of the people in an attempt to sanctify (*qdš*) Israel (37:27). Ezekiel, the priest, had harsh words about behavior in the temple during its final days, and his vision in chapters 8–11 depicts Yahweh abandoning the Jerusalem temple to destruction. While Yahweh was a sanctuary for the exiles only in a small way (11:16), a place for seeking him on the high mountain of Israel had been promised to those who would experience the new Exodus (20:40). Now Yahweh promised to put his sanctuary in their midst *forever.*

The sanctuary is the fourth and most significant of the everlasting gifts that Yahweh was promising to Israel. His "tabernacle"—a technical term for Yahweh's house going back to Israel's earliest days, but used only here in Ezekiel[24]—would be above them, almost, I would propose, as a sign of the covenant. The promise of a tabernacle in any case leads directly into the covenant formula: "I will be their God and they will be my people." Note the striking parallel in Leviticus 26:11–12: "And I will make my abode [tabernacle] among you, and my soul shall not abhor you. And I will walk among you, and will be your God, and you shall be my people."

According to chapter 36, the nations will recognize Yahweh when he manifests his holiness through Israel and before them (v. 23). Chapter 37 adds that these same nations will recognize that Yahweh is sanctifying

Israel (v. 28) by giving them the land, by installing David "my servant" as their prince, by making a covenant of wholeness with them, and, finally, by putting his sanctuary in their midst *forever*. Five times the word *forever* has occurred in this brief pericope, each time serving like an exclamation point to emphasize the promise to which it is attached. But the final promise, reinforced by the fourth and fifth *forevers* emphasizes that the sanctuary will always be at the center of Israel. For the priest Ezekiel this is the climactic promise.

CONCLUSION

We have seen that Ezekiel, through a creative use of formulaic expressions in 36:16–37:28, announced to exilic Israel a well-rounded picture of the future. The answer to almost every possible need is included in these gracious promises, which depend for their fulfillment on the holiness of Yahweh. The future depends, however, not on Israel's own claim to holiness, but solely on Yahweh and his word and his efforts to maintain—or better, recapture—his reputation and name.

The themes of chapter 37 can all be seen as outworkings of a theme first sounded in 36:16–38: Yahweh sanctifies his name. He does this by enlivening Israel (37:1–14), by unifying Israel (37:15–24a), and by sanctifying Israel (37:24b–28). This final theme can also be seen as the goal toward which all the other themes are pressing. Yahweh's sanctification of his name has its ultimate conclusion in his sanctification of Israel. And surpassing all his benefactions—of Exodus and gift of land, of purification from uncleanness and idol worship, of new obedience, of fertility in grain, fruit, and other produce, of rebuilt ruins and repopulated cities, of increased population, of new life for an Israel spread over the graveyard of exile, of unity, of land possession, of monarchy, and of covenant—surpassing all of these benefactions is the final gift that sanctifies Israel, the placing of his sanctuary in their midst. What that greatest of all promises might mean is spelled out in considerable detail in the last nine chapters of the book (see chapter 10 below). The nations who recognize Yahweh's sanctifying characteristics (37:28) are absent from those final chapters; the last appearance of the nations in Ezekiel, in chapters 38–39, is therefore, the subject of our next chapter.

NOTES

1. The MT of 36:18 defines the offense of uncleanness as the shedding of blood in the land (violence) and as impure behavior with idols (cf. 22:4), but the clause is lacking in the LXX and probably secondary.

2. Second Isaiah records a trial speech against Israel in which Yahweh accuses the people of wearying him with their sins, but he also announces that he will blot out their transgressions "for his own sake" (Isa. 43:25).

3. In its description of the new covenant, the book of Jeremiah says that Yahweh will write his law on Israel's hearts and that people—from the least to the greatest—will all know (acknowledge and obey) Yahweh (31:31–34).

4. The covenant formula has similar connotations of inescapable obedience in 11:20; 14:11; and 37:23.

5. This promise is expressed through the metaphor of Yahweh "calling" for the grain. (cf. Hos. 2:21–22).

6. For a study of the use of "building" and "planting," especially in Jeremiah, see Robert Bach, "Bauen und Pflanzen."

7. Rüdiger Bartelmus, "Ez 37, 1–14, die Verbform wĕqatal und die Anfänge der Auferstehungshoffnung," argues that the term *vision* in this case refers more to the content of the passage than to its genre. In his judgment, the genre of the pericope is an instruction to a prophet to proclaim a word of salvation. Because of unusual verb forms in vv. 7, 8, 10, the role of the prophet and the spirit in vv. 8b–10a, and the word *slain* in v. 9, he isolates an original pericope from the time of Ezekiel (vv. 1–6, 7b–8a, and 10b–14), which spoke of the revivification of the nation Israel, and a subsequent redactional insertion from the time of the Maccabees (vv. 7a, 8b–10a), which announced hope for the Maccabean martyrs. Despite the ingenuity of his argument, his conclusion seems unlikely. He is probably inaccurate in identifying *the* spirit in v. 9 with a supernatural entity (see below), and if this refers only to the wind or the breath, the alleged divergent role for the prophet also disappears. The lateness of his proposed redaction presents a difficulty, since the present shape of the passage was known by the LXX. It also does not seem clear to me that a Maccabean reader would draw the assurance from the passage that he proposes.

8. The prophet is transported in other visions as well (3:12, 22; 8:1, 3; 11:24; 40:1–2.

9. See Michael V. Fox, "The Rhetoric of Ezekiel's Vision of the Valley of the Bones," 10–11. Fox makes a number of perceptive comments about this pericope, but it is doubtful that he is right in claiming that Ezekiel presents himself more as a spectator than a messenger with divine authority (pp.8–9). Note the three messenger formulas in the pericope. Is not a claim to have a vision an argument from authority?

10. Fox, "The Rhetoric," 10, detects here a reinforcing of the centripetal movement of the overall imagery.

11. Though the rabbis seem not to have used this passage as a proof text for resurrection, it is clearly so understood in the paintings from Dura Europas. Ezekiel's use of resurrection imagery might suggest that he was acquainted with the idea even if we have no biblical evidence for this notion in Israel at this time. Fox, "The Rhetoric," 11–12, proposes that the audience of Ezekiel would have regarded corporeal resurrection as basically absurd: "He depicts the extreme case of unpredictable salvation in order to enable the people to expect a salvation that though unlikely is yet less radical, the return of the nation from exile."

12. Adrian Graffy, *A Prophet Confronts His People*, 84, suggests that only v. 11a is the interpretation and that vv. 11b–13 are an originally separate disputation word (the quotatin of the people is in v. 11b and the refutation and a recognition formula in vv. 12–13). He

views v. 14 as a redactional unit that ties the disputation word more closely to the vision itself.

13.   Aelred Cody, *Ezekiel*, 176.

14.   The verb '*lh* is used of the exodus from Egypt in 1 Sam. 12:6 and Hos. 12:14, and finds a modern equivalent in the noun describing Jewish immigration to Israel, *alia*.

15.   The reference to "my people" in v. 12 is lacking in the LXX and the Syriac; the reference in v. 13 is lacking only in the Syriac.

16.   In v. 17 this leads to an unusual expression: "They [the two sticks] will be 'ones' in your hand." The word *one* however, occurs in the singular in the parallel v. 19.

17.   Does this refer to tablets or even scepters? See the discussion by Zimmerli, *Ezekiel*, 2:273.

18.   Public witnesses are frequent in the symbolic actions cf. 4:12–13; 12:3–7; 21:6).

19.   So Zimmerli, *Ezekiel*, 272, 275, though, as he notes, it is an almost necessary part of the text. The issue in the interpretation, however, is more the protection of the newly gathered people from schism than the reunification process itself.

20.   See the excursus on "Israel" in Zimmerli, *Ezekiel*, 2:563–65. It is to the whole nation of Israel that Ezekiel was summoned to preach. Two espressions denoting the unity of Israel—namely the land ('*dmt*) of Israel and the mountains of Israel—are only found in our prophet.

21.   Jacob is also mentioned in 20:5, an oath of election sworn to the seed of the house of Jacob, and in 39:25, which speaks of the restoration of the fortunes of Jacob.

22.   Note the use of "king" in vv. 22, 24. This distinctive vocabulary and the close ties with 28:25–26 and Lev. 26 are appealed to by Zimmerli, *Ezekiel*, 2: 273, 276–79, in support of a late date for vv. 24b–28.

23.   Cf. Ralph W. Klein *Israel in Exile*, 86. In 16:60 Ezekiel does speak of Yahweh remembering the covenant made with Israel in its youth.

24.   The only other occurrence of the noun *tabernacle* in Ezekiel (25:4) is a secular reference to the dwellings of the "people of the East."

NINE

NO LONGER A PREY TO THE NATIONS

(EZEKIEL 38–39)

The hopeful words of chapters 33–37 climax in 37:24b–28, a passage which promises everlasting possession of the land, an everlasting Davidic prince, an everlasting covenant, and an everlasting sanctuary in the midst of Israel. One would expect that this thematic paragraph would be followed immediately by the vision of chapters 40–48, which provides a detailed description of the temple, its rites, and the distribution of the land in a restored Israel, or by a transitional account leading up to the restoration. Instead, in chapters 38–39 we leap ahead to a time after Israel has already been restored to the land, when it is threatened by a mysterious invasion from the north.

This chronological difficulty and the perception of differences in content, form, mood, and genre from the normal message of Ezekiel have led some scholars to deny these chapters in their entirety to Ezekiel.[1] But the chaotic conditions in northern Mesopotamia, presupposed in this account, and the picture of Israel dwelling in its land argue against a late date for these chapters. The Persian empire under Cyrus brought stability to the ancient Near East, especially after its defeat of Babylon in 539, and this stability would seem to make subsequent fears of a great eruption from the north groundless. In the depiction of Israel after its restoration to the land in chapters 38–39, there is no knowledge of the edict of Cyrus that allowed the Jews to return home, nor any specifics about the delay in rebuilding the temple or the meager living conditions that plagued the first years of the restoration;[2] in short, these chapters antedate 539 BCE. If a relatively early date is to be assigned to these chapters, in whole or in part, the possibility of interpreting them as coming from the prophet himself needs to be pursued.[3]

FREEDOM FROM FOREIGN ATTACK?

The defense of Israel against a foreign invasion by Gog or anyone else would seem to fulfill directly a promise repeatedly made by the prophet. In 34:25, for example, he assured the people in Yahweh's name: "They will dwell securely in the desert and sleep in the woods." This idyllic picture guarantees freedom from the fear of wild animals, by which the prophet may have meant an enemy attack as well as, or in addition to, the danger of the animals themselves. Verse 27 repeats the promise about living securely on the land, as does verse 28, and the latter adds: "They will no longer be a prey to the nations, nor shall the animals of the earth eat them up."

People in Ezekiel's audience may not have found this an easy promise to believe. First, they might worry that foreign nations in the future might misconstrue the events of 587, conclude from them that Jerusalem fell because of Yahweh's weakness, and seek to take advantage of the prevailing power vacuum. Even some within Israel apparently shared these doubts about Yahweh's power. As I wrote in another context, "One function [of the Deuteronomistic redaction of Jeremiah] is to defend Yahweh against the charge of neglect, powerlessness, or unfairness."[4] Ezekiel reassures his audience through an oracle concluding with two consecutive recognition formulas: Just as the house of Israel would come to know Yahweh as their God from the day of Gog's defeat onward (39:22), so also the nations would learn that it was because of Israel's iniquity and rebellion that they went into exile (39:23); it was not because Yahweh had failed in his ability to defend them.

A second reason for the exiles to doubt the promise about perpetual secure living in the land might stem from Israel's own prophetic tradition. Jeremiah had warned of an invasion by a mysterious northern enemy who would bring great destruction. Accompanied by clouds, this enemy's chariots would be like the whirlwind (Jer. 4:13). The prophet's depiction of this attack was replete with overtones of a return to chaos (4:23–26), and the cruel, merciless disposition of this enemy from the north compelled him to urge the people to bitter lamentation (6:22–26). The attack of the enemy from the north would make the cities of Judah desolate, a lair of jackals (10:22; see also 13:20). The identity of this enemy is by no means clear. The proposed equation with the Scythians,[5] based on a passage in Herodotus, faces numerous historical difficulties, not least of which is the silence of the prophet about the invader's identity. Jeremiah, at least in his early years, does not seem to have identified the nation from the north with Babylon. The author of Jeremiah 50–51, who is surely not the historical Jeremiah, made Babylon the *object* of the northern attack and identified the northern enemy itself with the Medes (Jer. 51:11, 27–28).[6]

Because of uncertainty about the identity of the fearsome northern enemy, and because even Babylon's attack in the early sixth century did not seem to bring about the total desolation and chaos that Jeremiah had announced, some within Ezekiel's audience might have wondered whether the prophetic word about an impending foreign attack might still be fulfilled on Israel *after* its restoration to the land. Ezekiel seems to anticipate this fear in a divine oracle: "Thus says Lord Yahweh, you [Gog] are the one I promised in former days—by the hand of my servants, the prophets of Israel, who prophesied in those days—to bring against them" (38:17; cf. 39:8). But Ezekiel also proposed that this coming attack need not finally be feared. His reasons for this confidence are spelled out in chapters 38–39.

The Invasion of Gog

The description of the attack of Gog and his total defeat are presented as a word revealed in Ezekiel (38:1). Yahweh instructed the prophet to set his face against Gog,[7] prophesy to him (cf. 38:14, 17; 39:1), and announce to him divine opposition (cf. 39:1).

"Gog" seems to be a cipher coined for the northern enemy by Ezekiel and is perhaps a reflection of Gyges, the famed king of the northern country of Lydia, who died in 644 BCE.[8] By giving the name of a powerful king from the previous century to the northern enemy, Ezekiel admits the dangers associated with a northern attack, although his ultimate purpose in this account is consolatory for Israel. Gog's country, Magog, is unidentified, though it also appears in the table of nations (Gen. 10:2; cf. 1 Chr. 1:5) as the second "son" of Japheth.[9] In that same list Gomer (Ezek. 38:6), Tubal, and Meshech are listed as "children" of Japheth. The latter two are identified in Ezekiel as the countries of which Gog is the chief prince (38:2, 3; 39:1). Both Tubal and Meshech are mentioned elsewhere in Ezekiel (27:13, as trading partners of Tyre; 32:26, as violent nations of the past now confined to an unfavorable part of Sheol), and they appear also in Akkadian documents (Tabal, in Cilicia, and Musku, in Phrygia), especially as opponents of Assyria.[10] Gomer is Ezekiel's word for the Gimirrai, a people from southern Russia who attacked Urartu from the north in the eighth century, and who are known as the Cimmerians in classical sources.[11] Gomer and Beth-togarmah (cf. 27:14),[12] a people coming from a city in Asia Minor called Til Garimmu, are among the allies ascribed to Gog in verse 6. The fearsomeness of these people is underscored by the mention of their "hordes"[13] and the many peoples who accompany them (38:6, 9, 22), and by their identification as enemies from the north (38:6, 15; 39:2).[14]

Throughout 38:1–9 Yahweh is presented as the controlling agent who will bring Gog against Israel,[15] but only verse 3 indicates that this act has negative consequences for Gog: "I am against you." The time of his conscription is set in an indefinite future—"after many days"; "at the end of years"—but it will clearly be after Israel, which had been scattered to many lands, is again restored to its land to live in apparent security (v. 8; cf. vv. 11, 14) in fulfillment of prophecy (28:26; 34:25, 27–28). Gog's attack is compared to a storm and a cloud, recalling some of the metaphors used by Jeremiah to describe the enemy from the north (Jer. 4:13).

WHY WILL GOG BE DEFEATED?

The next paragraph (vv. 10–13) describes the subjective motivations that led Gog to attack and that necessitate his defeat from a moral perspective. A divine speech quotes Gog's thoughts about the undefended character of Israel in its land—"no walls, bars, or doors"—and its complacency—"they dwelled securely." In addition to contemplating aggression against those who are defenseless, Gog has a greedy desire for their possessions, according to Ezekiel; he wants to seize spoil and carry off plunder.

By referring to Israel's many possessions and to its living on the navel of the earth, Gog tacitly admits how favored Israel has been by its God—and thereby he compounds his own guilt. The renowned trading nations of Sheba, Dedan, and Tarshish (cf. 25:13; 27:12, 20, 22, 25) ask about Gog's purpose with both amazement and admiration, echoing the vocabulary of his own thoughts: "Are you coming to seize great spoil and carry off great booty?" (cf. v. 12).

Yahweh's motivations for defeating Gog are spelled out in 38:14–16 and 38:17. In a pointed question Yahweh suggests that Gog is planning to attack "*my* people Israel" while they are dwelling securely and at ease, and then he goes on to charge Gog directly with plans for marching against "*my* people Israel" and against "*my* land." The tone of the question and the three uses of the possessive pronoun *my* suggest divine outrage at Gog's behavior toward the elect. Though Gog stirs himself, comes from his place, and goes up like a cloud against Israel—three verbs connoting his own self-propulsion—the real controlling power behind his attack is solely Yahweh: "It is I who will bring you." By bringing Gog to the land for judgment, Yahweh will prove to the nations his own holiness.

Verse 17 indicates that Gog's coming moreover fulfills the prophetic word about an invasion from the north. As the rest of the account progresses, and as was already hinted by the notice about Yahweh's opposition to Gog in verse 3, that fulfillment is ultimately going to be good news for Israel.

Verses 18–23 put the destruction of Gog into a cosmic, apocalyptic perspective.[16] Since they are the first unit in this chapter not structured as an address to Gog, and since they seem to make unnecessary or even impossible the one-to-one battle against Gog that Yahweh carries on in 39:1–5, it is possible that they represent a secondary expansion.[17] They function within the canonical context, however, to provide a third reason for Gog's defeat, namely, the wrath of Yahweh against him (cf. 7:19; 21:31; 22:21, 31; 35:11). The great earthquake that will rattle the land, terrifying the animals and creating a panic in all humankind, in which warriors will kill one another (cf. Judg. 7:22), will also make the mountains, terraces, and walls fall.

Yahweh's entering into a legal process with Gog (v. 22; cf. 17:20; 20:35–36) will take the form of plagues, blood, rain, hailstones, and fire and brimstone, reminding the reader of the divine attack on Sodom and Gomorrah (Gen. 19:24–28). The paragraph concludes with a triple assertion of Yahweh's purpose: "I will magnify myself, show myself to be holy, and make myself known to the many nations who witness Gog's fate—so that they will recognize that I am Yahweh." In exercising his wrath against the perilous world powers, Yahweh proves his true identity.

DIVINE ACTIONS AGAINST THE INVADER

The announcement of Yahweh's defeat of Gog in 39:1–5 takes the form of a battle account between two champions (cf. David and Goliath). Though Gog is still called a chief prince from the farthest north—with all the ominous overtones of the noun *north*—four verbs assert that Yahweh is the sole ultimate power behind the attack: "I will turn you around, and I will lead you by the nose,[18] and I will bring you up, and I will bring you in." With a quick "one-two" Yahweh knocks the bow and arrow from the hands of Gog, and forces him and all his accompanying hordes to fall. As unburied casualties, perhaps like those "slain by the sword" in chapter 32, their corpses will be food for the carrion birds and the wild animals (cf. Matt. 24:28). Confidence in this victory rests on a double appeal to Yahweh's word: "I have spoken"; "an oracle of Lord Yahweh."

Verses 6–8 extend this defeat to Gog's homeland and to his allies. Fire from Yahweh will move out against Magog and against all those "living securely" in the distant islands/coastlands (cf. 26:15, 18; 27:3, 15, 35). This adds an ironic, almost sarcastic, note since Israel's own defenseless "living in security" had prompted Gog to launch his attack in the first place (38:11; cf. 38:8, 14). In three ways this paragraph affirms Yahweh's holiness. First, Yahweh promises to make his holiness known in the midst of "my people Israel"; cf. 38:14–16), presumably by defending them. Second, he will no longer allow his holy name to be profaned by the nations. This sentence confirms our earlier suggestion that one purpose of the Gog chapters was to counter the fears that the nations might misconstrue the events of 587 BCE as a sign of Yahweh's weakness and his inability to defend his people. Third, a recognition formula in verse 7 promises that the nations will recognize through this defeat of Gog and his allies that Yahweh is the holy one in Israel.

Note the words of certainty with which this paragraph ends: "It will come about and it will happen" (v. 8; cf. 21:7). This oracle of Yahweh is the fulfillment of his previous word: "This is the day I promised." This assurance differs dramatically from 38:17, however, for the latter verse saw the attack of Gog as the fulfillment of prophecy, while this verse finds the fulfillment in Gog's defeat.

Isaiah is the prophet who spoke most clearly about the destruction of the invading enemy within the land of Israel. According to Isaiah 14:25, Yahweh would break the Assyrian in "my land" and trample him under foot on "my mountains." The references in Isaiah to "my land" and "my mountains" seem to be echoed in Ezekiel (38:16, "my land"; 38:8; 39:2, 4, 17, "mountains of Israel"). In 17:12–14 Isaiah promised a sudden end to the terror wrought by the unnamed invading peoples: "[Yahweh] will rebuke them, and they will flee far away." Finally, a judgment oracle against Assyria threatened that nation with the same type of attack that Yahweh would wage against Gog: "The Assyrian shall fall by a sword, not of man; and a sword, not of man, shall devour him" (Isa. 31:8; cf. Ezek. 39:1–5).

Bernard Erling has suggested that the only account that would fulfill these words is the legendary defeat of Sennacherib by the angel of Yahweh (2 Kgs. 19:32–36; Isa. 37:33–37).[19] While controversy has swirled about how the account of Assyria's defeat in Isaiah is to be interpreted, it is clear that Sennacherib did gain the upper hand in his attack of 701, and that Assyria did not come to an end in Palestine as these passages seem to predict.[20] However one understands the words against Assyria in Isaiah, they do not apply *directly* to the promise of the enemy from the north announced in Jeremiah. Yet it is not hard to imagine that someone could take the unfulfilled words of Isaiah about the defeat of the dread invader and the unfulfilled words of Jeremiah about the invasion of the enemy from the north and put them together. Thus: Yahweh would indeed bring in a foe from the north, now given specific identity under the name of Gog, in fulfillment of his earlier word (38:17), but at the same time he would also fulfill another prophetic word that the great invading nation would be utterly destroyed (39:8).[21]

The defeat of Gog (39:1–5) and the destruction of his homeland Magog (vv. 6–8) are to be followed by the burning of his weapons (vv. 9–10). A number of other biblical passages use the motif of weapons destruction to emphasize Yahweh's superiority over the nations or the foolishness of trusting in or fearing weapons (Pss. 46:9; 76:3; Isa. 9:3; Hos. 2:18). Ezekiel changes this motif by allowing the people themselves to engage in the destruction of weapons; in fact, this task and the burial discussed below are their only real participation in the whole contest. As the account makes clear from beginning to end, the coming of Gog and his defeat are totally under Yahweh's control.

The potential danger of Gog, suggested already by the prophecies of Jeremiah, is underscored by the massive armaments ascribed to him in Ezekiel—despite the fact that he is attacking a people living in pastoral peace. So many weapons will be left lying on the ground that they will supply Israel with enough fuel for domestic uses for seven full years (39:9)! The promise that Israel will despoil those who despoiled them and get booty from those who took booty from them (39:10) offers a dramatic surprise ending that is exactly opposite to the intentions of Gog himself (38:12–13).

Destruction of weapons is followed in the present text by the burial of the enemy dead. While this serves the important functions of keeping the land pure from ritual pollution (39:12, 14, 16) and of emphasizing again the enormity of Gog's defeat—since the burial process goes on for seven months and requires the appointment of a kind of permanent burying task force—it is hard to see how this action can be coordinated with 39:4 and especially with 39:17–20, which have the wild animals feasting on the dead soldiers. It seems likely, therefore, that verses 11–16 are secondary.[22] The irony of this passage is that Yahweh gives Gog a burial place in the land rather than the land itself. While the people get a name for themselves through their ghoulish burial task—burial and burning of weapons exhaust the extent of their contribution—this day (39:11, 13; cf. 38:10, 14, 18, 19) will ultimately be a time for the deity's own self-glorification (cf. 28:22).

Verses 17–20 provide Yahweh's own solution of what to do about the many soldiers killed from Gog's army. Yahweh invites every kind of bird and every kind of wild animal—that is, the entire nonhuman family—to a great sacrificial banquet which he hosts. Such imagery is not unusual in the context of ancient holy war and also within Israel (cf. 29:3–5; 32:4–5; Isa. 34:5–8; Jer. 46:10; Zeph. 1:7). The feast is obviously conceived as a victory banquet, with the invited guests stuffing themselves on the carcasses of heroes, on the blood of princes, and on horses and cavalry—in addition to the rams, lambs, goats, bulls, and fatlings of Bashan which we might expect to be part of a sacrificial victory meal. When David brought the ark to Jerusalem, he hosted a banquet and generously provided food for all the women and men of Israel (2 Sam. 6:19). Similarly, Yahweh's largesse may be suggested by the abundance of food and drink available, though the modern reader is shocked by the picture of carrion animals stuffing themselves and even getting drunk on the fare. Clearly the author is more interested in celebrating the victory of Yahweh than in worrying about proportionality in battle casualties. That the author himself may have intended some exaggeration in order to emphasize the totality of the victory may be suggested by the fact that he allows the animal guests at the banquet to eat the fat and the blood, which were normally reserved in a sacrifice for Yahweh alone (cf. 44:7, 15; Lev. 3:16–17).

Through this overwhelming defeat of Gog the house of Israel[23] will recognize Yahweh as God from that time onward (39:22). As we saw earlier, the Gog pericope does not appear to suggest that the present order is coming to an end—except, perhaps, for 38:18–23, which is probably secondary (cf. Rev. 20:7–10). The victory over Gog will be an occasion for the nations to see Yahweh's glory (39:21; cf. 13) and to realize his justice: the greedy enemy rushing to plunder defenseless, unoffending Israel, will himself be plundered. The nations will also recognize that the reason for Israel's defeat had nothing to do with Yahweh's weakness or inability to defend them. Rather it occurred because of their own uncleanness and rebellions (vv. 23–24).

The proof saying in 39:25–29 returns the reader to the status quo that existed before the beginning of the Gog account.[24] The promise here to restore the fortunes of Jacob recalls similar promises made to Sodom and Samaria (16:53) and even to Egypt (29:14). The promise to have mercy on the house of Israel marks the only occasion in the book where the prophet uses either the verb *to be merciful* or its nominal equivalent,[25] but Yahweh's passion for the sake of his holy name in these verses has a number of close parallels elsewhere (e.g., 20:9, 14, 22; 36:22–23). Restoration to the land will lead to serious reflection on the reasons that led to their departure from the land in the first place. As a result they will draw the shameful consequences[26] of their treachery (cf. 16:53–54). Even though Israel will in fact be restored to full security in the land, with no one able to make them afraid,[27] the ultimate purpose of such salvation is to cause them to know/acknowledge/obey Yahweh. He who had hid his face from his people in 587 (39:24) would never do so again (39:29), since he had poured out his spirit on them (cf. 36:27; 37:14).

Conclusion

Israel had once been a prey among the nations (34:8; cf. 36:4–5), and had been so with divine approval, because of improper behavior by its leadership and the faithlessness of the people themselves. But Yahweh had promised to save this flock and never to allow a repetition of their former punishment: "They shall no more be a prey to the nations, nor shall the beasts of the land devour them; they shall dwell securely, and none shall make them afraid" (34:28; cf. 34:22). Even the most fearsome of all imaginable nations, a country like Gog, whose chances for success might seem to be enhanced by the existence of unfulfilled earlier words of Yahweh, need not be feared. In Gog's own mind and in the thoughts of its rival mercantile powers, the taking of booty from Israel might seem both right and possible (38:12–13). But Ezekiel uses the account of Yahweh's defeat of Gog's invasion in chapters 38–39 to underscore once more the finality and the irreversibility of the divine promise for the future of Israel.

Ezekiel's oracles against the individual foreign nations (see the discussion in chapter 7 above) indicted them for a wide range of offenses and announced their ultimate destruction. But these oracles never dealt with the question of a great world power, present or future, Babylon or its successor, that might descend upon Israel. Ezekiel's ideal Israel of the future was to be a holy people, protected against sinning, and therefore never requiring the sending of divine punishment nor the kinds of announcement of judgment that characterized the preexilic prophets. But might some nation desirous of personal gain invade the holy land with success, thereby calling into question the long-range future of the people of God? In his account of Gog of the land of Magog, Ezekiel provides an elaborate and convincing denial of any such possibility. Israel will never again be a prey to the nations.

NOTES

1. See most recently Reuben Ahroni, "The Gog Prophecy and the Book of Ezekiel"; Walther Eichrodt, *Ezekiel*, 519. John Wevers, *Ezekiel*, 286, attributes only 39:1–4, 6 to the prophet; Georg Fohrer, *Ezechiel*, 212, believes 38:1–4, 6–13 and 39:1, 3–5, 9–10, 17–22 are from Ezekiel.

2. Cf. Zimmerli, *Ezekiel*, 2: 302–04. He argues for an original account consisting of 38:1–9; 39:1–5; and 39:17–20, assigning the rest to several secondary hands. Ahroni, "The Gog Prophecy," 20, claims that the lack of specificity suggests a time of composition later than Haggai and Zechariah.

3. Ahroni, "The Gog Prophecy," 9–10, concludes that a resumption of hostilities and subsequent reassertion of Yahweh's superiority have no logical place in Ezekiel's scheme of the future. As I hope to show, however, it is possible to understand the theological logic of this passage within the era of Ezekiel. Whoever put the passage in its present position—either Ezekiel or one of his successors—did not find an insuperable conflict with the logic of the rest of the book.

4. Ralph W. Klein, *Israel in Exile*, 57. Cf. Isa. 43:9–10; 48:3, 5 and my interpretation of these passages on pp. 101–02. Note also the frequent questions about the cause of the exile in the Deuteronomistic History and in the Deuteronomistic portions of Jeremiah. See *Israel in Exile*, 24–25.

5. R. P. Vaggione, "Over All Asia? The Extent of the Scythian Domination in Herodotus." See *The Interpreter's Dictionary of the Bible Supplementary Volume*, 797–8.

6. John Bright, *Jeremiah*, 359–60, dates most of chrs. 50–51 to the exilic period prior to the fall of Babylon.

7. On two other occasions the prophet is instructed to set his face against individuals (13:17, against prophetesses; 29:2, against Pharaoh).

8. Zimmerli, *Ezekiel*, 2: 301. Wevers, *Ezekiel*, 284, lists twelve identifications for Gog that have been proposed, including Gyges, but he believes that Gog and Magog are only a "rhyming pair" and that the solution to the name Gog is still unknown.

9. Zimmerli, *Ezekiel*, 2: 301. Wevers, *Ezekiel*, 286, believes the reference to Magog is secondary in any case; see Fohrer, *Ezechiel*, 213.

10. Zimmerli, *Ezekiel*, 2: 65; see Wevers, *Ezekiel*, 208.

11. Zimmerli, *Ezekiel*, 2: 306. Fohrer, *Ezechiel*, 213–14, notes that the Cimmerians were destroyed by Ezekiel's time, though their name was still used for Cappadocia.

12. In Gen. 10:3 (1 Chr. 1:6) Togarmah is called a "son" of Gomer.

13. *'gp* is a word used only by Ezekiel in the Bible (outside of this context it only appears in 12:14 and 17:21). Note also the great assembly of troops described with different vocabulary in 38:5, 15.

14. Since Cush (Nubia) and Put (Libya) are North African nations, it seems inappropriate from a Palestinian geographical perspective to mention them as "northern" enemies, and they are probably a secondary addition denoting well-known mercenary troops who might also support Gog. Zimmerli, *Ezekiel*, 2: 285, also sees the reference to Persians as part of a secondary addition. See Fohrer, *Ezechiel*, 213.

15. Yahweh plans to put hooks in his jaws and so give him very limited options (38:4; cf. 19:4). Gog and his many allies will actually be in the service of Yahweh ("you will be for me a guard"), though their efforts are directed against Yahweh's people (38:7 LXX).

16. Aelred Cody, *Ezekiel*, 184, finds the following apocalyptic elements in these chapters: a great battle pitting malicious forces against Israel in Palestine, taking place at a chronologically undefined moment, and accompanied by cataclysmic happenings in nature.

17. Zimmerli, *Ezekiel*, 2: 314, notes that the person who added this apocalyptic paragraph inadvertently included negative consequences for Israel in Yahweh's defeat of Gog.

18. The translation follows Zimmerli, *Ezekiel*, 2: 290.

19. Bernard Erling, "Ezekiel 38–39 and the Origins of Jewish Apocalyptic," 112.

20. John Bright, *A History of Israel*, 298–309, proposed that Sennacherib conducted two campaigns against Judah, the first of which was successful, the second basically a defeat. Recent scholarship, however, has largely discarded this view and his sought to resolve the literary conflict in different ways. See Brevard S. Childs, *Isaiah and the Assyrian Crisis*, and Ronald E. Clements, *Isaiah and the Deliverance of Jerusalem*.

21. Zimmerli, *Ezekiel*, 2: 296–98, 312, 325, understands the Gog pericope in this way, but he deems both 38:17 and 39:8 to be secondary.

22. So Zimmerli, *Ezekiel*, 2: 298. He also discusses and refutes scholars who hold 39:17–20 to be secondary. A series of etymological etiologies dealing with the Valley of the Travelers and with the Valley of Hamon-Gog and a number of the geographical references in ch. 39 are not clear.

23. This is the only time in Ezekiel that Israel is explicitly identified as the active subject in a recognition formula.

24. For this reason Ahroni, "The Gog Prophecy," 24, believes these verses are a redactional supplement inserted in the process of incorporating the Gog pericope into the text.

25. This is a contributing factor in Zimmerli's assigning these verses to a secondary hand. (*Ezekiel*, 2: 320).

26. Literally: "They will bear their shame." Many commentators emend the verb to "forget," i.e., "They shall forget their shame" (RSV). But Ezekiel never uses the word *forget*, though he frequently speaks of "bearing shame"; cf. Zimmerli, *Ezekiel*, 2: 295.

27. These were the conditions that Gog seized upon as signs of weakness and as an opportunity for aggression.

T E N

THE NAME OF THAT CITY:

YAHWEH IS THERE

(EZEKIEL 40–48)

At the end of chapter 37 Ezekiel put special stress on the importance of Yahweh's sanctuary for a future, restored Israel. Yahweh's promise to sanctify Israel by putting his sanctuary in the midst of his people was repeated twice and punctuated with the emphasizing word *forever*. This promise receives extensive elaboration in the final nine chapters of Ezekiel. The intervening chapters 38 and 39 have at once resolved a potentially threatening problem—the invasion of a northern enemy—and heightened anticipation for the climax of the book.

I suspect that many readers of Ezekiel 40–48 are initially overwhelmed or even disappointed. Detailed architectural measurements, disputes about rank among the clergy, and a description of a renewed division of the land among the twelve tribes seem to have little to do with a theology of divine presence, let alone the concerns of the modern reader. But what first strikes the reader as a mass of confusion and obscure detail about the temple, liturgical regulations, and the land actually plays a crucial role in the priest/prophet's message for his original audience and for readers today.

The chapters are a mixture of visionary sights and legislative materials. Some have wanted to prune the chapters down to what is purely visionary, or they have used what they perceive as literary or factual tensions and contradictions to sort out later additions from materials that can be assigned to the prophet himself.[1] Still others have denied these chapters in their entirety to Ezekiel.[2] The difficulty with such reductionist procedures is that they often impose our standards of consistency and order on an ancient document in which the literary or factual "tensions" may not have been seen as inappropriate. In addition, the results of such pruning have been anything but unanimous. Scholars in our generation are more inclined than our immediate predecessors to give the benefit of the doubt to the received text when the evidence for secondary materials is ambiguous or in doubt. In my judgment only those passages that make a sharp distinction between the priests and the Levites and charge the latter with idolatry are clearly from a later hand (e.g., 40:46b; 44:6–31; 43:19a; 48:11b; cf. 45:1–8; 46:19–24).[3] This exoneration of the Zadokites seems out of character with the Ezekiel we have studied, who reproved Israel for offenses that were going on in the temple precincts (chs. 8–11), and who claimed that the priests themselves did violence to the law, profaned Yahweh's holy things, made no distinction between the holy and the common, the unclean and the clean, and disregarded the sabbaths (22:26). But even these secondary passages do not seem to violate in principle what Ezekiel was trying to do in these final chapters.

What was he trying to do? Susan Niditch recently characterized the mixture of mystical speculation and pragmatic planning in these chapters as reasonable in such a document.[4] In addition to parallels in later Jewish literature, she proposed that the Buddhist mandala, in which a visionary experience is accompanied by a detailed architectual plan, forms an analogue to Ezekiel 40–48. Both the verbal images and the actual rebuilding of the temple in wood and stone, which the prophet surely expected to be carried out, are real and valid mirrors of a heavenly realm; the vision and the rebuilding itself need not preclude each other.

Niditch also finds in these plans for the future the same kinds of cosmogonic, ordering, categorizing emphases as are present in Genesis 1–11.[5] Through words and visions Ezekiel maps reality: the temple at the center, the fructifying river in chapter 47, the holdings of the tribes, the boundaries between sacred and profane, the role of the prince, and even the relationships between priests and Levites. Thus, even the materials that are probably secondary—also in her opinion—fit in with the cosmogonic character of these chapters.[6]

Jon Levenson has stressed the practical program implicit in Ezekiel's description of the temple, its liturgy, and the community: "The order defined by the vision is still a goal to be effected through human striving and was understood as such by the tradition."[7] Ezekiel 40–48 contains the only legislation in the Hebrew Bible that is not placed in the mouth of Moses. Ezekiel's vision of the future temple recalls the "pattern" *(tabnît)* of the tabernacle shown to Moses (Exod. 25:9; cf. the pattern given Solomon by David, 1 Chr. 28:11–19). Like Moses, Ezekiel is allowed to "see" the land, but only in a vision. Levenson also sees Ezekiel's tour of Zion as a foretaste of ultimate redemption, much like the sabbath in Judaism or the eucharist in Christianity.[8] We will need to return later to this eschatological orientation and the significance of its seeming nonfulfillment.

The Ezekiel whose words are contained in these chapters is a literary figure rather than a public speaker. While the distinction between what Ezekiel said and the way he or his followers arranged his materials into literary form is often difficult to make in the rest of the book, these chapters are clearly meant to be read. Menahem Haran's outline indicates their coherent structure:

I. 40:1–44:3. The temple's form—its layout, dimensions, parts, and furnishings

II. 44:4–46:24. Temple procedures, cultic regulations, and administrative rules that ought to be practiced

III. Chapters 47–48. The land—its flourishing, frontiers, divisions, and capital city.[9]

In his vision of the future Ezekiel is guided around the temple environs much as he was guided through the sinful temple of Jerusalem in chapters 8–11. A man accompanies him and makes measurements and occasional comments until the deity himself speaks in 44:5. The vision takes place on a very high mountain, recalling the promise of Isaiah 2 and Micah 4 that in future days Jerusalem would be established as the highest of the mountains. There are elements of the cosmic mountain here, as well as remembrances of Sinai, Eden, and, of course, Zion.[10] As Ezekiel tours the temple compound, he notes a variety of measurements, almost always only of length and width and not of height.[11] They are made according to the long cubit (41:8), a cubit plus a handbreadth—that is, the Egyptian royal cubit. The symbolic significance of these measurements will be discussed after we have finished a description of the tour.

40:1–44:3: THE TEMPLE AND ITS ENVIRONS

A wall around the temple area (40:5) separates the sacred area from the profane (42:20). According to 22:26 earlier priests had not properly maintained the distinction between the sacred and the profane, while according to 44:23 the teaching of this difference was to be one of their major tasks in the future. Each side of the walled-in temple area measured 500 cubits (42:15–20).

Within the walled area Ezekiel was taken on a tour of six gates; first he visited the outer gates on the east, north, and south (# 1, Figure 8), and then he was taken to the inner gates on the south, east, and north (# 2, Figure 8; cf. 40:6–7). These six gates are not military in function, replete with towers, but serve primarily to ward off impurity from the holy region. Each gate leads to a progressively higher area. The outer gates are approached by seven stairs (40:6, 22), while the inner gates have eight stairs (40:34, 37). An additional ten stairs lead into the temple itself (40:49). The gates consist of six separate buildings, and it may well be that Ezekiel saw the temple (# 4, Figure 8) as a seventh building and the goal of his guided trip through the temple area, much as the seventh or sabbath day is the goal of Genesis 1.[12]

The descriptions of the gates are detailed enough to permit the drawing of a schematic plan. The overall dimensions are 50 by 25 cubits (40:21, 25, 29, 33, 36). Extending through the center of each gate was a passageway lined on each side by three bays (# 3, Figure 9). The passageway of the outer gates ended in a vestibule (# 5, Figure 9) next to the exit into the outer court; the inner gates have their vestibule toward the outside and the threshold (# 2, Figure 9) abuts the inner court.

Archaeologists have demonstrated that this particular style of gate reproduces the architectual style of the tenth century, the era of Solomon. The remains of such gates have been discovered at Hazor, Megiddo, and Gezer, and it is reasonable to hypothesize that there would have been similar gates in Jerusalem as well (cf. 1 Kgs. 9:15).[13] Ezekiel's knowledge of this archaic style suggests that he had access to old records in Babylon. It also shows how he reused items from the tradition and adapted them to fit his particular theological agenda. Thus he changed the gates from a military to a liturgical use, and he transferred them from the city walls to the outside wall of the temple complex and to the border around the inner court.

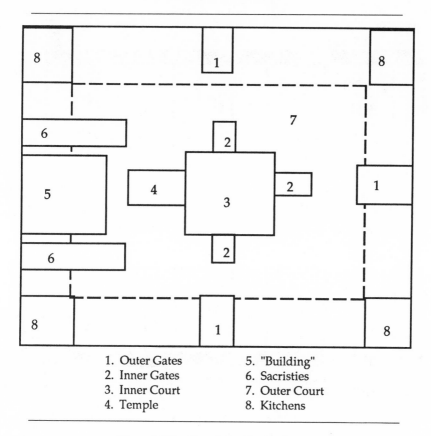

1. Outer Gates   5. "Building"
2. Inner Gates   6. Sacristies
3. Inner Court   7. Outer Court
4. Temple   8. Kitchens

Figure 8: The Temple and its Environs

The inner north gate was as far as lay people could go, and it was there that preparations for sacrifices were carried on (40:38–43). Two priestly vestries located in the vicinity of the inner north and south gates were set aside respectively for those who performed service at the altar and for those who did more general service in the temple (40:44–46). Both groups of cultic officials were called "priests" by the original author of these chapters; a later hand identified the altar priests as Zadokites (40:46b).

The three inner gates guarded the approach to an inner court of the temple (#3, Figure 8), measuring 100 by 100 cubits, in which was located

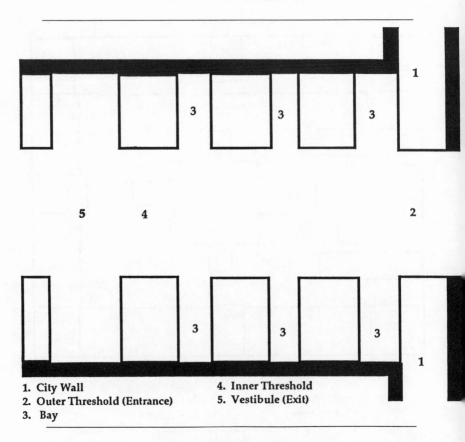

1. City Wall
2. Outer Threshold (Entrance)
3. Bay
4. Inner Threshold
5. Vestibule (Exit)

Figure 9: The Outer Gates

an altar for burnt offerings (40:47; 43:13–17). The altar was composed of a base surmounted by three layers of stone, each smaller than the layer below.[14] One approached the altar on steps from the east so that the officiant would be facing the temple. Ezekiel also records the sacrifices that were to be offered to purify the altar and prepare it for use (43:18–27). Presumably the temple itself was dedicated by Yahweh's arrival in it (see below), and the priests needed no new dedication ceremony since they merely continued the pre-exilic line.[15] In the Pentateuch's account of the wilderness shrine, the dedication of the altar in Leviticus 8–9 is reported separately from the dedication of the tabernacle itself (Exod. 40). Ezekiel's separate altar dedication rite, therefore, is another example of his dependence on tradition.

The temple itself (#4, Figure 8) consisted of three rooms: the vestibule *('ûlām)*, the nave *(hêkāl)*, and the innermost room *(pĕnîmâ)*. The internal measurements of these rooms are similar to those of the temple of Solomon, 20 by 12 cubits for the vestibule, 40 by 20 for the nave, and 20 by 20 for the most holy place (cf. 1 Kgs. 6).[16] As usual, Ezekiel only lists length and breadth. The overall length and width of the temple, counting the structures on each side and the rear, are 50 by 100, the significance of which we will note below. Each entrance in the temple gets progressively narrower as one gets closer to the place of Yahweh's presence. The entrance to the vestibule of the temple is 14 cubits wide (40:48), the entrance to the nave 10 cubits (41:2), and the entrance to the innermost room 6 cubits (41:3). Though Ezekiel himself did not enter the innermost room, his guide did and remarked: "This is the holy of holies" (41:4).

A series of annexes is noted on both sides of the temple, as well as a "building" (#5, Figure 8) with no specific function in the rear. (41:5-15a). The latter may have taken the place of the equally obscure "parbar" from first temple times (1 Chr. 26:18).[17] In any case, the presence of a building west of the temple and the absence of gates on the western side would make it impossible to approach the temple from the west with one's face toward the east. This may be an attempt to prevent a repetition of the fourth sin in 8:16-17, where twenty-five men stood between the vestibule and the altar and worshiped the sun as they faced east. The "building," its walls, and the surrounding open place to the east formed a square of 100 by 100 cubits (41:15). The next verses describe the decorations on the interior walls of the three temple rooms and the doors of the nave and inner room (41:15b-26). When Ezekiel saw "something like an altar" (cf. 1 Kgs. 6:20-22) in the nave, his guide commented: "This is the table which stands before the face of Yahweh" (41:22). We cannot be sure if this was an incense altar or a table for the showbread (cf. Exod. 25:23-30).[18]

To the north and south of the temple, along the western side of the sacred enclosure, Ezekiel saw sacristies (#6, Figure 8), in which the priests could eat their share of the cereal offering, the sin offering, and the guilt offering, and in which they could change their holy garments that had been used in the sanctuary before they reentered the outer court (#7, Figure 8; cf. 42:1-14; 44:19). These buildings are perhaps intended as a replacement for the vestries located near the inner north and south gates (40:44-46; see above). The guide notes, "These are the sacred chambers where the priests who approach Yahweh eat the sacred gifts" (42:13). Because these buildings duplicate the vestries of 40:44–46, and because they seem to mark degrees of holiness within the community that go beyond the basic distinction between the holy and the profane (42:20), they may well be secondary.[19]

At the end of this first part of the vision Ezekiel saw the glory of the God of Israel return from the east (43:1–5), accompanied by the noise of many waters and great light. This is explicitly identified in 43:3 with the glory that came to destroy the first temple in chapters 8–11 and with the divine appearance that was the centerpiece of his call vision in chapter 1. Appropriately, the prophet fell on his face (43:3; 44:4; cf. 1:28). Yahweh entered through the east gate, through which he had left in 10:19. After Ezekiel had been lifted up by the spirit and taken to the inner court, he noted that the glory of Yahweh had refilled the temple (43:5; cf. 44:4; Exod. 40:35).

Yahweh announced from within the temple: "This is the place of my throne and the place of the soles of my feet, where I will dwell in the midst of the people of Israel for ever" (43:7). Significantly, these words suggest that there is to be no ark on which Yahweh would be enthroned in the postexilic temple (cf. Jer. 3:16–17).[20] Yahweh also indicated that in the community centered about the new temple the sins of former days would not be perpetuated, neither the defiling of the divine name, nor the people's harlotry and idolatry, nor the inappropriate burial of kings (or erecting memorial stelae)[21] close to the sanctuary (43:7–9). The palace of the first temple period had been placed next to the temple (2 Kgs. 11), and King Manasseh for one was buried in the garden of his house (2 Kgs. 21:18), that is, in proximity to the temple. Ezekiel's plans for the future mention no palace for the prince at all. In fact, the city is far removed from the temple, and the prince's land and, presumably, his residence were to be outside the 25,000 by 25,000 area called the Whole Portion (see below). For a second time Yahweh promises, "I will dwell in their midst forever" (43:9).

Yahweh instructed Ezekiel to describe the temple and its plan to Israel so that the people would be ashamed of their iniquities (43:10). The various devices that we have noted to ensure the distinction between the sacred and the profane and protect the temple and its God from any impurity would remind the people of their previous defiling of the sacred. In 16:54 Jerusalem's restoration in the midst of a restored Sodom and Samaria was also designed to make Jerusalem bear its disgrace and feel ashamed over its previous evil deeds. The gift of the sisters Sodom and Samaria to Jerusalem as daughters would also lead her to remember her ways and be ashamed (16:61). According to 20:43, Israel would remember her ways and loathe herself in response to Yahweh's leading her back into the land (see also 36:32). The very fact that exilic Israel stands in need of a new gift of the land or of a new sanctuary presupposes that the old gifts were lost on account of sin, and so calls for the people to undergo appropriate reflection and repentance. Hence, both the proclamations of judgment and the proclamations of salvation are to lead people to repentance.

In order that the people might show proper remorse at the description of the temple, Ezekiel is ordered to write down its exits and entrances and its ordinances and laws so that they may be observed (43:11). The exits and entrances refer both to the six gates described in chapter 40 and to the movements of the prince and the people in connection with various kinds of sacrifices in chapter 46. The ordinances and laws include at least the various cultic regulations in these chapters. The torah, or instruction, about the house is then summarized: The whole territory on top of the mountain is most holy (43:12).

After the descriptions of the altar (43:13–17) and its dedication (43:18–27) were given, Ezekiel was brought back to the outer east gate of the sanctuary, which had now been closed. His guide instructed him: "This gate shall remain shut" (44:2). The explicit reason for this is to prevent anyone from traversing the same path Yahweh took into the temple. Implicit in the closure and in the guide's comment is the assurance that Yahweh would never leave through this gate again. Thus the divine promises of 37:26, 28 and 43:7, 9—that Yahweh would dwell in his sanctuary forever—are reinforced by the permanent closing of the gate itself. The only exception to the ban on the use of this gate is a partial one: the prince will eat his sacrificial meal in the outer gate (44:3), but even he enters by the vestibule (#5, Figure 9) facing the outer court and leaves by the same route. The outer door of the gate is never to be opened.

44:4–46:24: TEMPLE PROCEDURES

The second major section of chapters 40–48 begins with an admonition for Ezekiel to mark well the ordinances and laws of the temple and to mark those who are to be admitted to or excluded from the sanctuary (44:5; cf. 40:4).

To be excluded are foreigners who formerly participated in sacrificial rites. These people, branded as uncircumcised of heart (i.e., stubborn in spirit) and flesh, are often identified with the Gibeonites.[22] The offense of admitting them to the temple in the past is branded as a breach of the covenant (44:7; cf. 16:59).

The list of those admitted to the sanctuary, on the other hand, includes Levites and Levitical priests, with the latter here also called "sons of Zakok." The Levites themselves are to be admitted in a decidedly inferior position: they will supervise the gates and assist the laity with their sacrifices (44:11; 46:21–24). Such an inferior position for the Levites is also attested in the Priestly parts of the Pentateuch and in the books of Chronicles.[23] What is astonishing about this passage is that the exclusion of the Levites from priestly rites in the narrow sense is based on their idolatry (44:12) and on their involvement with abominations (v. 13).[24] The historical reason for the lower rank of the Levites may, in fact, go back to ancient rivalries between priestly houses[25] and/or to the effects of the Deuteronomic reform, which closed down local shrines without securing a place for the priests from these shrines in the Jerusalem temple (Deut. 18:6–8; 2 Kgs. 23:9). The moral reason provided by Ezekiel for this demotion cannot be validated or falsified on the basis of current data. Needless to say, it does reflect an intense dispute within priestly ranks. In the exoneration of the Zadokite priests as those who remained loyal to Yahweh when the people of Israel as a whole went astray, verses 10–31 go much beyond what Ezekiel himself is likely to have said and so are to be attributed to a later hand.

Verses 17–27 of chapter 44 provide the rules for the Zadokite priests. Included are instructions on what they can wear in the inner and outer court, on hair styles (they cannot shave their heads or let their locks grow long), on drinking alcohol (wine is forbidden while they are on duty in the inner court), and on whom they can marry (only virgins, or widows of priests).[26] The rules mandate them to teach people the difference between the holy and the common, the unclean and the clean, to serve as judges in disputes, and to observe all feasts, including the sabbaths. Contact with the dead is prohibited except in the case of certain close relatives. When defiled in these exceptional cases, they must offer a sin offering on returning to the temple.

Verses 28–31 make provision for priests' income (cf. Num. 18:8–19). They are to receive no inheritance or possession in Israel, though they may eat what has been offered as a cereal, sin, or guilt offering. "Devoted things" and a variety of offerings are also designated for them. They may not eat any living creature that has died of itself or that has been torn by a wild animal.[27]

The first eight verses of chapter 45 outline the portions of the land set aside for the temple, the priests, the Levites, the city, and the prince, but our discussion of them can be delayed for the fuller treatment of the land division in 48:8–22 below.

Rules for the Prince

The monarch of the coming era is always called "prince" *(naśî̄)* in chapters 40–48, a title from ancient Israelite tradition here suggesting the limited status of the king after the exile. A discussion of the prince's property in 45:7–8 ends with an admonition for him not to expropriate land belonging to the tribes. This leads in turn to a general prohibition for the princes of Israel not to engage in violence, oppression, and injustice (45:9). The prince, therefore, is to be the diametric opposite of his preexilic forebears. Ezekiel had charged earlier: "Her princes[28] in the midst of her are like a roaring lion tearing the prey; they have devoured human lives; they have taken treasure and precious things; they have made many widows in the midst of her" (22:25).

The following verses (45:10–17) require the prince to maintain right measurements and weights, for these determine the amount of the portions given to the prince by the people (v. 16).[29] It is from these portions contributed by the people that the prince is to provide burnt offerings, cereal offerings, and drink offerings on the feasts, new moons, and sabbaths in order to make atonement for the house of Israel. The next paragraph, verses 18–25, indicates the prince's sacrifices on the annual days of purifying the temple (on the first and seventh days of the first month) and on the pilgrim feasts of the first (Passover) and seventh (unleavened bread) months.[30] The annual purifying of the sanctuary serves somewhat the same function as the Day of Atonement, though the latter festival is not mentioned in the book of Ezekiel.[31]

The inner east gate, just like the outer east gate, is to remain shut except for the sabbath day and the day of the new moon (46:1). On these days of worship the prince enters through the vestibule of the gate (the vestibule of the *inner* gates faces the *outer* court; cf. #5, Figure 9), takes his stand by the post of the gate, near the threshold (cf. #2, Figure 9) that adjoins the inner court, and leaves again via the vestibule into the outer court. The people of the land worship only at the entrance to this gate, thus showing their position inferior to the prince in the temple (46:2–8). At the so-called "appointed feasts," the people enter the outer court by the north gate and leave by the south, or vice versa. In either case the prince enters and leaves in their midst (vv. 9–10). The sacrifices of the prince for the sabbath (vv. 4–5), the new moon (vv. 6–7), the feasts and appointed seasons (vv. 11–12), and the daily offerings (vv. 13–15) are also regulated in this law.[32]

Another paragraph sets limits on what the prince may do with his property. If he cedes some of it to his sons, it becomes part of their inheritance. But if he cedes some of it to his servants or staff, it remains theirs only until the year of liberty—the jubilee—when it reverts to the prince (46:16–17). Again, the law forbids the prince from taking any of the inheritance belonging to the people (46:18; cf. 45:8). While the prince must be provided land in the restored Israel, very careful provisions are made that the self-aggrandizing activities of many of the earlier kings will not be repeated. The prince is to be first among the worshipers, enjoying the right of closest access to the inner court of anyone except the priests themselves. He is also responsible for providing animals from his income for many of the sacrifices. But nowhere in these chapters does Ezekiel say anything about his political power. He would hardly have joined Isaiah in saying, "The government shall be upon his shoulder" (Isa. 9:6).

As a final part of the ordinances and laws in this section dealing with temple procedures, the guide took Ezekiel to the north set of priestly chambers (#6, Figure 8) where cooking space for their offerings was provided. Boiling and baking were to be done inside these facilities so that the priests would not have to take the sacrifices into the outer court and thereby "communicate holiness" to the people (46:19–20). In the four corners of the outer court were kitchens where cultic personnel, presumable the Levites, could boil the sacrifices of the people (#8, Figure 8; 46:21–24).[33] Twice at the end of chapter 46 the guide tells Ezekiel the purpose of what he shows him (vv. 20, 24).

47:1–12: THE LIFE-GIVING STREAM

The third section of chapters 40–48 opens with Ezekiel viewing a stream of water coming forth from the temple. Led out of the temple through the north gate by his guide, the prophet discovered the water issuing from the east gate and growing progressively deeper. At first the water reached only his ankles, and then his knees. After another thousand cubits the water reached up to the loins, and after still another thousand cubits one could only swim in it. His guide asked Ezekiel, "Mortal, have you seen this?" (47:6; cf. 8:12, 15, 17).

Along the banks of the river the prophet saw very many trees that would bear a new crop of fruit every month of the year and whose leaves would be good for healing purposes (vv. 7, 12). The guide notes that after the water passed through the barren Judean wilderness, it emptied into the Dead Sea, turning those stagnant waters fresh. Many kinds of fish thrived in the Dead Sea, and fishermen flourished along the whole southern half of the sea (from En-gedi to En-eglaim; vv. 8–10). Various swamps and marshes, however, would not be changed by the water of the river; from them salt could still be extracted (v. 11).

As Greenberg points out, this stream links the account of the temple and its rites to the forthcoming description of the land. In the ancient Near East in general, and also in the Bible, the home or the temple of a god was often situated by a river or stream. El's home in the Ugaritic texts is located by the source of the two rivers, in the midst of two seas' pools.[34] From the garden of Eden, sometimes called the garden of God in Ezekiel (28:13; 31:9), flowed a mighty river, which divided into four streams and watered the whole world (Gen. 2:10–14). The psalmist, when faced with impending chaos from tottering mountains and threatening sea, reassured himself with the knowledge that there is a river that makes glad the city of God. Since God is in the midst of this city, it will not be moved (Ps. 46:4–5). According to Isaiah 33:20–24 a sacred stream from Zion would bring physical healing for humans ("No inhabitant will say, 'I am sick' "), as well as spiritual nurture ("The people who dwell there will be forgiven their iniquity").

Thus, Ezekiel has drawn on a common tradition about the divine dwelling place to spell out the significance of Yahweh's return to the temple in Jerusalem. His presence in the center of the land would mean a transformation of the physical world, a new creation. The Judean wilderness stretching from Jerusalem east to the Dead Sea is one of the most barren areas in all of Palestine, and the name Dead Sea accurately expresses the lifelessness of that great body of water. Such dead places of the land, however, will be re-created by Yahweh's dwelling in Jerusalem. Three pieces of evidence for the extent of the new creation are cited: ever-bearing fruit trees, abundant and varied fish in the Dead Sea, and the tree leaves that cure human ailments. In short, the vision of the stream suggests that there is nothing that can escape change when Yahweh is present with his people.

Later prophecy continued and developed this picture. According to Zechariah 14:8, the waters emanating from Jerusalem would flow to both east and west, thus explicitly embracing the whole land, and they would continue winter and summer—making this stream more than a seasonal wadi. The prophet Joel connected the presence of God in the temple with the abundance of nature ("The mountains shall drip sweet wine and the hills shall flow with milk"), and with a fountain from Jerusalem that would water the valley of Shittim, an unknown locale full of acacia trees, probably situated east of Jerusalem (Joel 3:18).

William Farmer proposed that the reason why the Essenes founded their community on the desolate shore of the Dead Sea was because they eagerly anticipated the coming of God's new age, in which the stream from the temple would give life to the Dead Sea.[35] Their opportune location would enable them to be the first to see the fish jump!

The unfulfilled expectations about the stream from the temple may also find an echo and a reinterpretation in the Gospel of John. According to John 2:19–21, Jesus identified his own body with the temple of God. The evangelist also reports that those who come to Jesus and drink will never thirst, for "as the Scripture has said, 'Out of his heart [the heart of Jesus] shall flow rivers of living water' " (John 7:37–38). The stream of Ezekiel 47 may even provide a new level of meaning to an incident at the crucifixion of Jesus, when a soldier pierced his side with a spear and at once there came out blood and water (John 19:34). If God's presence in his temple means new life for his people, John's symbolism would suggest that the body of Jesus is now that temple, and that God was never more "with" his people than when Jesus hung on the cross. Hence those who believe in him should expect that there is nothing that now cannot be changed.

An explicit reference to Ezekiel's stream appears in Revelation 22:1–3. From the throne of God and the Lamb flows a stream that passes through the city. Trees of life on its banks bear twelve different kinds of fruit, with a new crop each month, and their leaves provide healing for the nations.

These later passages aside, the stream in Ezekiel is a powerful statement during the Exile of the transformative power of Yahweh's presence in Jerusalem. As we have seen, Ezekiel's picture of the temple area is no mere restoration of preexilic conditions; it is also a transformation, indicating that in the future the temple and its rituals will be free from impurity and abuses, and that Israel will not be threatened by the possibility of Yahweh departing again from his shrine. In the final two chapters of his book Ezekiel makes clear that this transformation affects the whole people and the whole land, not just the temple and its rites. And yet this transformation is inextricably connected to the one who has again taken up residence in the temple. When he is there, everything can be transformed—the Judean desert, the Dead Sea, the frailness of human bodies, and the equitable settlement of the tribes on the land.

47:13–48:29: THE DIVISION OF THE LAND

The borders of the land described to Ezekiel extend from Lebo-hamath in the north to the Brook of Egypt in the South, and from the Mediterranean Sea up to the Jordan River (47:15–20). The most remarkable aspect of these boundaries is the exclusion of the Transjordanian region, where the tribes of Reuben, Gad, and half of Manasseh lived according to Joshua's division of the land.

Here as elsewhere Ezekiel shows acquaintance with archaic traditions and a willingness to alter them to fit the needs of coming times. His picture of the land resembles that in Numbers 34:2–12, which also excludes the area across the Jordan, and both passages reflect a knowledge of the old Egyptian province of Canaan.[36] Ezekiel chose this picture, although he theoretically could have followed the outlines of the original division and extent of the land in Joshua, or even the extent of the land under David and Solomon.

His choice, we suspect, did not result primarily from a feeling for what were the most ancient or authentic boundaries of the land. Rather, he also knew that the Transjordanian region was associated with dangerous temptations. The two and a half Transjordanian tribes built an altar by the Jordan and swore an oath that they would never fall away to idolatry. This ceremony indicates the danger to the faith that was perceived to be present in Transjordan (Josh. 22:26–29). The same land east of the Jordan was unwisely chosen by Lot when he and Abram divided the land (Gen. 13). The men of Sodom among whom Lot lived were wicked, great sinners against Yahweh (Gen. 13:13). The land east of the Jordan was also the region of Moab and Ammon, the eponymous ancestors of the countries of the same names, whose conception was attributed in the tradition to an incestuous relationship between Lot and his daughters (Gen. 19:30–38). Ezekiel's expectation of the future was that Israel would be freed from idols, and that the people would walk in God's statutes and ordinances (36:25–27). It is hardly surprising, therefore, that even the borders of the land make such sinning less likely.

Ezekiel suggests another reform by announcing that resident aliens should receive an inheritance in the same way as native-born Israelites (47:22–23). In his accusations against Israel, Ezekiel had scored the extortion practiced on the resident aliens (22:7); such inequity would not be permitted after Yahweh's return. Humane treatment for aliens is widely urged in the Pentateuch (Exod. 22:21; 23:9; Lev. 19:10, 33–34; 23:22; Deut. 14:29; 24:14–15, 17–22). The prophet moves beyond this to suggest that full rights stem not from whether one is by blood an Israelite, but rather that all who live within the territory of Israel are Israelites. This view may show his acquaintance with a similar principle enshrined in the Holiness Code. According to Leviticus 17:15–16, both a native Israelite and an alien become unclean when they eat an animal that had died by itself. That is, aliens are treated like Israelites because they dwell in the land. In Deuteronomy 14:21, on the other hand, something that dies of itself, while forbidden to Israelites, could be sold with impunity to aliens or foreigners.

The distribution of the land itself also marks a major change from Israel's past (see Figure 10). While the tribe of Dan still gets the northernmost territory, the principle of arrangement for the tribes as a whole is not determined primarily by historical memory. In the middle of the land is the Whole Portion, where the priests and Levites live and where the temple and the city are located (48:8–22; see below). North of the Whole Portion are seven tribes, while five tribes are to the south of it, an appropriate imbalance since the region north of Jerusalem is larger than the south. The first four tribes north of the Whole Portion are Judah, Reuben, Ephraim, and Manasseh, whose eponymous ancestors were born to Jacob's full wives, Leah and Rachel. The first four tribes south of the Whole Portion are Benjamin, Simeon, Issachar, and Zebulun, whose eponymous ancesters were also born to Jacob's full wives. The remaining northern tribes, from south to north, are Naphtali, Asher, and Dan, born to Bilhah and Zilpah, handmaidens of Jacob's wives, while the remaining southern tribe is Gad, the son of Zilpah. The system of distribution is based on zones of holiness: the temple, its priests and the Levites at the

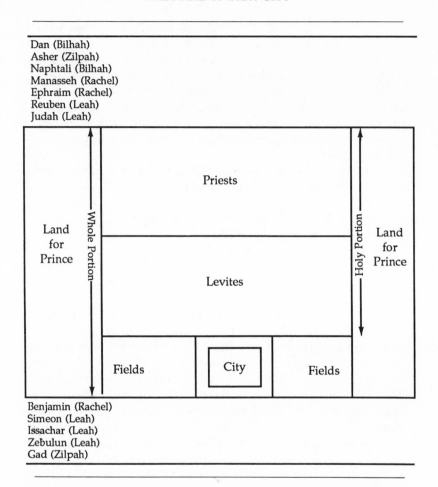

Dan (Bilhah)
Asher (Zilpah)
Naphtali (Bilhah)
Manasseh (Rachel)
Ephraim (Rachel)
Reuben (Leah)
Judah (Leah)

Benjamin (Rachel)
Simeon (Leah)
Issachar (Leah)
Zebulun (Leah)
Gad (Zilpah)

Figure 10: The Division of the Land

center; then four tribes to the north and four to the south descended from
the patriarch Jacob and one of his full wives; then three tribes to the north
and one to the south descended from the handmaidens of the wives.[37]

No northern or southern borders are listed for each of the twelve
tribes, but the territory of each extends "from the east side to the west."
This suggests that each tribe gets the same amount of territory directly
north or south of its neighboring tribe. Note that 47:14 speaks of dividing

the land equally and that each of the tribes gets exactly one portion (48:1–7, 23–27). Such equality would guard against a stronger tribe oppressing a weaker one, or even against a stronger tribe absorbing completely a weaker one and so reducing the total number to less than twelve. The proposed layout of the land, of course, was new to those in exile, but the promise of the land itself stems from the most ancient Israelite tradition. That old promise, Ezekiel indicates, is still valid: "I [Yahweh] swore to give it to your fathers, and this land shall fall to you as your inheritance" (47:14).

Within the Whole Portion a smaller area, the Holy Portion (or the portion for Yahweh, 45:1), consisting of two sections measuring 25,000 cubits by 10,000 cubits, is assigned to the priests and to the Levites.[38] The present text reasserts the superiority of the Zadokite priests who kept Yahweh's charge and the disobedience of the Levites. The superiority of the priestly territory is indicated in that it is called a most holy part of the land (45:4), whereas this evaluation is not given for the portion assigned to the Levites. Their territory is treated as their "possession," which may mark a loss in nobility (45:5).[39]

To the south of the territory of the priests and the Levites is the territory assigned to the "city." The lack of a name for the city may mark a reform designed to move beyond the old name Jerusalem or its history as the city of David. According to Ezekiel's plan the city will belong to the whole house of Israel and will be inhabited by representatives of all of the tribes (48:19). Just as in the era of Solomon, the city will be situated south of the temple, though the distance between city and temple is much greater in Ezekiel's design so that the possibility of the city corrupting the temple is made virtually impossible. Note the previous bad effect of the proximity of the temple and the palace (43:7–9). The city itself has sides of 4,500 cubits, with a belt of open land extending 250 cubits in each direction. Thus the overall dimensions of the city itself and its open land are 5,000 by 5,000. This leaves rectangular fields of 10,000 by 5,000 cubits on the west and east sides of the city, which produce food for the support of the workers in the city. This self-sufficiency of the city would make any kind of taxation to support it unnecessary and so, presumably, would reduce the possibility of the capital city exploiting the general population. The entire allotment for the city and its adjacent territories is 5,000 by 25,000 cubits.

Alongside the Holy Portion and the portion of the city (i.e., alongside the Whole Portion), to both east and west, land is to be set aside for the prince. As 45:8 makes clear, this land grant is to supply the needs of the prince so that he will have no cause for oppressing the tribes by depriving them of land. Again we see that Ezekiel announces not just a new Israel, but a renewed Israel, with the causes or temptations for sin and oppression removed.

The vision itself took place in the twenty-fifth year of Ezekiel's exile (on 10 April, 574), fourteen years after the fall of Jerusalem. Surprisingly, almost all of the dimensions listed in these chapters are also multiples of 25:

> The Whole Portion 25,000 × 25,000
> The portion of the Priests and Levites 25,000 by 10,000
> The city itself 5,000 × 5,000
> The city and its adjacent territories 5,000 × 25,000
> The temple complex 500 × 500
> The temple itself 100 × 50
> The gates 50 × 25
> The inner court 100 × 100
> The distances between the outer and inner gates 100
> The total number of steps 25

Does the number 25, contained in the date of the vision and suggested by the various measurements, carry symbolic importance? Did Ezekiel believe the reestablishment of Israel would be a kind of fiftieth year of jubilee (cf. 46:17), with the prominent mention of the number 25 in the date and in the measurements implying that by the twenty-fifth year of his call Israel could count itself halfway to the new day when the temple would be reestablished in the renewed land? Though one can never be certain of such a symbolic message, the convergence of the numbers on the figure 25 is very suggestive.

THE CITY RENAMED

The final paragraph in the book of Ezekiel (48:30–35) may not stem from the prophet himself, but it accurately points to the guiding theological motif in the final chapters as well as in the book as a whole.

The paragraph lists the twelve gates or exits of the city, assigning each of them to one of the tribes. The Leah tribes of Reuben, Judah, and

Levi are on the north, while the Leah tribes of Simeon, Issachar, and Zebulun are on the south of the city. To the east are the Rachel tribes of Joseph and Benjamin, plus Dan, the descendent of Rachel's maid Bilhah. On the west, the least favored direction in chapters 40–48 (cf. 43:1–5; 44:1–3; 46:1–3), are descendants of the handmaids, Gad, Asher, and Naphtali. Naturally, the arrangement in a square rather than in the vertical direction of 48:1–7, 23–29 caused a certain amount of dislocation, but the author of these verses retained the tribe of Levi as a full member of the twelve tribes and collapsed the tribes of Ephraim and Manasseh into the tribe of Joseph.[40]

An even larger departure from the scheme in Ezekiel is the name given to the city. In Ezekiel's view (45:6; 48:15–20) the city is a necessary part of any future Israel, but the city has a limited role, like the prince, and it is populated by representatives from all the twelve tribes; it has no name. In his earlier indictments Ezekiel had called it a bloody city (22:2), full of tumult (22:5).

In postexilic times Jerusalem or Zion was sometimes renamed in prophetic texts to indicate its new glory. Instead of names like Forsaken and Desolate, for example, the city would be called Hephzibah (My delight is in her) and Beulah (Married; see Isa. 62:4). A very late passage in Jeremiah renames Jerusalem "The Lord is our righteousness" (Jer. 33:16), a name given to the messianic figure by the prophet himself (Jer. 23:5–6). The final paragraph in Ezekiel would seem to reflect a similar honoring of the holy city. In distinction from the original prophecy, Jerusalem is no longer sharply differentiated from the temple complex, the place to which Yahweh's glory had returned. Rather, the city itself is the locus of the divine presence and, possibly, of the temple itself. The final sentence of the book reads: "The name of the city henceforth shall be, 'Yahweh is there.'"

CONCLUSION

The theme of Yahweh's presence with his people is the central motif in Ezekiel 40–48. Already signaled by the double promise to dwell with Israel forever in 37:26–28, the promise of divine presence takes shape in the final nine chapters through a description of the reconstituted temple complex, with great care being exerted to protect the ritual sanctity of the temple. Climaxing this part of the vision is the return of Yahweh to the temple, the prophet's awe in the divine presence, and the measures taken to make sure that no one would tread on the path taken by Yahweh and that Yahweh would never leave the temple again. The rights and duties of the prince, the priests, and the Levites in and around the temple are carefully defined. A symbolic stream issuing from the temple signals the total transformation of the land and the abolishing of illness as a result of Yahweh's presence. Finally, the land is equally divided among the twelve tribes, arranged in rank according to whether their ancestral mother was a full wife of Jacob or only one of the handmaids of his wives.

The book of Ezekiel opened with the call of the prophet in the context of a dramatic vision which made clear that Yahweh was indeed present in Babylon. The end of Jerusalem was later depicted by the inexorable, if reluctant, departure of the glory of Yahweh from the city. As the community that read Ezekiel waited eagerly for the promised new day when Yahweh would return to his temple and restore the land, they added a final paragraph (48:30–35) and gave a name to the previously unnamed city. The name—that is, the identity, meaning, and significance—of the city could now be wrapped up in the words "Yahweh is there." Perhaps for them the city was in fact the home of the temple. In any case, their emphasis on Yahweh's presence accurately reflected the center of the prophet's own theology.

Those readers who can see beyond the numerous architectural and liturgical details of these chapters catch a glimpse of the hope connected with the presence of God in the theology of Ezekiel. They know that when God is truly present with his people, nothing that is negative or less than perfect can remain impervious to change and transformation. Such hopeful news is also a summons for readers of this book to join the whole people of God in implementing renewal in church, society, and world.

Given the times we live in, we—like Ezekiel—know that only such a radical word will do.

Notes

1. Hartmut Gese, *Der Verfassungsentwurf des Ezechiel (Kap 40–48)*; Georg Fohrer, *Die Hauptprobleme des Buches Ezechiel*, 36–37; Zimmerli, *Ezekiel*, 2: 549.
2. G. Hölscher, *Hesekiel, der Dichter und das Buch*, 208; V. Herntrich, *Ezechielprobleme*, 125.

3. Other possible secondary passages include at least 42:1–14 and 48:30–35. See the discussion below.

4. Susan Niditch, "Ezekiel 40–48 in a Visionary Context," 209. Steven Tuell, "The Temple Vision of Ezekiel 40–48: A Program for Restoration?"denies that these chapters are either a program for restoration or a vision of the age after the eschaton. Instead, they represent for him the experience of a present, ongoing reality. Ezekiel sees Yahweh's glory as it enters the real heavenly sanctuary.

5. Niditch, "Ezekiel," 217.

6. Niditch, "Ezekiel," 221, finds that the book of Ezekiel as it now stands, including chs. 38–39 and 40–48, conforms to an ancient mythic pattern: 38:10–13 challenge/hubris; 39:1–10 battle and victory; 39:11–16 establishment of order; 39:17–20 feast; 39:25–29 procession/return; chs. 40–48 building.

7. Jon Douglas Levenson, *Theology of the Program of Restoration of Ezekiel 40–48*, 7.

8. Levenson, *Theology*, 18.

9. Menahem Haran, "The Law-Code of Ezekiel XL-XLVIII and Its Relation to the Priestly School," 51, 53. Greenberg's outline, "The Design and Themes of Ezekiel's Program of Restoration," 189, is similar if different in detail:

I. 40:1–43:12. Vision of the future temple

II. 44:1–46:22. Enterings and exitings—rules governing access to the temple and activities in it

III. 47:13–48:35. Apportionment of the land among the people

Other passages play an intermediate function. 43:13–27, describing the altar and its dedication, is attached formally to the preceding materials but links this static vision with the activity in 44:1–46:22. 47:1–12, the account of the fructifying river, links the temple (parts I and II) to the discussion of the land (part III).

10. Cf. Levenson, *Theology*, 5–53.

11. The wall in 40:5 is an exception: it is 6 cubits wide and 6 high.

12. Zimmerli, *Ezekiel*, 2: 362. The function of the 30 chambers, 40:17, is not given. See Zimmerli, *Ezekiel*, 2:352, for a discussion of how such chambers were used in the preexilic temple.

13. Zimmerli, *Ezekiel*, 2: 352–53.

14. The top layer was 12 × 12 cubits, the second 14 × 14, and the third 16 × 16. The base itself was 18 × 18. For a drawing see Aelred Cody, *Ezekiel*, 223, or Th. A. Busink, *Der Tempel von Jerusalem von Salomo bis Herodes*, vol. 2, *Von Ezechiel bis Middot*, 73, fig. 182.

15. See Greenberg, "Design and Themes," 194.

16. In 1 Kgs. 6 the vestibule measures 10 × 20, the nave and inner room together 60 × 20. Ezekiel seems to have tried to follow the Solomonic internal dimensions as much as possible, though his external dimensions fit in with his overall scheme in which measurements are multiples of 25. See Zimmerli, *Ezekiel*, 2: 358.

17. Zimmerli, *Ezekiel*, 2: 380; John Wevers, *Ezekiel*, 306.

18. Haran, 'Law-Code," 64, sees it as an incense altar; Zimmerli, *Ezekiel*, 2: 388–89, opts for the showbread table; Greenberg, "Design and Themes," 191, lists both as possibilities.

19. Note the distinction between regular priests and altar priests. Zimmerli, *Ezekiel*, 2: 399, also notes that one of the numbers in the dimensions of these sacristies, 70 × 100, is not a multiple of 25.

20. The Bible is silent about the final end of the ark. Was it destroyed by the Babylonians when they burned the temple, or had it been removed by an earlier king such as Manasseh? Cf. Menahem Haran, *Temples and Temple-Service in Ancient Israel*, 277–88. The account in 2 Macc. 2:4–8 of Jeremiah's preserving the ark in a cave seems to be without historical value.

21. Zimmerli, *Ezekiel*, 2: 417.

22.   Levenson, *Theology*, 135–40, notes that the evidence indicating that the Gibeonites were in fact circumcised is quite minimal, and he also observes that the role of the Gibeonites as hewers of wood and drawers of water did not include sacrificial tasks. He prefers to interpret this reference to the sacrificial role of foreigners as an allusion to Israel's involvement in the syncretistic rites of Beth-Peor (Num. 25; cf. Deut. 4:1–40). G.A. Cooke, *The Book of Ezekiel*, 2: 479, believes that the foreigners were originally prisoners of war presented by the kings of Judah to the temple as slaves. Zimmerli, *Ezekiel*, 2: 454, admits that the offense cannot be defined precisely.

23.   The Chronicler makes efforts, however, to show favor to the Levites as much as possible, without changing their exclusion from performing altar sacrifices.

24.   Levenson, *Theology*, 139, suggests that the Levites were the ones who admitted the foreigners into the sanctuary in violation of the covenant. Behind this polemic, in his view, is a critique of the Mushite priests who were responsible for the incident at Beth-Peor and a critique against contemporary rivals to the Zadokites from sanctuaries like Bethel. These opponents are called Levites. In my judgment, he errs in connecting the demoting of the Levites to their supposed role in admitting foreigners into the cult. In 44:7–9 Israel as a whole is criticized for having tolerated the admission of foreigners in the past. The lower rank of the Levites in comparison with the Zadokites in vv. 10–31 does *not* result from their admitting foreigners to the sanctuary.

25.   Frank M. Cross, *Canaanite Myth and Hebrew Epic*, 195–215.

26.   According to Lev. 21:14, the high priest cannot marry a divorced woman, a harlot, or a widow, but only a virgin. According to Levenson, *Theology*, 141, priestly laws for the high priest have been extended by Ezekiel to all the priests. No high priest is mentioned in Ezekiel. For other contrasts between Ezekiel and the Torah cf. 45:18 and 46:6–7 with Num. 28:11, and 45:20 with Lev. 7:25. See Levenson, *Theology*, 38.

27.   In Exod. 22:31 this rule is applied to all Israelites. Cf. Lev. 22:8.

28.   The reading follows the LXX; see *BHS*. The MT reads "a band of her prophets."

29.   Haran, "Law-Code," 57.

30.   In Exod. 23:16 and 34:22 this last feast is called the feast of ingathering; in Deut. 16:13, 16 and Lev. 23:34, it is called the feast of booths.

31.   Haran, "Law-Code," 65.

32.   According to the Priestly laws, there was to be a daily sacrifice in both the morning and the evening. See Exod. 29:38–42; Num. 28:1–8.

33.   The dimensions of these kitchens are 40 × 30 cubits, a rare exception to the phenomenon that almost all measurements in these chapters are multiples of 25.

34.   The translation is from Michael David Coogan, *Stories from Ancient Canaan*, 95.

35.   William R. Farmer, "The Geography of Ezekiel's River of Life." He identified En-eglaim with Ain Feshkah.

36.   See Yohanan Aharoni and Michael Avi-Yonah, *The Macmillan Bible Atlas*, maps 50 and 166.

37.   Not every aspect of the distribution can be explained. The location of Judah north of the temple and Benjamin south of the temple is one of the most difficult problems. Greenberg, "Design and Themes," 200, suggests that Judah is assigned to the former place of Benjamin, one of the smallest tribes, in order to humble it. Zimmerli, *Ezekiel*, 2: 541, wonders if the old connection of Jerusalem and Benjamin, in whose territory Judah lay, led to the juxtaposition of Benjamin and the city. In the land division under Joshua, Issachar and Zebulin were both in the north, with Zebulun located to the north of Issachar. In Ezekiel's plan both are placed in the south, with Issachar to the north of Zebulun. Perhaps, as the older of the two brothers, it merited the position closer to the temple.

38.   While Zimmerli, *Ezekiel*, 2: 535 fig. 7, puts the Levites on the north and the priests to their south, building on the suggestion that the temple "in the midst" should be as close to the center as possible, Greenberg, "Design and Themes," 202, places the priestly portion on

the north, which seems to be implied by the rest of chs. 47–48, which always describe territories from the north to the south. The priestly territory in 48:10–12 is mentioned before that of the Levites in 48:13–14.

39. Zimmerli, *Ezekiel*, 2: 470.

40. The order of the tribes about the tent of meeting in the wilderness forms a partial analogy. There the Leah tribes of Zebulun, Judah, and Issachar are on the east, the Leah tribes of Reuben and Simeon are on the south, together with Gad, the descendant of Leah's handmaiden Zilpah. The Rachel tribes of Manasseh, Ephraim, and Benjamin are on the west, while on the northern, least favored side are Asher, descended from Leah's handmaiden Zilpah, together with Dan and Naphtali, descended from Rachel's handmaiden Bilhah. Three Levitical clans and the Aaronites form the innermost ring around the tent of meeting, with the Aaronites being on the most favored eastern side (Num. 2; 3:21–28).

BIBLIOGRAPHY

Aharoni, Yohanan, and Michael Avi-Yonah. *The Macmillan Bible Atlas*. New York: Macmillan, 1968.

Ahroni, Reuben. "The Gog Prophecy and the Book of Ezekiel." *Hebrew Annual Review* 1 (1977): 1–27.

Albright, W. F. *Archaeology and the Religion of Israel*. Baltimore: Johns Hopkins Press, 1956.

———. *From the Stone Age to Christianity*. Garden City, NY: Doubleday Anchor Books, 1957.

Bach, Robert. "Bauen und Pflanzen." In *Studien zur Theologie der alttestamentlichen Überlieferungen*, edited by R. Rendtorff and K. Koch. Neukirchen-Vluyn: Neukirchener Verlag, 1961.

Barrick, W.Boyd. "The Straight-Legged Cherubim of Ezekiel's Inaugural Vision (Ezekiel 1:7a)." *CBQ* 44 (1982): 543–50.

Bartelmus, Rüdiger. "Ez 37,1–14, die Verbform *wĕqatal* und die Anfänge der Auferstehungshoffnung." *ZAW* 97 (1985): 366–89.

Bewer, J. A. "Beiträge zur Exegese des Buches Ezechiel." *ZAW* 63 (1951): 193–201.

Bitter, Stephan. *Die Ehe des Propheten Hosea*. Göttinger Theologische Arbeiten 3. Göttingen: Vandenhoeck & Ruprecht, 1975.

Boadt, Lawrence. *Ezekiel's Oracles Against Egypt: A Literary and Philological Study of Ezekiel 29–31*. Biblica et Orientalia 37. Rome: Biblical Institute Press, 1980.

Bright, John. *A History of Israel*. 3rd ed. Philadelphia: Westminster, 1981.

———. *Jeremiah*. Anchor Bible 21. Garden City, NY: Doubleday, 1965.

Broome, E. C. "Ezekiel's Abnormal Personality." *JBL* 65 (1946): 277–92.

Brownlee, W. H. *Ezekiel 1–19*. Word Biblical Commentary 28. Waco, TX: Word, 1986.

Brueggemann, Walter. "A Cosmic Sigh of Relinquishment." *Currents in Theology and Mission* 11 (1984): 5–20.

Busink, Th. A. *Der Tempel von Jerusalem von Salomo bis Herodes*. Vol. 2. *Von Ezechiel bis Middot*. Leiden: Brill, 1980.

Carley, Keith W. *Ezekiel Among the Prophets*. Studies in Biblical Theology, 2nd Series 31. Naperville, IL: Allenson, 1974.

Cassem, N. H. "Ezekiel's Psychotic Personality: Reservations on the Use of the Couch for Biblical Personalities." In *The Word in the World: Essays in Honor of Frederick L. Moriarty, S.J.* Cambridge, MA: Weston College Press, 1973.

Childs, Brevard S. *Isaiah and the Assyrian Crisis*. Studies in Biblical Theology, 2nd Series 3. London: SCM Press, 1967.

———. *Old Testament Theology in a Canonical Context*. Philadelphia: Fortress, 1986.

Christensen, Duane L. *Transformations of the War Oracle in Old Testament Prophecy*. Harvard Dissertations in Religion 3. Missoula, MT: Scholars Press, 1975.

Clements, Ronald E. *Isaiah and the Deliverance of Jerusalem*. JSOT Supplement Series 13. Sheffield: JSOT Press, 1980.

Coats, George W. *Genesis, with an Introduction to Narrative Literature*. The Forms of the Old Testament Literature 1. Grand Rapids: Eerdmans, 1983.

Cody, Aelred. *Ezekiel*. Old Testament Message 11. Wilmington, DE: Michael Glazier, 1984.

Collins, John J. *The Apocalyptic Vision of Daniel*. Harvard Semitic Momographs 16. Missoula, MT: Scholars Press, 1977.

Coogan, Michael David. *Stories from Ancient Canaan*. Philadelphia: Westminster, 1978.

Cooke, G. A. *The Book of Ezekiel*. 2 vols. International Critical Commentary. New York: Scribner's, 1937.

Crenshaw, James L. *Samson*. Atlanta: John Knox, 1978.

Cross, Frank M. *Canaanite Myth and Hebrew Epic*. Cambridge, MA: Harvard University Press, 1973.

Daube, David. *Studies in Biblical Law*. Cambridge: The University Press, 1947.

Davies, P. R. *Daniel*. Old Testament Guides. Sheffield: JSOT Press, 1985.

Däniken, Erich von. *Chariots of the Gods?* Translated by Michael Heron. New York: Putnam's, 1970.

Driver, S. R. *An Introduction to the Literature of the Old Testament*. New York: Meridian Books, 1960 (1897).

Eichrodt, Walther. "Der Sabbat bei Hesekiel." In *Lux tua veritas. Festschrift für H. Junker*, edited by H. Gross et al. Trier: Paulinus Verlag, 1961.

———. *Ezekiel*. Translated by Cosslett Quin. Philadelphia: Westminster, 1970.

Eissfeldt, Otto. "Schwerterschlagene bei Hesekiel." In *Studies in Old Testament Prophecy*, edited by H. H. Rowley. Edinburgh: T. & T. Clark, 1950.

BIBLIOGRAPHY

Erling, Bernard. "Ezekiel 38-39 and the Origins of Jewish Apocalyptic." In *Ex Orbe Religionum*. Studies in the History of Religions 21. Leiden: Brill, 1972.

Farmer, William R. "The Geography of Ezekiel's River of Life." *Biblical Archeologist* 19 (1956): 17-22.

Fohrer, Georg. *Die Hauptprobleme des Buches Ezechiel.* BZAW 72. Berlin: Töpelmann, 1952.

―――. *Ezechiel.* Handbuch zum Alten Testament 13. Tübingen: J. C. B. Mohr [Paul Siebeck], 1955.

―――. *Die symbolischen Handlungen der Propheten.* 2nd ed. ATANT 54. Zürich: Zwingli, 1968.

Fox, Michael V. "The Rhetoric of Ezekiel's Vision of the Valley of the Bones." *HUCA* 51 (1980): 1-15.

Garscha, Jörg. *Studien zum Ezechielbuch.* Europäische Hochschulschriften 23. Bern: Herbert Lang, 1975.

Gese, Hartmut. *Der Verfassungsentwurf des Ezechiel (Kap. 40-48).* Beiträge zur historischen Theologie 25. Tübingen: J. C. B. Mohr [Paul Siebeck], 1957.

―――. "Ezechiel 20:25f. und die Erstgeburtsopfer." In *Beiträge zur Alttestamentlichen Theologie*, edited by Herbert Donner, Robert Hanhart, and Rudolf Smend. Göttingen: Vandenhoeck & Ruprecht, 1977.

Geyer, John B. "Mythology and Culture in the Oracles Against the Nations." *VT* 36 (1986): 129-45.

Good, E. M. "Ezekiel's Ship: Some Extended Metaphors in the Old Testament." *Semitics* 1 (1970): 79-103.

Gowan, Donald E. *Ezekiel.* Knox Preaching Guides. Atlanta: John Knox, 1985.

Graffy, Adrian. *A Prophet Confronts His People.* Analecta Biblica 104. Rome: Biblical Institute Press, 1984.

Greenberg, Moshe. *Ezekiel, 1-20.* Anchor Bible 22. Garden City, NY: Doubleday, 1983.

―――. "Ezekiel 17 and the Policy of Psammetichus II." *JBL* 76 (1957): 304-09.

―――. "Ezekiel." In *Encyclopedia Judaica* 6: 1078-96.

―――. "The Design and Themes of Ezekiel's Program of Restoration." *Int* 38 (1984): 181-208.

―――. "The Vision of Jerusalem in Ezekiel 8-11: A Holistic Interpretation." In *The Divine Helmsman: Studies on God's Control of Human Events, Presented to Lou H. Silberman*, edited by James L. Crenshaw and Samuel Sandmel. New York: KTAV, 1980.

Gruber, M. "Akkadian *laban appi* in the Light of Art and Literature." *Journal of the Ancient Near Eastern Society* 7 (1975): 73-83.

Halperin, David J. "The Exegetical Character of Ezekiel X 9-17." *VT* 26 (1976): 129-41.

Haran, Menahem. *Temples and Temple-Service in Ancient Israel.* Oxford: The Clarendon Press, 1978.

———. "The Law-Code of Ezekiel XL-XLVIII and Its Relation to the Priestly School." *HUCA* 50 (1979): 45–71.

Heider, George C. *The Cult of Molek: A Reassessment.* JSOT Supplement Series 43. Sheffield: JSOT Press, 1986.

Herntrich, V. *Ezechielprobleme.* BZAW 61. Giessen: Töpelmann, 1932.

Heschel, A. J. *The Prophets.* New York: Harper, 1962.

Hölscher, G. *Hesekiel, der Dichter und das Buch.* BZAW 39. Giessen: Töpelmann, 1924.

Houk, C. B. "A Statistical Linguistic Study of Ezekiel 1:4–3:11." *ZAW* 93 (1981): 76–85.

Howie, Carl Gordon. *The Date and Composition of Ezekiel.* JBL Monograph Series 4 (1950).

Jacobsen, Thorkild. *The Treasures of Darkness: A History of Mesopotamian Religion.* New Haven: Yale University Press, 1976.

Jenni, Ernst, and Claus Westermann, eds. *Theologisches Handwörterbuch zum Alten Testament.* Vol. 1. Munich. Chr. Kaiser Verlag, 1971.

Joyce, P. M. "Individual Responsibility in Ezekiel 18?" In *Studia Biblica I. Papers on Old Testament and Related Themes.* JSOT Supplement Series 11 (1979): 185–96.

Keel, Othmar. *Jahwe-Visionen und Siegelkunst.* Stuttgarter Bibelstudien 84/85. Stuttgart: Katholisches Bibelwerk, 1977.

———. *The Symbolism of the Biblical World.* New York: Seabury, 1978.

Kilpp, Nelson. "Eine frühe Interpretation der Katastrophe von 587." *ZAW* 97 (1985): 210-20.

Klein, Ralph W. *1 Samuel.* Word Biblical Commentary 10. Waco, TX: Word, 1983.

———. "Expository Article on Jeremiah 23:1–8." *Int* 34 (1980): 167–72.

———. *Israel in Exile.* Philadelphia: Fortress, 1979.

Klostermann, A. "Ezechiel. Ein Beitrag zu besserer Würdigung seiner Person und seiner Schrift." *Theologische Studien und Kritiken* 50 (1877): 391–439.

Koch, Klaus. "Is There a Doctrine of Retribution in the Old Testament?" In *Theodicy in the Old Testament,* edited by James L. Crenshaw. Philadelphia: Fortress, 1983.

———. *The Prophets.* Vol. 2 *The Babylonian and Persian Periods.* Translated by Margaret Kohl. Philadelphia: Fortress, 1984.

Kreuzer, S. "430 Jahre, 400 Jahre oder 4 Generationen—Zu den Zeitangaben über den Ägyptenaufenthalt der 'Israeliten.' " *ZAW* 98 (1986): 199–210.

Kutsch, Ernst. *Die Chronologischen Daten des Ezechielbuches.* Orbis Biblicus et Orientalis 62. Freiburg: Universität's Verlag, 1985.

Lang, Bernhard. *Ezechiel.* Erträge der Forschung. Darmstadt: Wissenschaftliche Buchgesellschaft, 1981.

BIBLIOGRAPHY

————. *Kein Aufstand in Jerusalem: Die Politik des Propheten Ezechiel.* 2nd ed. Stuttgart: Katholisches Bibelwerk, 1981.

Levenson, Jon Douglas. *Theology of the Program of Restoration of Ezekiel 40–48.* Harvard Semitic Monograph Series 10. Missoula, MT: Scholars Press, 1976.

Long, Burke O. "Divination." *The Interpreter's Dictionary of the Bible,* Supplementary Volume. Nashville: Abingdon, 1976.

Lust, J. "Ez., XX, 4–26, une parodie de l'histoire religieuse d'Israel." In *De Mari à Qumran,* edited by H. Cazelles. Gembloux: J. Juculot, 1969.

McGregor, L. J. *The Greek Text of Ezekiel.* Society of Biblical Literature Septuagint and Cognate Studies 18. Atlanta: Scholars Press, 1985.

Menes, A. "Tempel und Synagoge." *ZAW* 50 (1931): 268–76.

Mettinger, T. N. D. *The Dethronement of Sabaoth.* Coniectanea Biblica Old Testament Series 18. Lund: CWK Gleerup, 1982.

Miller, J. W. *Das Verhältnis Jeremias und Hesekiels sprachlich und theologisch untersucht.* Assen: VanGorcum, 1955.

Miller, Patrick D., Jr. *Sin and Judgment in the Prophets: A Stylistic and Theological Analysis.* Society of Biblical Literature Monograph Series 27. Chico, CA: Scholars Press, 1982.

Mosis, Rudolf. "Ez 14,1–11–Ein Ruf zur Umkehr." *Biblische Zeitschrift* n.s. 11 (1975): 161–94.

Newsom, Carol A. "A Maker of Metaphors–Ezekiel's Oracles Against Tyre." *Int* 38 (1984): 151–64.

Niditch, Susan. "Ezekiel 40-48 in a Visionary Context." *CBQ* 48 (1986): 208–24.

Parunak, H. Van Dyke. "The Literary Architecture of Ezekiel's *Mar'ôt 'Elôhîm.*" *JBL* 99 (1980): 61–74.

Pritchard, James B., ed. *Ancient Near Eastern Texts Relating to the Old Testament.* 2nd ed. Princeton: Princeton University Press, 1955.

————. *The Ancient Near East in Pictures Relating to the Old Testament.* Princeton: Princeton University Press, 1954.

Rad, Gerhard von. *Der heilige Krieg im alten Israel.* 3rd ed. Göttingen: Vandenhoeck & Ruprecht, 1958.

Roberts, J. J. M. "Amos 6.1–7." In *Understanding the Word,* edited by James T. Butler et al. JSOT Supplement Series 37 (1985): 155–66.

Saggs, H. W. F. "The Branch to the Nose." *Journal of Theological Studies* 11 (1960): 318–29.

Smend, Rudolf. *Die Bundesformel.* Theologische Studien 66. Zürich: EVZ, 1963.

Terrien, Samuel. *The Elusive Presence: Toward a New Biblical Theology.* San Francisco: Harper, 1978.

Torrey, C. C. *Pseudo-Ezekiel and the Original Prophecy.* Prolegomenon by Moshe Greenberg. New York: KTAV, 1970 [1930].

Tov, Emmanuel. "Recensional Differences Between the MT and LXX of Ezekiel." *Ephemerides theologicae lovanienses* 62 (1986): 89–101.

Tuell, Steven. "The Temple Vision of Ezekiel 40–48: A Program for Restoration?" *Proceedings of the Eastern Great Lakes Biblical Society* 2 (1982): 96–103.

Vaggione, R. P. "Over All Asia? The Extent of Scythian Domination in Herodotus." *JBL* 92 (1973): 523–30.

Van Dijk, H. J. *Ezekiel's Prophecy on Tyre (Ez. 26,1–28,19: A New Approach.* Biblica et Orientalia 20. Rome: Pontifical Biblical Institute, 1968.

Vogt, Ernst. "Der Nehar Kebar: Ez 1." *Biblica* 39 (1958): 211–16.

――――. *Untersuchungen zum Buch Ezechiel.* Analecta Biblica 95. Rome: Biblical Institute Press, 1981.

Westermann, Claus. *Genesis 1–11.* Translated by John J. Scullion, S. J. Minneapolis: Augsburg, 1984.

Wevers, John. *Ezekiel.* New Century Bible. Greenwood, SC: Attic Press, 1969.

Williams, Anthony J. "The Mythological Background of Ezekiel 28:12–19?" *Biblical Theology Bulletin* 6 (1976): 49–61.

Wilson, Robert R. "An Interpretation of Ezekiel's Dumbness." *VT* 22 (1972): 91–104.

――――. *Prophecy and Society in Ancient Israel.* Philadelphia: Fortress, 1980.

Zimmerli, Walther. "Der 'neue Exodus' in der Verkündigung der beiden grossen Exilspropheten." In *Gottes Offenbarung.* Theologische Bücherei 19. Munich: Chr. Kaiser Verlag, 1963.

――――. "Der Wahrheitserweis Jahwes nach der Botschaft der beiden Exilspropheten." In *Tradition und Situation. Studien zur alttestamentlichen Prophetie Artur Weiser zum 70. Geburtstag dargebracht* (1963); reprinted in Zimmerli, *Studien zur alttestamentlichen Theologie und Prophetie. Gesammelte Aufsätze* 2, Theologische Bücherei 51, Munich: Chr. Kaiser Verlag, 1974.

――――. *Ezekiel,* Vol. 1. Translated by R. E. Clements, Hermeneia. Philadelphia: Fortress, 1979.

――――. *Ezekiel,* Vol. 2. Translated by James D. Martin. Hermeneia. Philadelphia: Fortress, 1983.

――――. "The Special Form and Traditio-Historical Character of Ezekiel's Prophecy." *VT* 15 (1965): 515–27.

Author Index

Author Index

Scripture Index